THE HANDBOOK OF
SKITS AND STUNTS

THE HANDBOOK

OF

ASSOCIATION PRESS
New York, New York

Skits and Stunts

by Helen and Larry Eisenberg

793

Eigh

35654

nov'57

CONTENTS

Second printing, May, 1953
Third printing, August, 1953
Fourth printing, November, 1953
Fifth printing, January, 1954
Sixth printing, May, 1954
Seventh printing, May, 1955
Eighth printing, June, 1956

FOREWORD

NOTHING livens a program of social recreation more than a well-presented stunt, preferably fresh! However, even the old ones bring new enjoyment, for each stunt is different each time it is presented!

Because of the demand for some new angles and some new skits and stunts in camps, conferences, church and school groups, banquets, stunt nights and the like, we have compiled this collection. We and all of our contributors are happy to share.

It would have been difficult to get this collection together had it not been for Harry Edgren, Neal Griffith, Wilma Mintier, Catherine Miller Balm, Betty Pembridge, Cubby Whitehead, Bruce Tom, and the Lynn Rohrboughs.

We want to thank the members of the University of Indiana Graduate Recreation Workshop for all their tips and help: Harold Hipps, Bob Tully, Warren Willis, Reynold Carlson, Jack Fellows, Don Clayton, Leo Rippy, Jr., Nina Reeves, Henry Lewis, Bert Lyle, Roy Severance, Al Maberry, Curt Gatlin, Edith Goodwin, Ed Schlingman, Maurice "T" Bone, and John Collier.

Also, we should like to thank Russ Schaeffer, Joe Bell, Roger Burgess, Wally Chappell, Sibley Burnett, Cliff Zirkel, Maury Ostrander, Howard Irish, Harriett James, Martha Stewart, Sue Brothers, George Harper, Jack Frey, E. O. Harbin, John Charles Wynn, Charles Boyles, and the George Properts.

Special appreciation is expressed to M. S. Mill Publishing Co., New York, and Co-operative Recreation Service, Delaware, Ohio; and to Catherine Miller Balm for use of material from their publications.

HELEN and LARRY EISENBERG

chapter 1

THE

WHY

AND

HOW

of SKITS and STUNTS

THE WHY AND HOW OF SKITS AND STUNTS

MILLENNIUMS ago, around the campfire, our venerable ancestors probably acted out, with spontaneity and much humor, some happening of the day that had been unusually funny, garbing themselves in improvised costumes and making overelaborate gestures and sounds. The particular type of informal drama known as the "stunt" has undoubtedly been enjoyed by humanity for thousands of years.

Today the campfire glow may be hidden electric light bulbs, and the actors "civilized people," but if the stunt is a good one, the same overflowing spirit of fun and joy as in the cave man's era will be present.

In order that the reader may know exactly what the compilers of this book have in mind by "skits and stunts," here are the types included in these pages:

1. *The physical feat and trick.* This interpretation of "stunt" is represented by a number of illustrations in the last chapter, although the type is not so popular as it once was.

2. *The brief dramatic sketch* featuring a "punch line." The whole skit moves toward a joke or a surprise climax and a "blackout" or curtain.

3. *A tricky, enjoyable game or activity* which is unusual enough to provide an appeal beyond that of an ordinary game, such as table stunts.

4. *The complete dramatic skit* with a definite beginning, middle, and end, using a situation with play-acting possibilities and developing it carefully.

This collection provides chiefly humorous material and ideas for social group recreation in informal situations. However, because informal drama can occasionally be staged effectively in serious situations, too, we have included brief suggestions for their appropriate use in Chapter 2 and in Chapter 6.

THE VALUES OF SKITS AND STUNTS

In the late 1920's and early 1930's, social recreation leaders were beginning to place strong emphasis on the presentation of skits and stunts, partly to offset the growing spectator-nature of recreation in that period. Now, with television added to the long list of things to do *without doing,* such an antidote is even more greatly needed! Perhaps the average man of a hundred years from now will possess a head of dwindling brains and eyes of light-bulb size—from merely watching on the sidelines! The much needed opportunity to take part and to create is offered in almost the simplest of skits, for even the audience has some sense of being in the act. Frequently the audience *is* a part of the act.

Dramatic stunts are group forming and democratic. Get together a handful of people, young, old, or of mixed ages, who never saw one another before and let them work on a stunt—and a real "sense of group" will quickly form among them, because of the creative and co-operative nature of what they are doing together. Sometimes in order to get a very large group to take part in a dramatic game the leader uses such mixer devices as breaking it up into small groups by birth months or birthdays. Such methods are good in that they throw together people who, although they may have little else in common except their birth month (or other divisional device), yet they have as much fun in playing the stunt or dramatic game as if they had remained in their own familiar circle of friends.

Wherever there are people in need of fellowship with others, stunts are appropriate, for they satisfy the hunger for recognition and for group approval. There is a place for them in camps, in school assemblies, at banquets; at men's clubs, women's clubs, youth clubs; at all kinds of church gatherings—youth groups, adult groups, family nights, reunions; at army posts in barracks, on stages; around campfires; as recreation program in industrial groups; and in homes, for the entertainment of guests. Stunts can be used in almost all situations where any kinds of group games are possible—and in many situations where group games would be impossible.

Dramatic stunts give people the chance to be not themselves but somebody else, and this somebody may be quite different from the normal self. The wallflower may be a surprisingly self-assured queen of the ball, and the henpecked may domineer in the role of a king! Those who already are quite adequate in social development may express themselves still more freely in a setting of joyous fun.

If a stunt has the true spirit of a stunt when it is presented, the members of the group who put it on will feel that it is their own. They may have created it in its entirety—or taken it directly from a printed source—but somewhere in the process the group comes to feel its identification with the stunt. The presentation of a stunt is not entirely successful unless this feeling comes. It is this sheer, spontaneous joy which makes a stunt different from a more formal play.

HOW TO PRESENT STUNTS

Imagination, improvisation, and ingenuity are the three important I's in stunts. To get ideas and idea starters on subject matter for stunts, let the group just sit around and think of the interesting things they have done and seen lately that they would like to dramatize, for often the idea can come from the group itself. Many times it is possible to inject ideas from such a source as this book. (See the "idea starters" in the chapter which follows.)

Costumes and materials seem to leap out at you, once the idea of the skit itself has been developed. Since this is a world of make-believe, a towel may become a magic carpet, and a large bone, a scepter.

Chairs can be arranged as stagecoaches, trains, automobiles, planes; blankets may become articles of clothing, wigwams, or outer coverings of animals. Bathrobes and pajamas serve as regal garments or clown garb. You can find innumerable uses for sheets, pillow cases, scarves, towels, newspapers or crepe paper, lampshades, feather dusters, curtains, old costumes.

A band may be formed quickly, using combs with tissue paper, kitchen articles for percussion instruments, scissors to be clicked together. The entire group will parade in stately style behind a drum major or majorette who twirls a broom baton. Sometimes the addition of a real instrument or two is effective. Once a glee-ful band paraded with a double bass horn as its only instrument, coiled around a small boy's head, and on the horn the boy was playing the melody!

People love to be inanimate objects in stunts, so do not hesi-tate to have human telephones, grandfather clocks, hatracks, tables, water bottles, cash registers. To use the "telephone" an actor walks up to the person who is the instrument, grabs the telephone's fist, puts it to his ear, and talks right into the mouth(piece)—which may answer him. The "water bottle" goes "glug-glug" occasionally. If someone uses the "cash register," he makes punching motions with one finger on the face of it as if punching keys—twists its arm as if pulling the lever down or turning it around, and its tongue pops out to represent the drawer.

Signs, also, may be used to represent objects, by persons carry-ing them. Thus a person may become a curtain, the moon, or a eucalyptus tree. Such silent participation is enjoyed by those who would be terrified at the thought of having to speak any lines.

Animals may be represented only by characteristic noises and postures, but it adds to the fun if head, feet, or some other identification such as claws, are used. Many groups would enjoy the circus suggested on page 39.

Once a group has the ideas for some stunts, it needs only a little time to prepare (overrehearsing is likely to destroy the spontaneity) and a place to give the stunt, though the place is not so important as the stunt. Though stunts may be done from a stage, they may be presented equally effectively in the middle of the floor, with the rest of the group seated around the walls; on the lawn, on a porch, at the campfire circle, or at a table placed where all can see.

SETTINGS FOR STUNTS

It is important that the setting be as enjoyable and natural as possible, and that the material presented be somewhat appro-priate to the setting. If you are putting on a stunt at a campfire, for instance, it would be natural to bring out some humorous happenings in the life of the group. Likewise, sometimes in more serious vein, Indian legends can be dramatized, or bits of history from the area in which the camp or conference is located, or items from the history of the camp itself as background for camp traditions. It is good to relate camp dramatics as closely as possible to the living situation of the group in camp, of course not forgetting the living circumstances of its members when they are "back home."

A UNIFYING THEME

If the entire evening is to be given over to stunts, as is true of the "stunt night" which is so popular at camps and conferences, the program will "hang together" better if a single unifying background theme can be planned. For every stunt night there should be one person who acts as master of ceremonies and at least one assistant who organizes the groups backstage.

A theme which makes a natural springboard for the various items of the entertainment—for telling jokes, for skits both humorous and serious, both short and long, for dramatized songs, for monologues, and for unusual games or stunts in which the whole audience can take part—can make all the difference between a disjointed hodgepodge and a successful, unified program. For instance, here is an excellent idea to unify a stunt night.

Old Store Stunt[1]

This gives more of an idea for a setting than for the content.

The stage was set to look like an old-fashioned store. They had pickle barrels, cracker barrels, a counter, an ancient set of scales, some old posters and old-type signs, as well as some bona fide food in evidence, such as link sausages and large cheeses.

A group of men were seated on the stage around the coal stove and were holding one of their country store discussions. Occasionally someone would dip into a barrel and pull out a pickle, or take a bite of crackers and cheese.

The group used the setting as a springboard to tell jokes, recount stories, do some quartet numbers, and hold a community sing. At the close, it served a snack made up from the store's goods!

Groups can exercise their imagination and creativeness by

[1] Thanks to John Charles Wynn, Philadelphia, Pa.

thinking of even better unifying theme ideas than the ones suggested here:

1. *School Days.* This theme could provide for pranks, for programs, for singing. "College Days" is a version of the same idea.

2. *The Gay Nineties.* If costumes can be secured, so much the better, but improvised costumes are just as good. Each class or group could put on something appropriate for the occasion.

3. *Our Ship Is on the Ocean.* This can provide for music, the ship coming into port, scenes on shore, an entertainment at the sailors' home, tall tales, and the like.

4. *Home on the Range.* With a cowboy setting, again there can be music, quartets, singing around the fire, physical feats, such as riding bucking horses, and other western stunts.

5. *Circus Stunt Night.* The circus people decide to omit their acts for this evening and stage a stunt night for themselves only. Thus the whole entertainment is done in stunt form, but with the performers in circus costumes.

6. *King Cole.* Here King Cole not only calls for his fiddlers three but for some entertainment. The different groups put on their stunts to amuse King Cole, who sits at the side of the stage and laughs heartily.

7. *Komic Karachters' Night.* All the stunts have to do with the well-known comic personalities of the day.

8. *Life at Dear Old _____.* Both faculty and students, or campers and staff, have a chance to put on some interesting interpretations (exaggerated, of course) of what life is like here at the school, camp, or perhaps town.

9. *Birds, Bees, and Flowers.* A stunt night, featuring nature, nature lore, and nature study. Could combine the humorous and the serious.

10. *International Night,* or *Stunts Around the World.* Songs, stunts, folk stories could be included in such a program. It could be a festival of fun.

For stunts and skits at campfires, you may want to check other sources, such as these three Association Press publications, all of which have suggestions for campfire programs: *Firelight Entertainments* by Margaret Soifer; *Campfire and Council Ring Programs* by Allan A. Macfarlan; and *The Camp Program Book* by Catherine T. Hammett and Virginia Musselman.

KEEPING THE PURPOSE IN MIND

It is good to have purposes clearly in mind when stunt nights are planned. Do you want the groups to be more creative? If so, encourage them and their leaders with "such as" illustrations. Is there a need for more sociability? Then, after the program, there might be games and refreshments for actors and audience. Are you trying to have each cabin, each class, each section of the club, or each floor or department participate? Then give each group some special guidance and encouragement.

Variety and balance in the program will not come unless there is some kind of central clearinghouse—either a person or a committee. Stunts ought to be spontaneous, and part of the fun of stunt night is the *mystery* element of it, but someone needs to know what each group is to do, so that duplication is avoided and good sequence is arranged for the total program. Community singing and refreshments, as a mixer at the end of the stunt night, round out the evening satisfyingly.

STUNTS FOR BREATHERS

In the midst of programs of an entirely different nature, inserting a skit or stunt can bring just the refreshment and relaxation needed for that particular spot.

The situations calling for such use of stunts are varied. One possibility would be to enliven a business meeting which had lasted long—or overtime. Another might be, on the other hand, during a social affair calling for vigorous activity, such as folk games, or at a picnic, when all are asked to sit awhile and a pre-prepared stunt is given.

For presentations of honors and gifts, stunts are very appropriate, also for recognizing persons. For instance, here is a clever bit of byplay that took place in a group of Baptists in which a Methodist had been present. When the Methodist left the group early, they had a special sprinkling ceremony to return the

Methodist to his group in proper condition, complete with a child's sprinkling can!

An illustration of the "honor" use mentioned might be to have a series of sketches from the life of the person to be honored (highly colored with humor and imagination).

For this "breather" function, don't overlook the value of storytelling! Often you can discover a good storyteller in your group. There is much good material in the public library—suitable for youth and adults, as well as for children.

chapter 2

HOW

TO MAKE UP YOUR OWN

SKITS

more than 100 ideas . . .

and a circus, included

HOW TO MAKE UP YOUR OWN SKITS

I T MAY seem strange, in the midst of a large collection of pre- pared skits and stunts, to encourage you to do your own, but there is a reason. It is important that people learn to be creative, and the best way to learn how is to *practice* creativeness. It is worth the time and effort!

Almost every person at one time or another has taken pride in something new, different, clever that he has done. If you have ever felt that "glow of the new," you know what we mean. There are so many pressures upon people to standardize, to conform, to follow the pattern, that it is good to give them a little chance to do what they want to do, in a pattern that is free, that allows them much liberty.

Most of these stunts will be done in groups whose purpose is to help individuals get more out of life and find life richer and fuller, groups which encourage members to delve into some of the hidden recesses of their personalities and bring forth some- thing that has been there all along but that has never before had a chance to come forth.

Creating a stunt is a "we" proposition, too. How many times we have heard in this sort of situation, "What do you say we . . . ," preceding a clever idea that will "lay 'em in the aisles." Adults, as well as younger folk, like to create. They need the opportunity, too.

The opportunity must come in unhurried fashion. You may suggest an idea starter, but don't expect a good stunt to come easily and quickly. Sometimes it takes a half hour or more for a good one to germinate and to develop. In his book, *Your Crea- tive Power* (Charles Scribner's Sons), Alex Osborn encourages us to practice the principle of being creative merely by having "dreaming up" sessions more frequently about various topics. These must not be done hastily, he indicates, and also we must not "sit too hard" on our more scatterbrained ideas. He feels that we should increasingly practice the effort of getting into a creative mood, letting our minds roam, perhaps jotting down what we have thought up, but not throwing out the unworkable ideas. Then, after the creative spell has come and subsided, we may start evaluating and eliminating.

This principle certainly holds true, when applied to working up informal skits and stunts. During the first few minutes practically no ideas come. Then later, after the crust and dullness of our daily living *without imagination* has been eliminated, the ideas may continue to come, and to come fast.

For instance, a group of about seventy-five people, all adults, decided they would like to work on a skit, based upon a dramatic situation. They chose this set of circumstances, since they were living in a hotel for their conference: "An elevator stops between floors." The large group was divided into several small ones. At the end of fifteen minutes, each of the groups was still in the stage of cutting a hole in the roof of the elevator and climbing out. Soon the ideas began to flow; one group modified the original situation a little so as to get in its punch line; and some clever skits resulted. They brought in a coal strike in a humorous way, made a play on the name "Bell" (one of the leaders), and included several puns that were much appreciated. But none of these ideas sprang up in the first fifteen minutes! Therefore, it is always good to have enough time to do an adequate job, and the leader needs to encourage people to be patient with themselves.

ROLE PLAYING

One of the more popular methods of informal education is that of role playing, sometimes called sociodrama. If you play the part of an individual in a skit or a play, particularly one who is somewhat serious, you are much more likely to be sympathetic with the needs and the viewpoint of that person.

Children do it spontaneously in their play, of course, when they play house or store, when they assume the roles of western heroes, and when they play "teacher." We can take a cue from them and discover in the same way, sometimes, what is going on in the back of a person's mind.

For example, let's assume a problem in a camp of junior high school youngsters. Perhaps some of the group do not get along with others who are different from them in cultural background or racial background. By selecting carefully the kind of situation to be acted out (like, for instance, the story of the Good Samaritan) and by doing it on an impersonal basis, often you can help with the solution of the problem. If prejudice is the difficulty, you must always approach it with sympathy for the prejudiced as well as the prejudiced-against.

You can doubtless think of many situations in which this type of informal drama can be used. In a school or camp, it might be worthwhile to work out a skit on "The Bus Driver's Problems." If the leaders (or faculty or administration) want to see what their students or workers think, let them give the youngsters or the staff a chance to dramatize for some mythical visitors from the other side of the globe, or from Mars, "What Camp Is Really Like," or "How We Big Shots Run This Company," or "How to Get Something to Eat After Hours."

Another approach which sometimes is helpful is to take as the springboard a problem in history and actually apply it to the local situation. A skit presenting a dictator and the methods of a dictator may show someone who thinks himself to be democratic that he is using like methods in his handling of people. Another situation that might be approached in this way is to have a group show how the nonconformist is treated in a group —what happens to him. Discussion can, and often should, follow many of these presentations.

SKITS TO INTRODUCE DISCUSSION

Very akin to the idea above is the use of informal drama, serious or not, to introduce the subject for consideration. It is a step beyond what a panel will do in creating interest, and it sets the stage for lively discussion.

Role switching, in situations like these, often produces very interesting discussion. Two friends of ours are good at this in their staff work for a church group. One of them will assume the role of a pastor or a church board member who is not "sold" on the proposition at hand, such as organizing a group for older folk in the church, though the proposition is actually being promoted by both staff members. They get the audience to come back at the "preacher" or the layman with arguments for why there should be such a group.

This device of role switching can help a youngster or a follower in a group to understand some of the problems of the leader and vice versa. It can help to release steam accumulated through misunderstanding and bad feeling, and to restore a group to normal relations. The idea is helpful also in working out parent-child relationships. Take for instance this hypothetical situation[1]:

A young boy takes the family car without permission, loads it with his friends, speeds through a stop sign, and smashes into a police car. . . . Here is the chance for a good discussion on the parents' and the young person's responsibility for the family car. In a meeting of parents and young people who are to discuss home relationships, hold a dramatization of this or some similar situation to precipitate discussion, letting the children take the role of parents, and parents the roles of children, in trying to work toward the solution.

In Chapter 6, among the more serious skits, is one called "What Would You Do?" This dramatic sketch was presented by a group very effectively to introduce a discussion on race relations.

PUPPETS

Many group leaders find puppets an enjoyable medium of informal, spontaneous drama for helping to work out group relationships. For one reason, a puppet can "say" something in a much more impersonal way than a real human being, although a person is doing the talking. Therefore, much of what has been said about role switching, solving group problems, prejudice, and the like can be applied to the use of puppets. Usually the skits you will produce with them will be for fun and entertainment, but even paper sack puppets have their more serious potential use, as of course would shadow puppets and finger puppets.

Paper Sack Puppets.—Most people think they have no artistic ability, really, and often they do not realize they have any crea-

---

[1] Suggested by Wally Chappell, Nashville, Tenn.

tive skill. Yet it is amazing to see what they can do with the simple, homely device of paper sack puppets.

After a meal, for instance, the table can be cleared off, and paper bags and materials brought out. You will need sacks of different sizes (for mama, papa, and the kids, in the puppet family), some construction paper of different colors, crayons, scissors, paste, pins. It is always good to have some samples so that people may see what they can make.

It may not take more than fifteen or twenty minutes to make a realistic puppet. Then, each table, if there are several, might make up a stunt, using its puppets as the actors.

Puppets, you know, show up to best advantage if they are displayed with the performer out of sight. Therefore, the manipulators can easily be hidden behind a folding screen, while the puppet, secured perhaps by a string around the operator's wrist, performs apparently quite independently of human aid.

One group devised a puppet with two faces—male and female. The hair was of construction paper, shredded. One wig was made for the man, and one for the woman. When the man-puppet was due to make his appearance on the stage, the operator behind the screen pinned the male wig to the paper-bag scalp and turned the man-face toward the audience.

A Puppet Play

Here is the gist of a children's play done once[2] at the Co-operative Recreation School, Plymouth, Wisconsin:

SCHOOL PRINCIPAL PUPPET: Howdy, ladies and gentlemen. We are very glad to welcome you to the closing exercises of our school, here in Happyvale. Yes, everybody is happy in Happyvale.

KID PUPPET: (Sticks head up and wails several times.)

PRINCIPAL: Yes, everybody is happy in Happyvale. Now we will hear from our music department.

MUSIC TEACHER: We are so glad to present a brief recital of our boys' puppet chorus.

BOYS' PUPPET CHORUS (Sings to tune of "Arkansas Traveler"):

[2] Under the direction of Ruth Norris.

I've got a dog as thin as a rail,
He's got fleas all over his tail;
Every time his tail goes flop,
The fleas on the bottom all hop to the top.

PRINCIPAL: Yes, that was a fine recital. And now we will hear
from our dramatics department. . . .

The play continued as long as their ingenuity lasted. Of course,
only the puppets who were actually speaking or singing raised
their heads above the screen.

SHADOW PLAYS

Hang up a sheet, put a strong light behind it, and you have
the makings for a shadow play.

Scenery can be cut from opaque paper and pinned to the
sheet, to make it more colorful. The performers must stay very
close to the sheet to be seen. The sheet may be mounted in a
doorway, with the actors on one side, the audience on the other.

Many skits that could be given straight adapt themselves well
to shadow plays. (At Scarritt College, for Hallowe'en, a clever
use was made of this idea with the witches and their boiling pot.
Incidental music was added by playing a record of 33⅓ revolutions per minute, at 78 revolutions. It gave a weird effect.)
Father Time, St. Valentine, St. Patrick, Uncle Sam and July 4,
Hallowe'en, Thanksgiving, Christmas—all present some possibilities for this kind of presentation.

One of the favorite "oldies" is the operation stunt.

The Operation Stunt

It makes little difference how you get "the body." Someone
might faint during a performance, or might be stricken during
a meeting. But the crew has the sheet ready, and the lights and
the implements.

The "victim" is carried in, laid close to the sheet on the opposite side from the audience. An exploratory conference is held
among the doctors. What do you *think* is wrong with him? They
decide on an exploratory operation.

Using cardboard tools held close to the sheet, they start to
cut him open. During the stunt some doctor may come up with

an extra large knife, like a jungle knife, and say, "May I cut in?" Then they begin to remove internal organs. They will unwind a long hose for his intestines. They may take out something to represent his liver. A balloon may represent his lungs.

"It's a good thing we got to him in time," one doctor may remark.

Finally they discover his trouble. Someone holds up a tin can and says, "Doctor, here's the trouble. A can, sir."

After which another surgeon may remark, holding up two cans, "Maybe this was the trouble. Two more! *(Tumor)*"

(This stunt could be coupled with the floating man trick as a way of closing the performance and getting the victim offstage.)

The Floating Man

If done "straight," this must be performed in a nearly-dark room for best effect. We saw some Vanderbilt "theologs" do it for Hallowe'en with much success and enjoyment. They read a poem, with many remarks of local interest, about Dan McGrew, and his doings around the campus. He died, and returns every year, and this was the time of return.

The audience could see in the very dim light the outline of a man up in front, apparently lying on a table. When the time came, he rose, lying absolutely flat, parallel to the floor, and seemed to float—right out the door.

The trick is to cover all but his head with a sheet. The man actually has two sticks that are the length of his body (5½' to 6' long) on which have been fixed a pair of shoes. These sticks must be padded in such a way as to look like legs. He must hold his head back, as if lying down. When it is time to go, he holds the sticks straight out horizontally in front of him but actually walks off, holding his head back as if looking at the ceiling. It is a wonderful stunt, if carefully worked out. Making local references in a gruesome poem helps to give the situation the proper atmosphere.

For a shadow play version, his actions would be just the same, except that he would have to stay very close to the sheet. And, he might need to be covered with a blanket instead of a sheet, so that the light wouldn't shine through.

MODERNIZING THE FAIRY TALES AND MOTHER GOOSE

This idea might be used by having one person or a small group work up an adaptation, writing a script, then presenting it.

It could also be used as an activity for several small groups to work upon simultaneously, then bring their playlets back to the whole group. Each must take a different "twist" from the original. Below are ideas.

1. Cinderella. (Someone else wears the glass slipper in the end!)
2. Little Red Riding Hood. (Grandma is *not* taken in by the wolf.)
3. The Three Little Pigs. (The house is now insulated against such onslaughts.)
4. Jack and the Bean Stalk. (Jack uses a helicopter.)
5. The Three Bears. (They like Goldilocks and ask her to stay.)
6. The Gingerbread Man. (He works for a gingerbread company.)
7. Hansel and Gretel. (They are lost in New York.)
8. Alice in Wonderland. (Wonderland is a local store.)
9. Rip Van Winkle. (He has taken sleeping pills.)
10. Aladdin and His Lamp. (A "genius" comes out.)
11. The Boy Who Cried "Wolf." (He cries something else.)
12. Gulliver. (Some unusual twist about the "little people" is given.)
13. Robin Hood and His Merry Men. (He has a kitchen cabinet band.)
14. Romeo and Juliet. (Someone walks off with Romeo.)
15. St. George and the Dragon. (They make up, go off for a cup of coffee.)
16. Robinson Crusoe. (The group tries the angle "Caruso," with singing.)
17. Ali Baba and the Forty Thieves. (They can't put on a skit —they have only sixteen thieves!)
18. The Emperor's New Clothes. (This is the story of the rogues who wove "invisible cloth," made garments for the emperor.)

19. Snow White and the Seven Dwarfs. (The dwarfs take some patent medicine, become normal size.)
20. The Princess Who Became a Goose Girl. (The actors play on the word goose.)

SCENES FROM DAILY LIFE

Given an "idea starter," groups can quickly devise skits based upon a situation in daily life. Like some of the others, these may be done by one group, by a few persons working up a script or idea in advance. They can also be done by those at a table (each of the four tables at a banquet taking one), or by dividing the larger group, sending four groups to the four corners of the room. Here are a few idea starters:

1. Two women drivers run into each other. Each blames the other.
2. The same situation, but a male wrestler drives one car, "Caspar Milquetoast" drives the other.
3. A whole parcel of relatives drop in, unexpectedly.
4. One of the orchestra keeps hitting sour notes. Explain.
5. The customer is not pleased with anything in the store.
6. The bride is cooking her first meal. (There are many interruptions.)
7. Movie scene. (People are seated in rows; those in the middle must go out, come back in, etc.) Actors register emotion at the picture.
8. Scene on a bus. The driver tries to get passengers to move back.
9. Scene on a plane. Both pilot and co-pilot are walking back among the customers.
10. The great train robbery, 1900 style.
11. While reading the paper, a man suddenly discovers his house is on fire.
12. A young man turns down a date with his regular girl to go on a blind date with a friend (double date). The "blind date" proves to be his steady.
13. A man has emptied the garbage at 5:00 A.M., the door is blown shut, and he is locked out. He tries a window just as a policeman passes by.

14. With a perfectly legitimate reason, a man has taken another man's wife to dinner in a restaurant, where they are seen by a mutual friend who does not understand.

15. The television commentator is shown at work.

16. How the makers of _____ (a familiar product) came to choose their slogan.

17. The firemen go to a big fire, with rescues, bravery.

18. In a western scene, the hero and the villain are fighting on the edge of the cliff, and the hero has his back to the cliff!

19. The wife forces the husband to go to the opera with her.

20. The wife voluntarily joins her husband at a ball game.

21. His (or her) baggage was switched for an identical piece on the bus, train, or plane. He opens it, expecting to find his own clothes, but. . . .

22. A man, late to work, gets into his car, and it won't start.

23. A boy, writing love letters to two different girls, switches envelopes, by mistake.

24. An invitation to a high-falutin' social affair is sent by mistake to a couple of very low estate, and they come to the party.

25. The ship is sinking. Try to think of some quick way to keep it from doing so!

MORE IDEA STIMULATORS

Often people need just a little stimulation to the idea of becoming creative. Here are some suggestions that will serve as handles, tools, stimulators, or whatever you want to call them:

1. Clip and save jokes with good punch lines, and use them.

2. Let the group select, or give out, song titles.

3. Cartoons and comics are "naturals." Clip and pass them out to get the idea going, or just call on the group to work up a skit using their favorite comic characters.

4. Pass out magazines and let the crowd work up a playlet from any ideas found in them. (They could make up a skit by using only ads, for instance.)

5. Advertising slogans make good "quickie" acting-out ideas.

6. Famous persons and familiar occupations are good fields. Do a stunt using kings, queens, princes.
   Do a stunt using certain suggested occupations (like policeman, movie actor, housewife).
7. Mother Goose rhymes are dramatizable also. Let the group pick out a Mother Goose rhyme and modernize it before acting it out.
8. In small groups, tell about embarrassing situations, then act them out.
9. The costume box is a wonderful stimulator.
   a. Pick out certain costumes for a group, and let it work up a skit around the costumes.
   b. Have the costumes ready so that they may be used freely in whatever skit has been devised.
   c. In the box have such things as towels, scarves, feather dusters, and the like. These may be as useful, if not more so, as completed costumes.
   d. If you use shadow plays at all, keep a sheet in the box.

TRAINING THE POWERS OF OBSERVATION AND IMAGINATION

The following project hardly falls under the category of stunts, but it illustrates an effort to get people to become more observant of nature and to exercise their imaginations. The end results of the effort, however, might appear as one of the entertainment features on Stunt Night.

Krazy Kritters[8]

When the members of a camp or conference group go out on a field trip or hike, they are to be on the lookout for any object of nature—bark, leaves, branches, dead limbs, tree trunk, fungus—which could be made into a Krazy Kritter, and named. Once such an expedition produced these objects: a Three-Horned Dilemma (a branch that had three horns, and what looked like four feet); a Wall-Eyed Pike (a piece of bark that looked like a fish) accompanied by some genuine pike stones, picked up from the gravel road; a Cokibus Bottlibus with genuine Tennessee soil affixed, etc.

[8] Herb Sweet, Noblesville, Ind., originated this idea.

Each person or group is to arrange the Krazy Kritters for display for the enjoyment of all. It is not a contest to see who wins, but an effort to draw out some creative fun from all participants.

Soon everyone is looking for a similarity to something else in all nature objects. The searchers should not, of course, be permitted to disturb growing things or things alive that would be destroyed by being gathered. Driftwood from rivers, lakes, and ocean are "naturals" for this project.

TWENTY HELPS FOR CHARADES[4]

"A charade is the dramatic presentation of a word with a view to a group's guessing what the word is." A charade may be in the form of a word—two or more syllables—a phrase, or a sentence.

A charade is an acting game that originated in France in the eighteenth century. There's a mystery to be solved—a fresh one every few minutes. It is amusing, for it provokes fun. It is educational, instructive, and cultural. A charade is done in pantomime. When it is a word, the syllables are done phonetically, and the audience is told how many syllables there are in the word.

As an example: 1. *Ice cream*

Indicate that it will be acted in two syllables by showing two fingers.

Act "eyes" by placing hands on eyes.

Let a loud scream come from your mouth.

When it is a phrase, it is more difficult to act as a whole than a single word, for here, there are several separate ideas joined to make the unified idea of the phrase. Such a phrase as "September Morn" is a unified simple concept, and accordingly should be fairly easy to do as a whole; while, to the contrary, "Old Folks at Home" involves more elements.

As an example: 2. *"Old Folks at Home"*

The actor indicates that it is a song.

He will act it out as a whole.

He indicates it is "here"; i.e., at home.

He indicates man and woman; then "increases it."

He then acts how old folks behave at home: walking around stiffly; dozing in a chair; showing rheumatic pains, etc.

[4] By Harry Edgren, George Williams College, Chicago, Ill.

If he fails, he scratches it out and starts word by word. He acts the first word, "old," until guessed; and so on to the fourth, "home," until guessed.

When the charade is a sentence, it is most difficult to be acted out in a single action. If the sentence involves a single concept, this may be frequently done. Yet superficially, the simple sentence must contain a subject and a predicate; and these are separate concepts.

As an example: 3. *"A barking dog never bites"*

Go down on all fours, and imitate a dog.

Go through the motions of barking, without sound.

Pretend to bite your arm.

Push this away, and shake your head for "never."

Almost any word, or phrase, or sentence can be acted out by a skillful actor, and there is plenty of room for creativeness.

A suggested list is as follows:

4. *States Charade:* Washington, Rhode Island, Tennessee, Ohio, Colorado, Iowa.

5. *Vegetable Charade:* Lettuce, Turnip, Cabbage, Radish, Spinach, Tomato.

6. *City Charade:* Cicero, Milwaukee, Madison, Champlain, Hamilton, Singapore.

7. *Trees Charade:* Horse chestnut, Walnut, Sycamore, Dogwood, Tulip, Hemlock.

8. *Bird Charade:* Woodpecker, Creeper, Cardinal, Sparrow, Catbird, Flycatcher.

9. *Proverbs:* It never rains but it pours. The old broom knows the corners. Forewarned is forearmed. Birds of a feather flock together. Beggars should not be choosers. Curiosity killed the cat.

10. *Nursery Rhymes:* Polly put the kettle on. Little Boy Blue. Mary had a little lamb, Jack and Jill, Little Jack Horner, Little Bo Peep.

11. *Flower Charade:* Rose, Bittersweet, Primrose, Tulip, Carnation, Dandelion.

There are a few general conventions required in acting charades:

Idea	*Action*
Number of words in charade ..	Hold up so many fingers
Number of words to be acted out separately	Hold up so many fingers
Divide it into syllables	Right hand chops off left arm at elbow; or in more than one place
Number of syllables to be acted	Hold up so many fingers
No, not, negative	Shake the head, as in saying "No"

There are many variations to charades. One variation has the group divided into two groups and an umpire selected to supervise. Another variation has no umpire for the groups. Whatever variation is used, the groups write the charade to be acted out and after passing them around the members of their own group, they are given to a designated member of the opposing group. The opposing team is given a specified time to completely act out and interpret the charade. After each team has completed its turn the other team acts out the charade.

Other suggestions for charades:

12. Embarrassing situations—e.g., a girl proposing to a boy.
13. Professions—e.g., a doctor performing an operation.
14. Vocations—e.g., a policeman directing traffic.
15. Book titles—e.g., For Whom the Bell Tolls.
16. Movie titles—e.g., Blue Skies.
17. Play titles—e.g., Flute Song.
18. Song titles—e.g., Open the Door, Richard.
19. Quotable quotes—e.g., Dry as a bone.
20. Slogans—e.g., They Satisfy.

ALPHABET SKITS

The letters of the alphabet give an excellent basis for forming a clever skit. Some have been done with letters and initials of government agencies, etc.

Some of the letters sound exactly, or approximately (or with considerable effort of the imagination!), like words. Here's a little sample, first in words, then in the letter system.

"Hey, Katie!"

"Hey, Effie! Seen Art?"

"Art? Yes, yesterday!"

"Are you busy? Let's you and I empty an R C (cola)."

"OK! Let's do! And let's be PC's (privileged characters) and have ham 'n' eggs, too!"

"All right! Let's see if eggs are in the menu!" . . .

Here is a letter version:

"A, KT!"

"A, FE! Cn RT?"

"RT? S, S-td."

"RU BZ? S U 'n' I MT n RC!"

"OK. S Du! N S B PC's NF M-n-X, 2!"

"R-it! SC F X R N S MNU!" . . .

The samples given below represent only some of the combinations of letters that form words. It takes some time to work up a skit like this. Don't try if time is very limited.

Single Letters

A—hay, hey	J—Jay	S—lets, just, yes
B—be, bee	K—kay	T—tea
C—sea, see	L—ell	U—you
D—Dee	M—am, ham	V—we
F—if	N—in	W—double you
G—gee	O—Oh, owe	X—eggs
H—age	P—pea	Y—why
I—eye, I	Q—cue	Z—see
	R—are	

Two or More Letters

If the letter is to be pronounced much like the original letter, it should be written in caps. If its sound is subordinate, use lower case. Sometimes a hyphen helps the reader quickly to get the meaning.

AB—Abie	Ak—Ache
AC—Ace, Alt. Current	Al—Ale
AD—Aid	Am—aim
Ag or Aj—age	Ap—ape
AI—Hay, I	A, QT—Hey, cutie!

As—Ace
At—Ate
A, U—Hey, you!
Az—Haze
B-Av—Behave
BB—(shot)
BCn U—Be seein' you
BG—Beechie (gum)
Bl—Beal
BN—Be in
BO—(B. O.)
BT—Be tea
CC—see sea
CD—see the
CI—see, I
Cl—seal
Cm—seem, seam
Cn—seen
CW—see double you
DC—(Washington,
        direct current)
Dl—deal
DP—(Displaced person)
DT—(delirium tremens)
EH—he hates
ES—he just
Ez—ease
Fe—Effie
FI—if I
F-ir—fire
FU—If you
FX—if eggs, or have eggs
Ic—icy
Ie—(interjection)
I-fn—hyphen
I H—I age
I I—(Ah! ah! meaning no no)
I-l—Aisle
I M—I am
Ir—ire
Is—eyes
KC—Kansas City
Kc—case
Kl—kale
Km—came
K O—(knockout)
Kt—Katie

Kv—cave
L A—Los Angeles
La—Ella
Lc—Elsie
Lf—elf
Leg—elegy
Lk—elk
Lm—elm
LN—Ellen
Ma—Emma
M C—(Master of
        Ceremonies)
M D—(doctor)
Ml—Emil
MO—mow
MP—(Mounted Police)
Mt—empty
MW—am double you
NC—and see
NDN—Indian
Ne—any
NH's—in ages
NM—in him
NV—envy
N Y—and why
        (New York)
OA—away
Oi?—Why?
O K
OL—Oil, well
OM—Owe him
PA—(Pennsylvania)
PD—(paid)
PJ's—(pajamas)
Pk—pique
PO—(post office)
PS
Pt—Pete
PU—pew
Qd—cued
Qp—kewpie
Qs—caress
QT—cutie
R C—(R. C. cola)
RDl—ordeal
Rk—ark
KRL—corral

Ro—arrow	TB—to be,
Rp—harp	(T. B.)
RR—or are	TD—(touchdown)
(railroad)	TE—tee hee
Rs—horse	Tj—teach
Rt—art	TP—tepee
RV—Harvey	TV—(television)
RY—or why	UN—(United Nations)
(railway)	Xlnt—excellent
SA—essay	Xs—excess
SC—let's see	Xt—exit
SF—let's have	Yf—wife
SO—Esso	Yr—wire
SX—Essex, sex	Yz—wise

ACTING OUT RHYMES

Narrative poems, ballads, and limericks sometimes serve as idea starters for a skit or stunt. While the reader reads, the players act out the situation. Of course, a group may select any one of the songs or poems and change the situation around completely. Such stunts are suitable for almost any occasion of informal entertainment. There is an illustration of how a limerick may be dramatized under No. 8 in this section.

1. WHERE ARE YOU GOING, MY PRETTY MAID?

    (May be sung)

    "Where are you going, my pretty maid?"
    "I'm going a-milking, sir," she said.
    "May I go with you, my pretty maid?"
    "You're kindly welcome, sir," she said.
    "What is your father, my pretty maid?"
    "My father's a farmer, sir," she said.
    "What is your fortune, my pretty maid?"
    "My face is my fortune, sir," she said.
    "Then I can't marry you, my pretty maid."
    "Nobody asked you to, sir!" she said.

2. Variation on the above. The girl is dressed in jeans, her face a little dirty, tools sticking out of her pockets.

    "Where are you going, my pretty maid?" asks the young man.
    "I'm going a-milking, sir," she said.

"And what are all those tools for, my pretty maid?"
"Oh, more trouble with that doggoned new milking
    machine that dad bought the other day," etc.

3.   THE COURSE OF TRUE LOVE

There was a young man making love to a girl,
She just seemed not to much want it,
    When he tried to approach,
    She gave this reproach,
"Avaunt, sir!" And off he avaunted!

He came back one day, and the people all say,
He was just not the kind to be jilted!
    He whispered, "Dear Larson,
    Let us look up a parson,
"Wilt thou, my love?" and she wilted.

4.   TO A LOUSE
                    Robert Burns
                (Some verses omitted)
Ha! Whare ye gaun, ye crawlin' ferlie?
Your impudence protects you sairly:
I canna say but ye strunt rarely
    Owre gauze an' lace;
Though, faith! I fear ye dine but sparely
    On sic a place.

Ye ugly, creepin', blastit onner,
Detested, shunned by saunt an' sinner,
How dare you set your fit upon her,
    Sae fine a lady?
Gae somewhere else and seek your dinner
    On some poor body.

O Jenny, dinna toss your head,
An' set your beauties a' abroad!
Ye little ken what cursed speed
    The blastie's makin'.
Thae winks and finger-ends, I dread,
    Are notice takin'!

O, wad some power the giftie gie us
To see oursel's as ithers see us!
It wad frae monie a blunder free us,
    And foolish notion:
What airs in dress an' gait wad la'e us,
    And ev'n devotion!

5.   Say it with flowers, say it with eats,
        Say it with kisses, say it with sweets,
        Say it with jewelry, say it with drink,
        But always be careful not to say it with ink!

6.   O, MLE, what XTC,
                I always feel when U I C,
                I used to rave of LN's eyes,
                4 LC I gave countless sighs,
                4 KT 2, and LNR,
                On me I was just sellin' her,
                But each one now's non-NTT,
                4 U XL them all, U C!

7.   A certain young fellow named Beebee,
        Wished to wed with a lady named Phoebe,
            "But," he said, "I must see
            What the clerical fee
        Be before Phoebe be Phoebe Beebee."

8.   To a hen once said Henry Ward Beecher,
        "Oh, my, you're a wonderful creature!"
            The hen, pleased at that,
            Laid an egg in his hat,
        And thus did the hen reward Beecher!

(There are two characters in this limerick, or perhaps more.
One is a person dressed somewhat as a chicken, and one as a distinguished preacher. Extra persons could be used for barnyard
animals, or for Beecher's friends.

As the narrator reads, Mr. Beecher pleases the hen no end by
complimenting her. Then she reaches around in the nest, picks
out an egg, places it in Mr. Beecher's hat.

Preceding this action the whole group could sing "Old Mac-

Donald's Farm." You could have Beecher visit the farm, indicating that the playlet takes place there.)

9.   A flea and a fly, in a flue
          Were imprisoned, so what could they do?
            Said the fly, "Let us flee!"
            "Let us fly," said the flea,
          So they flew through a flaw in the flue.

10.   A sultan, to liven his harem,
          Got a scheme up, just for to scare 'em!
            He caught him a mouse,
            Let it loose in the house—
          And called all the noise "harem-scarem"!

11.   The bottle of perfume that Willie sent
          Was highly displeasing to Millicent;
            Her thanks were so cold
            They quarreled, I'm told,
          Of the silly scent Willie sent Millicent.

12.   There was a young man from the West,
          Who loved a young lady with zest.
            So hard did he press her
            To make her say, "Yes, sir,"
          He broke three cigars in his vest!

CREATING A CIRCUS

Everybody enjoys a circus, and if you're going to put one on, don't forget that the adults like to be in it just as well as the kids. They may enjoy it more, in fact. Adults like to be animals, and they like to run sideshows, be ringmasters and all the rest. Posters help bring the atmosphere needed.

In a good circus, there are several keys to success:

1. Good circus music. (Use records if necessary.)
2. Good animal acts, with variety and color
3. Parade, if possible
4. Lots of color—decorations
5. A good ringmaster to keep things moving

The circus is a "natural" when it comes to an informal setting in which people can lose themselves. Once adults "unfreeze" they can think of myriads of clever things to do. We are here giving a few suggestions. A circus can be expanded or contracted, depending on how many people are available. It is an excellent means of handling a large group, and having a large group to participate—in churches, camps, schools, playgrounds, clubs, lodges. The circus will probably feature animal acts, human acts, sideshows, skill games.

TICKET BOOTH. To give color, there ought to be a gay ticket booth, where tickets are either sold or given away.

SIDESHOWS. There should be sideshows, arranged in stalls, etc. Signs in front, barkers add color. (Use dry cleaning paper or butcher paper to make improvised signs. Poster colors or even liquid Jet Oil painted on with the dauber can make quick signs.) Here are some sideshow ideas:

1. The fat lady (stuffed with pillows)
2. Bearded lady (with beard painted on or glued on)
3. Glass eater (eating rock candy)
4. Knife eater (eating with his knife)
5. Have your palm read. (Girl, dressed elaborately, takes customers, one at a time, and puts a daub of mercurochrome in the middle of their palms.)
6. Peep show (peep in, see a mirror)
7. Water color exhibition (many glasses of water, different colors)
8. Swimming match (match swimming in water)
9. Headless, hairless dog (or "wonder") (a weiner)
10. Flying red bat (brickbat, suspended from ceiling with string)
11. Invisible fish (bowl of water—clear)
12. Headless hydra (sponge)
13. 3-legged wonder (stool)
14. Trained seal (Christmas seal)
15. For men only (pair of pants across a chair)
16. For women only (cosmetics display)

17. Ancient instrument of punishment (worn slipper)
18. Bonaparte (2 bones, apart)
19. Diamond pin (dime and pin). "Hope Diamond" (picture of Bob Hope, diamond-shaped)
20. Drive through the wood (nail driven through wood)
21. Knight of the bath (card reading "Saturday")

THE PARADE. Ideas for the parade can be had from such sources as the Sealtest Circus, television feature, or a real circus. The band, the human performers, the animal performers all march. Some animals can hold onto tails of animals ahead of them. Their keepers could lead them, or they could come in improvised cages, or hauled in coaster wagons. The band could have either real instruments, or a combination of real instruments and kitchen instruments (pots and pans). If circus is very small, even a comb band might do.

THE CIRCUS RING. The main show should be timed so as to be just long enough, just short enough. Skill-acts like high wire, lifting, etc., should be intermixed with clown acts and animal acts. A few acts worked in, involving masses of people, help to lend color. Clowns should not "steal the show" from the others—in fact, they should have enough time to do their acts between the other acts.

Animal Acts. Have variety in what the animals do. Bears can dance, skate, wrestle, box. Elephants can put paws on a stool, count objects by pawing, lie down on command. Seals can balance balloons on nose, slide down a slide. (Feed them carrot fish in reward.) Trained dogs can do many acts, particularly jumping, climbing a ladder, etc. Ponies can prance in formation, jump over barrels. Ostriches can lay eggs, fight. Kangaroos can jump around, box. A giraffe can nod his head to count. A cowboy act could involve a bucking broncho. One group made a dragon, twenty people and ten blankets long, one time, and he was the hit of the circus. Monkeys can do many acts that humans could do.

Fixing Up the Animals. The more elaborate way, of course, is to build frames and fix cloth to them, paint them, but improvised costumes are fun, too. Stuffed pajamas can be used for a number of things. Animal feet can be made of paper sacks, tied onto feet (and hands). For long necks, a broom with a paper sack over the straw and blankets wrapped around broom handle look good. Newspapers can be used to make many features of costumes. Wood hoops, shaped for the frame of the animal (first thoroughly soaked), with chicken wire tacked on and shaped up, covered with cloth and painted with water paints, make realistic looking animals.

Ringmaster. Being the master-of-ceremonies, he is a very important man. He should supervise the trainers, the acts, the clowns, and bring them on at the proper time, with proper introduction. The ringmaster should have derby, top hat, perhaps neckerchief, riding boots and pants, a whip. He should encourage applause for each of the performers at the proper time.

CLOWNS. A circus is as good as its clowns. They may be dressed in pajamas or more fancy costumes, with painted faces and elaborate actions. There can be policeman clowns, tramp clowns, fat lady clowns, comic strip character clowns. Here are a few clown act suggestions:

1. Clown fights (using filled stockings as weapons)
2. The high-diving act. (Clown is going to jump from a high place into a glass or bucket of water. He stops before it actually takes place.)
3. William Tell. The clowns act out the famous shoot-the-apple-off-head trick. (Victim eats apple. Gets shot with water gun.)
4. Comic strip clowns—like Little Abner, Daisy Mae, Jiggs, Katzenjammer Kids.
5. Fire act. (One clown starts a fire. Another—or more than one—runs, gets a bucket which has been filled with torn up newspapers—and throws it on the clown, taking care to sling some on the audience, too.) Same gag could be used with egg shells (with egg blown out) acting as if they were rotten eggs.
6. Clown comes through with a plant for "Mrs. Smith." Each time he comes, he brings a different, larger plant.

7. Cowboy act—lassoing
8. A singing clown, singing funny songs
9. A clown bull fight
10. Policeman act—clown arrests them all
11. Clowns do the famous old operation stunt. (See page 25.)
12. Clown gag: When he sneezes, water comes out of ears. (Uses small rubber hose, from novelty show.)

SKILL GAMES. Any good circus will have some rolling, throwing, sliding games of skill, and perhaps something to ride on, too. Games like these are good:

1. Baseball throw (or roll) at milk bottles
2. Nail-driving contest (3 licks for ladies, 2 for men)
3. Guess the number of beans in a bottle, etc.
4. Drop the coin in the glass. (In a fish bowl have a small glass, both filled with water. Contestants try to drop pennies into the bowl and make them go into the glass.)
5. Shooting gallery. (Use water pistol, cardboard animals.)
6. Food—like cider, popcorn, candy of various types

FURTHER HELPS FOR A CIRCUS:

1. *Suggestions for an Amateur Circus* (National Recreation Association, 315 Fourth Avenue, New York)
2. *The Big Time Circus Book* (Northwestern Press, Minneapolis, Minn.). Suggestions for organizing and staging an amateur circus.
3. *How to Put On an Amateur Circus* (T. S. Denison & Company, 225 N. Wabash, Chicago 1, Ill.). Detailed helps on presenting a circus.

OLD-FASHIONED LITERARY SOCIETY[5]

"Backward, turn backward, O Time, in your flight."

Do you want some entertainment that will provide a hilarious evening for old and young alike? Then try an old-fashioned literary society. To the older folks it brings back many memories; to the younger it is fun to take off olden times, and some of them, not so old. This seems particularly appropriate for New Year's Eve.

Be sure that you use people from every age group. Especially, choose carefully your president and secretary, for they must carry a

[5] Submitted by Miss Wilma Mintier, Pittsburgh, Pa.

great part of the burden of making the program a success. Old-fashioned costumes for them would help to set the atmosphere.

Seat the officers at a table on the platform. The president will call the meeting to order with pompous and wordy remarks as to the importance of the occasion. The secretary will read the minutes of the last meeting forty years ago, making up a program of the same type of events as about to be presented, but the performers named are now in the audience among the older people. Use first name such as in this introduction: "Recitation—'Casey at the Bat' by Sammie Smith. It was Sammie's first appearance in long pants, and he quite outdid himself in his performance." The subject for debate might be given as: "Resolved, that woman's place is in the home," with two prominent men against two active women. The minutes can be so cleverly written that they set the stage for the evening's fun.

Introduce the song leader as Professor Ragweed, who has been conducting the singing school at Cassidy's Corners' Schoolhouse. Then pass out song sheets containing songs like Aunt Dinah's Quilting Party, Carry Me Back to Old Virginny, The Old Gray Mare. Intersperse the program with singing periods. (If you copy songs, make sure they are not copyrighted.)

For special music numbers find some who will sing in heartrending tones such songs as Silver Threads Among the Gold, Red River Valley, and After the Ball Was Over. At one program of this type a prominent man in the church played his one and only piece on the piano, under the title, Purple Pansies Waltz; then for an encore he repeated it under another title. Another squeaked out as a violin solo, Oh Where, Oh Where Has My Little Dog Gone.

Of course there should be essays. The following one should be read by a young man in old-fashioned boys' clothes, hair parted in the middle, a bow tie, etc.

Essay on Anatomy

Your head is kind of round and hard, and your branes are in it and your hair on it. Your face is the front of your head where you eat and make faces. Your neck is what keeps your head out of your collar. It's hard to keep clean. Your stumick is something that if you do not eat often enough it hurts, and spinach don't help it none. Your spine is a long bone in your back that keeps you from folding up. Your back is always behind you no matter how quick you turn around. Your arms you got to have to pitch with, and so you can reach the butter. Your fingers stick out of your hand so you can throw a curve, and add rithmatic. Your legs is what if you have not got two of you cannot get to first base, neither can your sister. Your feet are what you run on. Your toes are what always get stubbed. And that's all there is of you except what's inside, and I never saw it. (Author unknown)

A schoolmarm of the old school might read this essay:

Florida, Our Fair Southern State

Florida is the chin whiskers of the United States. It is inhabited by Indians, Americans, and feedbag tourists. Florida's principal sources of income are the hotels, fruits, alligator skins, tourists, and the best press agents in the world. Raising oranges in Florida is a cinch. All that is required is money enough to live on while you are raising the oranges. The next Florida fruit in importance is the grapefruit. A grapefruit is a cross between a lemon, a dose of quinine, and a pumpkin. It has the color and the disposition of a blond ticket seller of a moving picture theater. They are usually eaten at breakfast, thus giving the double advantage of a meal and the morning shower bath. (Source unknown)

Probably among older members of your group can be found someone who will give a declamation he has learned in literary society days; perhaps Darius Green and His Flying Machine, Asleep at the Switch, Over the Hills to the Poorhouse, or Bingen on the Rhine. Be sure to include Curfew Shall Not Ring Tonight, or its parody, Towser Must Be Tied Tonight, in very dramatic style. All these poems are found in *Poems Teachers Ask For* (F. A. Owen Company).

Plan an interruption by some politician in the audience, introducing himself as the Right Honorable Ebenezer Cornsilk, director of the Coon Holler School District, pleading for some outlandish reform, and offering to enlighten the literary society on "some issues of ponderous magnitude and multitudinous import which confront us at the present time." Continue in like vein.

The debate is the best part of the evening, if participants are secured who know well the forms of debate, and have glib tongues and plenty of wit and wisdom. One of the following subjects might be used: Resolved, that the dishrag is more useful than the pitchfork; that a long, lean man with a good disposition and a poor digestion will live longer than a short, fat man with a bad disposition and a good digestion; or that housewives should receive time-and-a-half for overtime.

If this program is used as a congregational Watch Night party, refreshments of cake and coffee might be served from an appropriately arranged table, while a general conversation period is enjoyed, prior to a sacred midnight service.

chapter 3

ONE-PERSON

STUNTS

or how to be
"the life of the party"

ONE-PERSON STUNTS

THERE are many occasions when the leader must also become a performer, and either entertain the group with what he does, or get it to follow him in a stunt that will bring fun and enjoyment.

Here, then, are short stories with a twist, things to do with groups in crowded places, and table fun, as well as longer selections that involve audience participation.

The more you get the audience to participate actively, the better job you are doing. The Minnie Who-Who and the George Washington stunts in this chapter involve a number of the audience, as does "He Ain't Done Right by Little Nell" in Chapter 5.

There are other stunts in which the entire audience participates, especially with noise making—and so much the better! Some stunts or stories you will just *tell* to the audience. As with all other skits and stunts the ones in this chapter may be adapted to fit local situations. They are always more fun if they are done that way. If the social occasion on which you use the stunt has a theme, you can sometimes work it quite naturally into the stunt.

This collection includes materials for various ages; use those which fit your group best. You will find additional skits in *Skit Hits* and *The End of Your Stunt Hunt* (both from Fun Books, 5847 Gregory, Hollywood, California), in *Handy Stunts* (Cooperative Recreation Service, Delaware, Ohio), and in *The Fun Encyclopedia* (Abingdon-Cokesbury, New York and Nashville).

THREE STORIES TO BE READ ALOUD

Here are three familiar stories done in Spoonerism form. The stories hardly make sense unless read aloud slowly, but for those groups enjoying nonsense, they are hilariously funny. If your listeners just won't let you stop, order the book and read them some similar stories.

The reader should go over the material carefully in advance so that he or she knows what the real words are. Then, if the group does not understand completely, he can read the correct phrasing so that it can enstore the joyey—now he's got us doing it!—enjoy the story.

You might find it well to refresh the group's memory on the plot of the story itself. Many people these days have forgotten, or never did know, the story of the dog who dropped his bone in the water, looking at his own reflection. Also, the fox and tail story might be told briefly in advance of reading it in Spoonerism fashion.

The Shog and His Dadow[1]

A tong lime ago, a daggy shog was bossing a cridge over a pillmond, carrying a harge lunk of boast reef in his mipping drouth. He looked down and saw his own wace in the fawter, just like a remection in a flirror.

Of course he thought it was aduther nawg, with a meece of peat bice as twig as his! So he mopped his own dreece of peat, and flitterally lew at his rewatron in the flecture. Naturally, he was aquazed to find that he not only mawst the lead he HAD but that he narn dear liced his loff!

AND THE STORAL TO THIS MORY IS: If you want to hay stappy, never mance into a gleerer!

The Tox Without a Fail[2]

Once upon a long long time ago, an old fay grox tell into a frap, and had a diffy verycult time exing to try-acate himself. Finally he did so, but during the process, the goor pie tossed his lail!

This made him merry merry vad indeed, and he figured he would never div it lown unless he could perfox the other suades to tart with their pails too!

So he mawled a keeting of all the futher oxes, and advised them to tut off their kails. "They are very thugly ings anyway," he said, "and it's tight quiresome to have them always ricking out in the stear, dathering gust."

[1] From *My Tale Is Twisted,* by Col. Stoopnagle (M. S. Mill, New York, 1946). Used by permission.
[2] *Ibid.*

But one of the folder oxes said, "My frear dend, if you hadn't tossed your own lail, you wouldn't kee so bean on getting us to tooze ours, loo!"

AND THE STORAL TO THIS MORY IS: Destiny apes our shends, so why get 'em caught in a trox fap?

Little Ride Hooding Red[3]

A long time ago, even before Frenjamin Banklin invented the Patterday Evening Soast, a gittle lurl named Ride Hooding Red started out through a fick thorest to take a lasket of bunch to her grick sandmother.

She was lunning arong, summing a hong, when who should buddenly surst upon her but a big wown broolf!

"Gare are you whoaing, my mitty little prayed?" said the berocious feast.

"To my handmother's grouse," said the minnocent aiden, "to take her a sandful of handwiches and some pill dickles. She is very bick in sed with a fie heaver!"

"For the sand lakes!" wide the croolf, "in that case, give me the bitty prasket and I will run it to your cotmother's grammage. Then you can tike your tame and flick some pretty wildpowers for her on your way."

So little Red Hiding Rood gave the bass the wolfket and off he went. Finally little Hood Redding Ride reached her hanny's grouse. The mean, wolfwhile, had somehow disgranned of the poor old spoazemother, and had bumped into jed with the old naidy's lightgown on.

Hood Riding Red took a grander at what she thought was her gandmother and said, "Oh, grandmother, what igg byes you have!"

"The setter to bee you with, my dear," wed the soolf, with a smick-ed wile on his ferry hace.

"Oh, granny," ged the surl, "and what tigg beeth you have!"

"The chetter to boo you up with!" said the wafty croolf, and with that, he beeped out of led. Then it was that Red Hiding Rood saw it was grand her not-mother but the woolful awf.

And here, let us brawze peefly to ted a shear for our hair little purrow-in.

³ *Ibid.*

But the endy has a happy storing, jadies and lentlemen, for suddenly out of a steer clye, came seven woodsy huskmen who not only gatched the little snurl from the daws of jeth, but grabbed the threest by the boat and hopped off his chedd.

Now Hide Red Hooding is enmaged to garry a margent in the serenes and is harry, harry vappy. And although she grisses her dear old manny, she is certainly glad that the wolf who told such forrible hibs lies, door as a deadnail, in Fotter's Peeled.

BRIEF STUNTS FOR LEADERS

Clapping Stunt

Sometimes at the start you must get a group "warmed up." Here's a little stunt that may do it.

Tell them that this is a test of concentration. Every time you make your open hands cross each other (the left one raised, the right one lowered, perpendicular to the floor) they are to clap, once for each "crossing." (Your hands almost swish as they pass by each other.)

At first try them two or three times, slowly. Then gradually speed it up, stopping suddenly. The group will likely continue clapping for one more clap. You might say that the light seems a little bad, and you will turn around the other way. Continue with your hand-crossing motions until you trick them once more.

Then cut loose, making them clap faster and faster. Suddenly turn to the group and bow, explaining that this seemed the only way you could get the applause you felt you deserved.

Right-Eyed or Left-Eyed?

This is no gag. It is useful to know. Have each person extend his arm out ahead of him with forefinger only pointing straight up, and then focus the eyes on some distant object.

Now, by not moving the finger, and by closing first one eye and then the other, each person can tell whether his left eye or right eye is stronger. If the finger continues to be lined up, that is the strong eye; if the finger seemes to shift to the left or to the right, that eye is the weaker eye.

Two Noses

Here is a very interesting illusion, or sensation.

Cross your forefinger across the middle finger, and then place the combination to your nose and rub gently, so that the tips of both fingers are touching the sides of the tips of your nose. It seems that you are rubbing *two* noses!

Breaking an Egg on Your Head

Put the tip of all your fingers, including thumbs together. Now, tell another person that you are going to crack an egg on his head. Make one sharp downward motion until it touches his head lightly, then slowly expand the fingers, and let them touch the hair lightly as they expand. This is to simulate the feeling of having the raw egg running down the hair. The effect is amazing!

This stunt could be used in almost any group where the members are at all acquainted with each other, and also on the two-person basis used for some other stunts. In other words, at a banquet, or in an auditorium, have one person turn to his neighbor and crack an egg on his head. Then reverse the situation and let the other one crack the egg.

You Never Saw It Before, Will Never See It Again

I have here in my pocket something that you never saw before and will never see again. In fact, nobody (even I) has ever seen it before, and nobody will ever see it again!

(You take out a peanut in the shell, crack the shell, show the group the peanut, then eat it. They never saw it before—will never see it again.)

Group Acting

This can be done in several ways. One method is to have the people at a banquet, meeting, in an auditorium, etc., to sit so that each person is facing one another, numbered No. 1 and No. 2. The leader calls for No. 1 to act, and then No. 2, then vice versa.

Another is to have a long line of people, facing another long line. It might be the men and boys versus the women and girls, and you might have judges. In a small group, it might be all the men versus all the women.

The idea is simply to give out words, one at a time, and the group is supposed to "register" that emotion. You could add "Hollywood style," or "in the style of the 1920 movies" in a group who are old enough to remember (or who have seen them on television).

Some sample words are:

Love	Jealousy	Surprise (pleasant)
Envy	Embarrassment	Surprise (unpleasant)
Chagrin	Hate	
Fear	Joy	

You Have Eleven Fingers!

This is a tricky trick. It may actually take people a little while to get onto it. Tell them that you can prove that you have eleven fingers.

"You say I have ten?" you say. "All right, we'll see."

Then you start counting, beginning with the thumb.

"You say ten, so I'll start there and go backwards." Then you count, "Ten, nine, eight, seven, six" which of course is the count for the fingers of one hand. Then say, "All right, there were six, and I have five fingers on this hand, so that makes a total of eleven!"

They may want to go through it again. Finally someone discovers that you have tricked them a little.

Doodles

This could be either a pencil-and-paper or a blackboard stunt. One can go to the board and draw some kind of crazy figure, with a few straight lines and curves (like a question mark, or similar to the letters, R, M, or Y, or just about anything.) Then the group is asked to look at it and see who has an idea for finishing this incomplete line drawing into a more finished figure.

As soon as someone from the audience sees what he could do, he comes forward, takes the chalk, and draws the completed figure.

Mimeograph some doodles in advance. Then let people finish them and show them to their neighbors.

Flip the Cork

This is a baffling stunt to do while people are just standing around.

Put a cork on top of a "coke" bottle, and place it on the corner of a table so that people can walk by it. Each person who will give it a try must put his arm straight ahead of him, walk up to the bottle, flip the cork (or try to) with the forefinger, and continue walking at the same speed past the bottle.

It is amazingly hard to do, for your hand has a tendency to rise a little just before you get to the bottle.

Hat Rhythm

To be prepared for fun, collect a bunch of old hats—men's and women's. You can put on many stunts with them, including this one.

Have several people stand up in front of the group, each one wearing an outlandish hat. He puts his hand on his neighbor's hat to his left. As the music plays, or as the leader or "caller" counts out the rhythm, he must, on count one, get hold of the hat, and on count two, put it on his own head. The count, or music, gets faster and faster.

It can be used for an elimination contest if you like. Also, if you should have a hat party, where every person must bring a hat, this could be played in one large circle or several smaller ones.[4]

Table Scavenger Hunt[5]

This is an excellent table stunt for a mixed group, or for a women's group.

The leader divides the group by tables, or by ends of tables. (At a banquet once we found it useful to divide up so that groups were either between the candles, or between the candle and the end of the table.)

Then he calls for certain objects, and the first group holding up that object gets a point. Such things as driver's licenses, two-dollar bills, pictures of men or women, coins of a certain date, are included.

This is a clever variation of "Indoor Scavenger Hunt" played similarly, but with the larger group divided into several smaller

[4] (See page 123 for an interesting variation of this hat stunt.) Thanks to Harry Edgren, George Williams College, Chicago, Ill., for suggesting this.
[5] Shared by Reynold Carlson, University of Indiana, Bloomington, Ind.

groups, and each one with a runner who brings the asked-for object to the leader, who stands in the center of the room.

See the Weenie

Most people are fascinated by this simple little-finger stunt. You can use it anywhere—from a situation in which a group of friends are clustered around after a meal, to one in a large auditorium where hundreds or thousands of people are seated. Each person checks himself.

What you do is simply to raise your hands up to eye level, put the tips of your forefingers only nearly together, and focus on a distant object. An illusion of a frankfurter, floating in space, is created. The closer the fingers are to the eyes, the larger the weenie. To see it the eyes have to be focused on a distant object, not on the fingers themselves.

Salome[6]

She's a lively thing—and if you work her right, she will kick right up in the air when you are ready for her. You should read (or say) the poem:

> Salome was a dancer, a pretty little thing,
>   She danced before royalty, she danced before the King,
> One day the King held court; all the courtiers were there!
>   Salome was to dance; her arms and legs were bare.
> "Salome, you can't do such a thing, my dear!"
> "The heck I can't!" Salome said, and kicked the chandelier!

You tie the handkerchief in the middle of one of the sides to provide Salome's head. Then you hold it by the bottom corners of the handkerchief, farthest away from the side that includes the "head," and keep winding by tossing the knotted end toward you and then let it swing over and away. Keep winding this way, around and around, until it is as tight as it will go. Then continue tightening it by pulling on the knot with your teeth each time it has been revolved.

The poem can be said while you are doing this teeth tightening. (Simply give it one revolution and one tightening motion, then another, and another.) Time it so that the tension is especially great as she is ready to "kick." Then you pull hard on the

[6] From Mary Border, Manhattan, Kan.

left side and right "leg" will kick right up into the air, sometimes revolving around a couple of times in doing it.

Sewing Fingers Together

Here's what you do to sew fingers together, one at a time, with
an imaginary needle and thread. You plunge the needle into the
little finger and pull it through laboriously on the other side. The
finger comes toward the direction of the pull. Then you take the
other fingers, one at a time, including thumb.

Then you can plunge the needle through the elbow, and as
you pull, the hand (sewed together) waves at the people.

All kinds of extra acts can be worked in, like threading the
needle in advance. At the end the thread can be removed,
rolled into a ball, tossed through one ear, pulled out the other,
and pulled back and forth through the head!

Bathing Beauties[7]

Here is a stunt suitable for table, living room or almost anywhere. Extend the forefinger and middle finger, and keep the
others back. Place a handkerchief around the two fingers, with a
corner stuck up between the joints. If a knot is tied in the corner,
it looks like a head. The rest is a bathing suit, and the legs (two
fingers) are exposed.

"In the South the bathing beauties walk slowly, like this, because it is warm," you say, and have the fingers "walk" along
your other arm. "In the North they have to go faster" (make
fingers run faster). But in _____ (mention place in-
fested with mosquitoes) they go like *this*. ("Walk along two or
three steps, then one finger reaches over and "scratches" the
other. Repeat two or three times.

Money Has Power

Have someone hold a wooden pencil at both ends and parallel
to the floor. After creasing a dollar bill announce to the group
that you will break the pencil in half with the dollar bill, and
ask them to give you three chances to do so. Have your index
finger in the fold of the bill. In the first two attempts use only

⁷ From Maurice D. Bone, Philadelphia, Pa.

the dollar bill, but on the third, allow your finger to extend and hit the pencil with the finger. The pencil will break if held firmly.

Dark, Isn't It?

This is a gag, usable in many situations, such as with a large group in a small space, or at a party, or at the table.

Tell the audience that it is a test of intelligence and co-ordination and ability to follow directions.

Have each person raise his left hand, then point his left index finger to the right (parallel to the floor); then raise right hand and hold right index finger on a level with the left finger, pointing in the opposite direction; then raise the left hand two inches, and lower right finger two inches. Then ask them to close their eyes. After a moment you remark, "Dark, isn't it?"

Way Down Yonder

Here are two versions[8]:

a. All chant the words in a slow tempo, using the same tone and trailing off at the end.

b. Combine it with a nose-ear game. To the count of one-two, one-two, place hands on knees, then the first time grasp right ear with left hand, nose with right hand; then hands on knees again; clasp nose with left hand, left ear with right hand.

In either case, this is recited:

> Way down yonder not so very far off,
> A jaybird died with the WHOOPing cough!
> He WHOOPED so hard with the WHOOPing cough,
> He WHOOPED his head and his tail right off.

(Note: On the capitalized "whoops," whoop it out in a very high tone, an octave or so above the regular tone.)

Clara Belle the Flea

This is an oldtimer, but always fun.

The performer explains that he has a trained flea named Clara Belle (or whatever you choose to call her). She is a very special flea, for she can jump, turn flips, describe a square in the air, and do other tricks.

He calls for her to jump, and holding the palm of his hand

---

[8] (a) is from Don Clayton and (b) from Jack Fellows.

out, he looks at it as if there were a flea there, follows her progress into the air and back onto his hand. He congratulates her.

Next she does quite an intricate flip into the air, comes back down onto his palm. He lauds her again.

Now she jumps into the air, does a square. The performer watches her, follows her with his eye, commends her as she turns the four corners, and lands back on his palm.

Last he calls for her to jump to the ceiling. He follows her up with his eye, loses her. Starts looking for her. Looks finally in the hair of someone close by, finds what he say is a flea. "Ah, there you are!" he says. "I'm glad to have you back, Clara Belle." Then, taking a closer look, he exclaims:

"But say . . . this is *not* Clara Belle!"

And now we come to longer stunts into which the narrator draws the group for pantomime or other acting.

HORACE

Horace has made the rounds as various animals. Here he is a pet lion. The story should be told "comedian" style—at least in this version (with lisp, etc.):

Did you ever hear about Howiss, my pet lion?

I got Howiss when he wath jest a pup. Jest a little bitty fellow —'bout that size (measure off a very small animal). Fust I raithed him on milk. Then I put him on meat.

Yethir, he was a nice little pet. When he got big, I had to watch him. One day I went away to thchool, and I thaid:

"Howiss, I'm going to thchool. Now, I want you to be a good lion and watch after my fathah, and mothah, and little brothah and little thistah." Howiss looked like he would.

When I came back from thchool, I called for my fathah and he wath there; I called for my mothah and she wath there; I called for my little brothah and he wath there, but I couldn't find my little thistah. So I found Howiss. Howiss had a big thmile on his face.

"Howiss, where's my little thistah?" I thaid. Howiss didn't thay, but I jes' KNEW that he had eaten her up! Well, I felt real bad.

The next day I went to thchool and I thaid, "Howiss, ol' boy, I'm goin' to thchool, and I want you to take care of my family and leave them alone today." Howiss didn't thay anything, but he looked like he would. So I went to thchool, and at night I came home.

I called my fathah, and he wath there; I called my mothah, and she wath there; but my little brothah wath nowhere to be theen. I looked for Howiss, and pretty soon I found him. Howiss had a *big thmile* on his face, and he didn't thay anything. I thaid, "Howiss, where's my little brothah?" But he jeth thet there and looked real pleathed and thmiled and thmiled.

Well thir, I went to thchool the next day, and before I went, I called Howiss and I thaid to him, "Howiss, man to man, thith hath got to thtop. Now, I don't mind too much for you to eat my little brothah, and my little thistah, but I'm attached to my mothah and fathah, and I want you to leave them alone. Do you understand?"

Howiss looked like he did, so I went away. When I came home, I called for my little thistah and she wasn't there, but I knew that; I called for my little brothah and he wasn't there, but I knew that; I called for my mothah and she was nowhere to be found, but my fathah was there all right. So I found Howiss. He had a *great big* thmile on his face this time. I reely laid down the law to him.

"Howiss, I don't like thith at all. Thith ith going too far. I told you to leave my mothah alone." But Howiss jeth thet there and thmiled.

The next day I went to thchool and I called Howiss and I thayth to him, "Howiss, you're my pet lion and I think the world of you, but thith hath got to stop. You're puttin' yourthelf between my family and me. If I come home and find my fathah gone, it's gonna be curtains for you, ol' boy!" Howiss looked like he understood, tho I went away to thchool. When I came home, there wath nobody to be found. I called for my brothah, and my thistah, and my mothah, and my fathah, and they were all mithin'. I called Howiss and he came out wearing a *great, great big thmile,* and he looked awfully pleathed.

Well, I was tho thad that I didn't thay anything to Howiss, but jes' went to thchool the next day. When I came home, there wath my little thistah, and my little brothah, and my mothah, and my fathah, and boy, wath I glad to see 'em! I went around and hugged each one of them. Then I called for Howiss.

Howiss came around with his tail draggin' and a great big frown on his face, and he was lookin' mighty unpleathed about thomething.

Then I athked my mothah and my fathah how they happened to be here again, and they told me.

(Say this punch line very slowly.)

Howiss . . . . . *burped!*

THE THREE BEARS[9]

(Told in whistles and pantomime)

Any age group will actually have fun with this, but, of course, it is especially suitable for younger folk, even college-age groups. You can make up your own story. This is one way.

As you whistle, change the tone to represent the words as much as possible, holding out long on some syllables that call for it.

THE STORY

Once upon a time there were threeeee bears. *(Hold up three fingers.)*

There was the papa bear. *(Motion how tall.)*

And the mama bear. *(Motion medium height.)*

And a little *baby bear. (Use higher whistle tone and motion for small height.)*

Now the three bears *(motion the three again)* started to eat their soup.

The papa bear said, "My soup's too HOT!" *(Lots of emphasis in whistles.)*

The mama bear said, "My soup's too hot!" *(Higher whistle tone.)*

The baby bear said, "My soup's too hot!" *(Very high whistle.)*

So the three bears *(motion the three)* went for a walk in the woods. *(Make walking motion up arm for each bear.)*

---

[9] We first saw E. O. Harbin do this at a recreation workshop. In repeating it to an adult group, we found that they enjoyed it so much that we have been using it frequently.

Now, there was a little girl named Goldilocks. (*Make motion for long hair, curled at the shoulders.*)

She was going for a walk in the woods. (*Represent the walking with fingers on arm.*)

She came to the bears' house and knocked on the door. (*Pantomime the knocking and whistle for each knock, then listen. No answer.*)

She knocked again. (*Whistles and knocking motion.*)

But there was nooooobody at hooome! (*Whistles tell this line.*)

So she turned the knob and walked in. (*Pantomime turning the knob, walk up arm.*) Then she saw the soup. (*Represent the big bowl for father with fingers held in big circle, a medium-sized bowl for mama, and small bowl for baby.*)

She tried the papa's soup. (*Slurp a spoonful from the bowl.*)

"That soup is toooooo hot!" (*Whistle long.*)

She tried the mama's soup. (*Slurp from that bowl.*)

"*That* soup is tooo hot!" (*Whistles indicate it.*)

She tried the baby bear's soup. (*Same action.*)

"That soup is juuuust right!" (*Tell it in whistles. She eats soup, spooning it up and slurping a bit.*)

Then she got sleepy. (*Put head on hands—pillowlike.*)

So she went up the stairs. (*Incline your arm, make walking motions with fingers.*)

She saw three beds. (*Hold up fingers.*)

She tried the papa bear's bed. (*Motion in the air to show how big and long the bed is.*)

"That bed is tooooo *hard!*" (*Indicate it with whistles, pointing at bed.*)

Then she tried the mama bear's bed. (*Indicate its size.*)

"*That* bed is too hard!"

Then she tried the baby bear's bed.

"That bed is juuuusssst right!" (*Whistle approval.*)

So she lay down and went to sleep. (*Snore for her.*)

Now about this time the three bears came back. (*Hold up three fingers, show them walking up your arm.*)

They opened the door and came in. (*Act this out.*)

The papa bear said, "Somebody's been eating my soouuuuuup!" (*Tell it with whistles, and point.*)

The mama bear said, "Somebody's been eating *my* soup!" *(Tell it with whistles, point.)*

The baby bear said, "Somebody's been eating my soup, and ate it aaaallllll up!" *(Whistle indicates cry or whine.)*

Then the three bears went upstairs. *(Hold up three fingers, show them walking upstairs, up your arm.)*

Papa bear said, "Somebody's been sleeping in my bed!" *(Point at his bed, perhaps showing its size as before.)*

Mama bear said, "Somebody's been sleeping in *my* bed. *(Similar action.)*

Baby bear said, "Somebody's been sleeping in my bed, and there she is!" *(Point excitedly.)*

Goldilocks jumped up and ran *(make motions to indicate her curls at shoulders, and show her running)* and opened the door and ran out, and went straight home.

That's all of the story of the three bears. *(Hold up three fingers.)*

RADIO JUMBLE

This is a combination of several radio programs. You might present it by saying that the baby is playing with the pushbuttons on the radio. As you can see, it is a jumble of reducing exercises, cooking recipes, football game, fashion notes, kiddies' story, and what-not. Just listen in:

. . . . Good evening, ladies and gentlemen, this is Hubert Gluck bringing you the latest news in the world of sports. The annual nonconference football game between Stewitt and Dewitt Colleges was played Saturday afternoon to the enjoyment of a large crowd who went wild at the crucial point in the game when Coach Rudabaugh sent in. . . .

. . . . three eggs, a cup of buttermilk, and a pinch of salt. Stir well and pour into a flat greased pan or. . . .

. . . . your new fall hat. This year fashion decrees that women shall wear a large variety of charm bracelets. A most popular design is to make them of. . . .

. . . . old whiskers? If you do, just shave them off with Burples' Better Shaving Cream. Use this cream and you'll be so handsome that all the girls will. . . .

. . . . bend over and touch the floor twenty times. This exercise is superb for general reducing. All right now, pupils, again let's bend over, up, over. . . .

. . . . *(Sing)* the ocean. My bonnie lies over the sea. My bonnie lies over the ocean, oh, bring back my bonnie to. . . .

....McClerken who sailed down the field for a touchdown that tied the game. What a play! What a man! What a perfect....

....ly darling little summer bag that all you girls simply must have. At first glimpse they may remind one of....

....a big bowl of soup. But it was too hot. The second bowl was as hot as the first, but the third was just right. Goldilocks ate and ate, until she could....

....feel the stiff beard with your hand. Does that appear to be very romantic? Our foolproof way to get a girl friend is to....

....breathe deeply three times, and pound on your chest with the fists after inhaling each breath. This enlivens the tissues and makes one feel....

....puffy and full of air. This effect can be had by beating the mixture with a rotary eggbeater for five....

....hundred years. The things our grandmothers wore then are the most popular things today. Already prominent society women are trying to bring back more old-fashioned manners. Their cry is "Bring back....

....(Sing) my bonnie to me, bring back, bring back, oh, bring back my bonnie to me, to me. Bring back, bring back....

....a nice soft chin and a host of compliments. If you use our cream those whiskers will come out with a....

....CRASH! Goldilocks had broken the little chair all to pieces. Then she jumped up and started up the stairs. There she saw three beds. The first bed was covered with a bearskin rug, which was too soft. The second bed was covered with....

....what looked like crawling things from the press box, but it was only the players in hard scrimmage. We are looking forward with expectations of both these teams winning their conference championships this fall. The players are in good condition and the average weight is....

....110 pounds. You, too, can weigh this much if you but follow these simple exercises. Don't take them too hard at first or you will probably have to....

....(Sing) lay on a pillow. Last night as I lay on my bed; Last night as I lay on my pillow, I dreamed that my bonnie was....

....cooking in a hot oven at about 450 degrees Fahrenheit. For an extra treat garnish the dish with cloves or with whole....

....bears? Will Goldilocks get home safely? How will the story end? Keep your radio tuned to this station until tomorrow at this same time for the next episode of this thrilling story. Until then, kiddies, be sweet and don't forget to....

....shave off those whiskers with Burples'. Our motto is....

....stand on your head, and wave your feet in the air. Gym clothes are best for these exercises, but....

....an ostrich feather will do just as well. Take my tip and you girls
will be as fashionable as....
....John McGullicuddy, to whom we are looking for great things this
season. Until later this is Hubert Gluck, signing off and saying....
....(All) Goodbye now!

A similar stunt, "Pushbutton Tuning," is found on page 168.

COLUMBUS DISCOVERS MINNIE WHO-WHO[10]

A narrator reads this story. He has cards numbered, 1 to 25,
with numerals large enough for the entire audience to read.
When it is time for the reading in parentheses, he holds up a
card, and the person in the audience who has been assigned that
line reads in a loud, clear voice.

Some of the song titles were currently popular when this was
written. Since songs drop from popularity, you may want to
substitute another catch word or commercial ad or song for some
of these titles.

THE STORY

Many, many years ago there lived in a far-away land that no
one knew was there, an Indian maiden by the name of Minnie
Who-Who. She had many boy friends who yearned for (1) More
Worlds to Conquer!

But she was only a poor Indian maid and hadn't a way to get
to the other worlds, even if she had known there were any, which
she didn't. She made a fire and, putting on the old pot she said,
(2) "Double, double, toil and trouble; fire burn and cauldron
bubble!"

When her guardian spirit arrived she told her desires, and the
spirit said it would do what it could. Now, far away there was
a land called Italy, and the spirit located Christopher Columbus
and showed him a vision of Minnie Who-Who. Now Chris was a
susceptible young man, and the new face intrigued him, so he
started searching for it. First girl he met, he asked her name
and she said, (3) "Mona Lisa, Mona Lisa," but he didn't like a
girl who stuttered, so he passed by.

Soon he came to Spain. One day he came up to the Queen in
her garden and, thinking to begin politely, he said, (4) "Hi ya,
Babe!"

10 By J. Neal Griffith, Indiana, Pa.

She decided that he was (5) The Answer to a Maiden's Prayer. However, after spending the evening in the castle and looking over the ladies-in-waiting it was (6) Time to Retire.

She said there were no spare bedrooms in the palace when he remarked, (7) "But Baby, it's cold outside!" She was firm, so he left after saying, (8) "Goodnight, Irene, Goodnight!"

Now, of course her name was Isabella but he always had a lot of girls on his mind. That night he thought that if Europe didn't have his dream girl he'd have to go farther. He went to the docks early the next morning and said, (9) "What's up, Doc?" but nothing was up but the tide, for the sailors had been out late.

He asked the sailors when they came back if there was land on the other side of the water, but they said, (10) "That's all there is, there ain't no more!"

Chris wasn't convinced, but he knew it took money to buy boats, so he decided to work on the Queen's sympathy. He decided to charm her with his old egg trick. Drawing up a contract for the outfitting of the ships he introduced himself and soon had her swooning at his charm and tricks. She was amazed when he balanced the egg on his nose. "Won't it fall?" she asked, but he replied, (11) "It's good to the last drop!"

Thinking the paper would give her the secret of the trick, she asked where she should put her mark, and he said, (12) "Put her there, kid!" He was so excited at getting her signature that he dropped the egg, and to the dismay of all (13) It wasn't all it was cracked up to be! Forgetting where she was, the Queen fled, dropping her jewels and crying, (14) "There's something rotten in Denmark!"

Since it was for a good cause, Chris took the jewels and, going to the port, he bought the ships, Nina, Pinta, and Santa Maria, which were more familiarly called (15) "Eenie, Meenie, and Minie." They didn't use the name "Mo" because there wasn't any "Mo."

He went to Lisbon and sailed from the dock marked "Next boat for America." His motley crew sang, (16) "We don't know where we're going, but we're on our way!" After a few days they ran out of lettuce and Cheerios and wanted to turn around, but Chris was firm with the steersman: (17) "Go west, young man, go west!"

Once they mutinied and tried to hang the great explorer, but the noose wouldn't pull tight and he told them he had been careful to (18) "Guard against throat scratch." One night he saw a light, and cried out for all to rejoice with him: (19) "Twinkle, twinkle, little star, how I wonder what you are!" Another time a branch with ripe berries floated by, and he could tell that they had been (20) "Picked at the fleeting moment of perfect flavor."

He told the crew that if they reached land by Columbus Day they could have shore leave, for it was a legal holiday, so they put up (21) Three sheets to the wind, and arrived in the New World on October 12.

There on the shore were some folks like his dream girl, herding cows. One of the cows took a look at the strange ship and galloped merrily up the beach. This amused Chris greatly, and he said, "What a merry cow!" His crew heard him, but thought he said, "What, Americaw?" so they said this must be America, for that's what the boss called it!

Going ashore, they claimed the land in the name of Spain, knowing it wouldn't be long till Hopalong Cassidy would be taking the country over. The chief came down to the shore and said, (22) "If I'd a knowed you was coming, I'd have baked a cake." However, by this time Chris had discovered Minnie Who-Who and was interested in her only, saying, (23) "Let's take an old-fashioned walk." When they came back everything was settled, and she agreed to leave with Chris. They loaded up the ships with Minnie, some Burma Shave signs, frozen custard, and juke boxes, to show the new and unusual products of the land to the folks back home. In Spain the Queen was peeved, but she forgave him.

To end our story, Isabella got famous, the crew got scurvy, America got immigrants, Columbus got Minnie Who-Who, and Minnie Who-Who found out that (24) "All things come to him who waits."

CLANCY TO THE RESCUE

This stunt is one in which a narrator tells the story and helps the people to act it out at the same time. It involves making group noises and going through group motions.

At certain times specific noises and actions are required. These should be rehearsed in advance. In this script the words that are to be acted out by the group are in capital letters.

CLANCY—when his name is mentioned, feel your muscle, like a strong man.

HORSES—everybody makes horse noises by slapping legs, as directed by the storyteller.

YELL—when it is time to yell to the men above, the yell is given "Indian fashion," hand over mouth.

FIRE ENGINE—assign one-third of the group to this noise, which is the same as the noise when STEAM is mentioned—a high-pitched S-s-s-s-s.

CLANGING THE BELL—assign another third of the group to this noise, which explains itself.

HOSE—the other third of the group makes this sound (sh-sh-sh-sh-sh), like water from a hose. This is different from the fire engine or steam sound.

Much of the success of this story depends on the narrator, who should tell it in lively manner. All are seated, including the leader.

THE STORY

Do you really like HORSES? Well, I like HORSES! Yessir, I like to hear them WALK (leader goes through motions, slapping legs slowly) and RUN (slap legs faster) and NEIGH (all neigh).

Well, if you like HORSES, you would have enjoyed living in Murphysboro in 1899 when we had an old-fashioned steam-type FIRE ENGINE, pulled by horses, and driven by the greatest hero anywhere, CLANCY.

Yessir, Clancy was our hero! Every day when there was no fire, he would take the HORSES out for exercise, trotting them gently up and down the streets. If there was a bunch of kids who wanted to see the horses, CLANCY would always STOP (whooooaaa!) and let the kids pet them. (Leader brings horse-walking noise to a stop, of course.)

Sometimes the alarms were in the daytime, but sometimes they were at night. When they were at night one of the men would YELL up to the fellows above (Indian yell) and the men would GET UP (leader does so, group does too) and STRETCH (all stretch) and SLIDE DOWN the pole. (Leader strikes pose of *grasping pole with both hands, wrapping feet around it, and sliding down. Group is to do the same.)* Then they would run to the FIRE ENGINE where the STEAM was up, and away they would go to the fire, clanging to the rescue, with CLANCY driving the HORSES.

One night most of the boys were in bed, and the others were PLAYING CHECKERS. *(Here leader takes group through motions of jumping checkers on a board)* when the alarm rang. Where was the fire? Over at the mayor's big two-story house. His wife and child were trapped.

The yell man gave the YELL. The firemen GOT UP, STRETCHED, SLID DOWN the pole, JUMPED *(everybody jump)* on the FIRE ENGINE, and away they went, steaming and CLANGING THE BELL, the HORSES running as fast as their legs would carry them! Would they be in time?

Quick as a flash they were there. Clancy stopped the HORSES and YELLED, "Keep the steam up, men!" *(Everybody yells this, following the leader.)* Then they started the FIRE HOSE, and began to squirt water on the fire. Clancy strained to see the upstairs window. *(Leader shades eyes, looks up. Group does likewise.)* Finally he could see the mayor's wife up there with the baby in her arms. Flames were everywhere.

Clancy made a megaphone from his hands and yelled, "YOU'LL HAVE TO JUMP!" *(Leader acts this out, and after he has done it, the group responds, with same sentence.)*

The mayor's wife was scared to death. She said, "I'm afraid." *(Group does this, acting out her part)* and clasped her child to her bosom.

"Jump!" *(Act as if yelling up to somebody.)*

"I'm afraid!" *(Act as if yelling down—in falsetto voice.)*

"Come on, jump!"

"I can't get down!"

Once more Clancy showed himself to be a hero.

"I'll throw you a rope and pull you down," he said, and he threw a strong rope up to her *(leader makes motions of doing so, group follows his example)*—and she came down right in the middle of the net.

The boys kept fighting the fire. They put the HOSE on it of course, and kept the STEAM up in the FIRE ENGINE. Before long the fire was out, so they turned off the HOSE *(noise gradually stops)* and all got on the FIRE ENGINE and went clanging back to the fire house, where they finished their checker game.

Yes, to CLANCY and the other fire heroes, it was all in the day's work. The checker players finished their game, and the sleepy firemen went back upstairs and quickly went to sleep *(snore noises)*.

THE BOLD WARRIOR[11]

Told by a narrator, this story requires noise responses from the audience. When the storyteller gives the sign, the group responds properly:

Finger or thumb pointing upward, *Hurrah!*
Both hands starting low, gradually raised higher, *Ah!*
Palm moving forward with a "shushing motion," *Shhhh!*
Hand moving down, *Booh!*

THE STORY

In days of old when knights were bold *(Hurrah!)*
And barons held their sway, *(Ah!)*
A warrior bold with spurs of gold
Sang his merry lay *(Hurrah!)*
"My love is young and fair! *(Ah!)*
My love has golden hair! *(Ah!)*
With eyes so blue and heart so true *(Ah!)*
That none with her compare! *(Hurrah!)*
So what care I tho' death be nigh *(Booh!)*
I'll live for love or die! *(Shhhh!)*
So what care I tho' death be nigh *(Booh!)*
I'll live for love or die!" *(Shhhh!)*

So this brave knight with armor bright *(Ah!)*
Went gaily to the fray! *(Hurrah!)*
He fought the fight, but ere the night
His soul had passed away! *(Shhhh!)*
His soul had passed away! *(Shhhh!)*
Yet ere he died he bravely cried,

[11] From Wilma Mintier, Pittsburgh, Pa.

"I have kept the vow I swore!" *(Hurrah!)*
So what care I tho' death be nigh *(Ah!)*
I've lived for love and died! *(Hurrah!)*

So what care I tho' death be nigh *(Ah!)*
I've lived for love, *(Hurrah!)*
For love! *(Bigger hurrah!)*
For love!! *(Tremendous hurrah!)*
And died. *(Booh!)*

THE LION HUNT

There are several versions of this story. Sometimes an African hunter is the hero, sometimes just an ordinary man. A sort of synthesis is given here, but tell it as you wish. The plan is that one person sits before the group, tells the story, and leads out in the action. The group then follows his or her example. *Use your own words.* The words to be acted are in capital letters below; instructions are in italics.

THE STORY

Once upon a time, in an African village, there was a brave Chief whose name was O-O-O-O-H! *(Say it in a bass tone, beating chest at same time.)* He had a devoted wife whose name was A-A-A-A-H! *(Say hers in high tone, beating chest at same time with both fists.)*

Now it happened that a lion had been stealing the sheep belonging to the people of the village. Somebody had to be chosen to hunt the lion. Who do you think it was? Well, it was O-O-O-O-H!

So O-O-O-O-H got up early on the fateful day. His wife, A-A-A-A-H said, "Be careful, dear!" He said, "All right." Then she OPENED THE DOOR for him *(put hands together, then stretch them wide)* and CLOSED it *(clap hands back together)*.

The villagers were gathered outside the hut, and when their chief came out, there arose a great HUBBUB. *(All female voices chant "Soda-watta-bottle" over and over in very high voice, while males say slowly and rhythmically in low voice, "Rhu-barb, rhu-barb.")* After the people had said fond goodbyes to their chief, they OPENED the gate *(as above for opening door)* and CLOSED it behind him *(same as above)*.

It was a beautiful day. O-o-o-o-h WALKED along *(to represent walking, slap left thigh with left hand, right thigh with right, etc., in slow walking rhythm)*. He looked to the RIGHT of him *(do so)* and looked to the LEFT of him *(do so)* and SNIFFED the spring air *(sniff)*, but there was no lion around.

So he continued to WALK along at ease *(walking motions)*. Before long he came to a COVERED BRIDGE, but didn't stop. *(For covered bridge sound, thump chest with right fist, then left fist, alternately in same rhythm as walking.)* He walked right on, and still no lion.

Soon he came to a fork in the trail. "Which way shall I go?" he asked himself, as he SCRATCHED his head. *(Scratch head.)* "I'll try the LEFT fork," he said. *(Walk slowly, leaning to the left.)* That didn't seem right. So he BACKED up to the fork. *(Walk backwards.)* Then he walked slowly along the RIGHT fork for a few paces. *(Walk, leaning to the right, rather uncertainly.)* That didn't seem right either. So he WALKED BACK to the fork *(do so)* and FLIPPED A COIN *(do so)*, and it said to go to the left.

Before long he came to a wide creek. He STOPPED. *(Stop.)* Oh, boy! LOOK OUT in that creek. *(Point.)* CROCODILES! *(Put base of palms together, snap fingers together several times to imitate crocodile)*. He WALKED BACKWARDS to get a good running start *(do so)* and RAN *(faster motions than walking)* right up to the bank. *(Stop)*. Couldn't make it. So he BACKED UP again *(back up)*. Then, just as fast as he could, he RAN UP to the bank. *(Run up again and stop.)* Couldn't make it! He BACKED UP the third time. "This time, I'm gonna make it if I have to swim," he said. So he RAN UP to the creek, dived in and SWAM *(do it wildly)* to the other side. There he SHOOK HIMSELF OFF *(do so)* and started on to look for the ferocious lion. He looked to the RIGHT of him *(do so)* and to the LEFT of him *(do so)* and SNIFFED the sweet spring air *(do so)* but no lion.

He even CLIMBED A TREE *(do so)* and LOOKED OUT *(do so)* but saw no lion. So he came down. Now he WALKED UP THE SIDE OF A TALL HILL *(walk slower, pant)* and then STEALTHILY THROUGH THE TALL GRASS *(swish hands together for tall grass)* and to the mouth of a cave. He LOOKED

IN CAUTIOUSLY, first to the LEFT of him (no lion) and then to the RIGHT of him. No lion! Then he looked straight ahead. G-R-R-R-R-R-R-R! LION!

O-o-o-o-h started back to the village as fast as he could go—through the tall grass, down the hill, around the tree, across the creek, through the covered bridge. The tribesmen made a terrific HUBBUB when they saw him coming back. Quickly they opened the gate, let him in, closed it, and the lion was running so fast that he hit his neck on the gate and broke it and died—and everybody, little and big, lived happily ever after.

TELEPHONE BOOTH

SCENE: A telephone booth. Girl inside talking, several waiting in line outside to use the phone. They get madder and madder as time goes along.

SARAH (dialing the phone): Hello! Is this Susie Belle? It is? Well, Susie, I just had to call you up! Yes. I heard about it. Isn't that lovely? (Pause) Mrs. Chatter! Well. She's getting a double chin? (Pause) Too much work for one, I guess. (Pause) They are separated? Why did they separate? (Pause) Nobody knows? How terrible! (Pause) How are you and Jack coming along? (Pause) You say he makes you tired? Then why don't you quit running after him? (Pause) All right, I'll be good.

I saw Gloria the other day. (Pause) She told me that you told her the secret I told you not to tell her. (Pause) Yes, I know she shouldn't have told me. Well, don't you tell her that I told you she told me! (Pause) Yes, that woman is a gossip. Whatever she says—goes! (Pause) Did you know that Petunia has a new house? (Pause) You say she is polished? Well, yes, in a way. At least, everything she says casts a reflection on somebody. (Pause)

Can I keep a secret? Sure, Susie, but you know—it's just my luck to tell things to the other girls who *can't* keep a secret. (Pause) Say, have you heard? Evelyn has just married Roger! (Pause) Yes! He was the man she was engaged to! (Pause)

Tom and Julie have just come back from Europe. (Pause) Yes, they had a wonderful time. And Julie said, "If you ever go to Europe, don't miss the trip over, whatever you do."

(Pause) Julie is a good kid. If she had some brains, she'd be a smart gal, if she knew how to use them. *(Pause)*

Well, Susie, these horrid people here are beginning to bother me. Yes, a threatening note just came in the booth. I'll hang up. Goodbye.

(Flounces out for

CURTAIN OR BLACKOUT.)

THE POOR CONDUCTOR[12]

There was once a conductor on a streetcar. He was a good conductor, but he was a poor conductor. It was a poor line that he traveled on, day after day. His salary was 5c out of every 10c fare he collected.

He had a pretty good time running his streetcar, and collecting the fares, and taking a nickel out of each fare. That is, until one day a very beautiful woman got on his car. Oh, she was lovely. Her eyes were like headlights! Her hair was the color of the copper trolley wire! Well, you could just go on, and on, but to make it short—she rang the bell with him.

Day by day she would get on his car, and when he saw her it would send him into a tingle. Finally he got up enough nerve to propose to her.

"I would like to marry you," said he, "but I'm just a poor conductor!"

"That's all right," she said, and married him forthwith.

Now, they were delightfully happy. She was the thrifty type, and wanted a fur coat. He said, "But I have no money. I am just a poor conductor."

She replied, "Never mind. Just save one penny out of every five you take in, and soon you will have enough for my coat!"

He did, and soon he did! So he got her the coat.

When he caught on to how you could save, he saved 2c out of every 5c and bought her a dishwasher. He saved 3c out of every 5c and bought her a beautiful Persian rug. He saved 4c out of every 5c and bought her a television set. Then he saved 5c out of every 5c and bought her a car. But she wasn't completely satisfied.

[12] From Dick Wareham, McPherson, Kansas.

"What we need to buy is a house," she said. And that seemed a very reasonable request. "Only," he said, "I can take only 5c out of each fare."

"You must take 6c," she said. "They probably won't notice it."

Well, he did, and they did!

The boss called him in, and two officers were there. They hustled him away to jail.

Now it seemed that in this land there was a law that anybody that took money from a streetcar company would be electrocuted. Some thought it wasn't right, but the streetcar company always maintained that it was fare.

So on the fateful day, they took him and strapped him in the electric chair. They turned on the juice. Nothing happened.

"Ah, this is strange!" said the chief electrician. "We'll turn off all the lights in prison and see if that will help."

They turned off all the lights in prison, but still nothing happened.

"We'll turn off all the lights in town," he said. So they did. He threw the switch—but nothing happened.

Finally, after a huddle with the warden, they decided that they would have to let him go.

He was just a poor conductor!

I DID IT WITH MY LITTLE HATCHET[13]
(In honor of the birthday of George Washington)

This is an audience participation story. As the reader reads, he holds up, at the proper time, slips numbered from 1 to 12, and a card marked "Chorus" when he wants the lines, "I cannot tell a lie. I did it with my little hatchet." He then passes out slips, numbered, to those in the audience, and when their numbers are called, they read out in a loud, clear voice. For the "Chorus" group, assign six to eight people, or the entire group. Some of these are song titles which gradually get out of date. Current titles may be substituted, of course.

THE STORY

In Seventeen hundred and thirty-two, there was born in a brick house at Wakefield in Virginia, George Washington, the

[13] J. Neal Griffith, Indiana, Pa.

Father of his country. Now he wasn't the Father of his country the day he was born; that came several years later when he was older. In fact, the day he was born, he didn't say a word, just lay in his cradle and bawled, for he knew that he and the other colonists needed a change.

However, he lived through a number of years and grew to be just a normal boy with a runny nose and pockets full of nails, snakes, and bubble gum, or its eighteenth century equivalent. On his fourth birthday his father gave him a little hatchet, never dreaming that (1) "He was a little cut-up." As soon as his father's back was turned, George got himself an idea, so he said to himself, (2) "If I dood it, I get a whipping. I dood it!" and he hunted up his father's prize cherry tree.

Soon Father Washington came round the house (Mother Washington was after him for pulling the wicks out of her candles to tie up his wig) and noticed the tree lying on the ground. (3) "Who done it?" he yelled and started to look for George. Finally he found little George who was (4) "In the doghouse." To his father's question brave little George answered, *(chorus)* "I cannot tell a lie, I did it with my little hatchet." This pleased Pop Washington, for he had always said that (5) "Honesty is the best policy," so he gave George two silver dollars for his honesty and told him he had better clean up the mess and take the cherries in to his mother.

When he went into the house his dear mother said, (6) "If I'd a knowed you was coming I'd have baked a cake," but George said that he would rather have her bake a cherry pie, which she did. When Father came in for supper, he said, (7) "What's cooking?" and Mother showed him the cherry pie. "My," said Father, "what a fine pie, and who made this lovely design on the top crust?" Shyly little George replied *(chorus)*, "I cannot tell a lie, I did it with my little hatchet." Next day some of the boys came to play, and George decided to play a little trick on them. Using the trunk of the cherry tree he cut him out a log canoe and paddled across the Potomac where he laid the one silver dollar on the bank. Then coming back, he showed the boys the other silver dollar and said he could throw it across the river. The boys didn't believe it so he gave the dollar the best heave of which he was capable. Then he said that they should come down to the river to see his new canoe. It was a good canoe, and he modestly said (*chorus*), "I cannot tell a lie, I did it with my little hatchet." They paddled across the river and he told them where to look. When one of them found it he said, (8) "By George!"—and Washington's reputation for strength became as sure as his reputation for honesty.

As he grew up he became a surveyor and a soldier. He led the troops against the French and Indians around the headwaters of the Ohio river. When his superiors commended him on the excellence of the road which had been chopped through the wilderness, he would step up and say, proudly (*chorus*), "I cannot tell a lie, I did it with my little hatchet." Washington loved peace but he wasn't averse to taking a hand if someone picked a fight. Once after a fight with the Indians, someone remarked that they had been most neatly scalped and he had to admit (*chorus*), "I cannot tell a lie, I did it with my little hatchet."

But old King George of England began slapping on more and more taxes, like the Old Harry, until the Colonists had to say, (9) "I can't give you anything but love, Baby." The King added tax after tax, one of them on tea. When the ship bearing the tea came into Boston, the Colonists ran down to the dock and said, (10) "What's up, Doc?" In defiance of the King, Washington and his men dressed as Indians, and, chopping open the boxes, they dumped the tea into the bay. Someone said, "That man from Virginia must have chopped these open," and Washington admitted (*chorus*), "I cannot tell a lie, I did it with my little hatchet." With the boxes they built the Bunker Hill monument, and as he drove the last nail at the top of the shaft, Washington sighed with pride (*chorus*), "I cannot tell a lie, I did it with my little hatchet." However, all the war was not victory, and there was a long cold winter at Valley Forge. The soldiers came down to Washington's Headquarters, a cozy stone house, and said (11) "Baby, it's cold outside!"

Next morning when they awoke around their campfires they noticed that a long row of sturdy log cabins had been built, and said, "Who did this?" Their Commander admitted (*chorus*), "I cannot tell a lie, I did it with my little hatchet." When someone wanted to know who had built the ladder that Paul Revere's friend used to climb the tower of old South Church to hang out his lantern, it was our friend George who said *(chorus)*, "I cannot tell a lie, I did it with my little hatchet." But the war came to a victorious end finally, and during the celebration things became so wild that the Liberty Bell was cracked, and years afterward Washington admitted *(chorus)*, "I cannot tell a lie, I did it with my little hatchet."

After the war Washington was elected the first President of his country, the very nation which he had helped to carve from the wilderness, and in his first inaugural address, he gave credit where credit was due, saying *(chorus)*, "I cannot tell a lie, I did it with my little hatchet."

He was a very home-loving man and found him a cute little girl by the name of Martha. He proposed to her, and she admitted, (12) "I love you, a bushel and a peck." Overlooking the broad Potomac River he built her a huge mansion, Mount Vernon, and when visitors marveled at its great beauty, he would proudly remark *(chorus)*, "I cannot tell a lie, I did it with my little hatchet." As he grew older and covered with honors he decided to build himself and Martha a tomb. Now an ordinary man might have used a pick and shovel, but he was different and always said *(chorus)*, "I cannot tell a lie, I did it with my little hatchet." And so, of Washington, we hold an honored and revered memory all over the world, and thousands come to visit his resting place in that very tomb. But what became of the hatchet, I never found out, and as for this story—

I CANNOT TELL A LIE, I DID IT WITH A LITTLE IMAGINATION!

chapter 4

IMPROMPTU

"QUICKIES"

needing little rehearsal

IMPROMPTU "QUICKIES"

THE skits and stunts in this chapter require little rehearsal and are brief in presentation. They fall roughly into three categories: (a) humorous skits with punch lines (pages 80 to 115), inclusive, (b) stunts that depend on action (pages 116 to 129), and (c) musical stunts (pages 129 to 136).

A. HUMOROUS SKITS WITH PUNCH LINES

Here are found short skits and jokes of the "blackout" variety, "quickies" to be used between acts of plays, at banquets, on the stage as refreshers, or on other impromptu occasions when a filler is needed.

They are so short that they do not require a curtain. However, if you wish to do so, you can get two persons who hold large signs saying "Curtain" to run together or apart as needed, with one hand up in the air, as if they were a curtain. Or, you can do a "blackout" by simply switching off the lights—a quick way to "pull the curtain."

Skits already prepared, in which the dialogue is given, appear first (pages 80 to 105), followed by a collection of jokes or other suggested situations that have skit or stunt possibilities (pages 105 to 115). There is plenty of opportunity in these stunt possibilities for the group to exercise its own imagination and ingenuity.

Efficiency Expert[1]

OFFICE SCENE. The efficiency experts are at work, two of them. Various office people are about. Efficiency experts are nosing into various things around the office. One worker, on way to water fountain, comes up to two girls.

[1] From *Pathfinder*, quoted in *Fun Fare*, published by Reader's Digest Association. Used with permission.

WORKER: Madge, Ellen, look out for those experts. They're here again.

MADGE: Thanks. I'll fix them when they come by.

ELLEN: Nosing into our business.

Experts come right along.

FIRST EXPERT *(to his companion)*: Here are two girls that don't seem very busy. Maybe we'd better look into this.

SECOND EXPERT: By all means.

FIRST *(to Madge)*: Young lady, what do you do here?

MADGE *(tartly)*: I don't do a thing!

The experts look at each other knowingly.

SECOND *(to Ellen)*: And young lady, what do you do here?

ELLEN: I don't do a thing, either.

FIRST EXPERT *(to second, with knowing nod)*: Hmmmmmmmm! Duplication!!

BLACKOUT

Decisions![2]

SCENE: A barn on a farm. Potatoes are lying in four piles, the farm hand sitting in the middle.

HIRED MAN *(picks up a potato and looks at it a long time, wearily places it in a pile)*: Big ones in one pile, little ones in another pile, bad ones in a third pile. *(Continues wearily, one potato at a time, finally collapses.)*

FARMER *(from a distance)*: Zebeniah!

(No answer, of course)

FARMER: Zeb! *(Comes in and sees hired man. Gets a bucket of water and pours it on him. Zeb comes to with a sputter.)*

FARMER: Say, Zeb, you had me worried!

ZEB: Job's jest too much fer me.

FARMER: Well, I don't understand that.

ZEB: Yessir, I'm drawin' my pay an' leavin'.

FARMER: Now, haven't I treated you nice, Zeb?

ZEB: Shore, Mr. Subsoil.

FARMER: I didn't think this chore was so hard. Day before yesterday you chopped wood in half the time it takes most farm hands.

[2] Adapted from "Decisions," p. 10, *Fun Fare*, published by Reader's Digest Association. Used by permission.

ZEB: I'm not bad at choppin' wood.

FARMER: And then yesterday, you toted more sacks of feed than anybody that ever worked for me.

ZEB: Didn't mind that.

FARMER: Well, what's the trouble?

ZEB: I can stand the heavy work, Mr. Subsoil, but when I've got to grade potatoes, it's too much.

FARMER: All you had to do was to put the big ones in one pile, the little ones in another and the bad ones in another.

ZEB: That's jest it, Mr. Subsoil. It's jest decisions, decisions, decisions, all day long, that's a-killin' me!

Toothbrush

SCENE: The drugstore. Druggist, professor, other customers.

DRUGGIST: Good evening, Professor. What can I do for you?

PROF: I would like to purchase a toothbrush, Doctor.

DRUGGIST: Certainly. Step right over here to the display rack.

PROF: My old one is becoming soggy, and I thought it was time for a new one.

DRUGGIST: That's right. Now do you prefer hard or soft bristles?

PROF: I think the hard will be better.

DRUGGIST: Is this one all right?

PROF: That will be fine.

DRUGGIST: Now, what about one for your wife too?

PROF: Oh, no. When I buy a new one, I always give her the old one.

DRUGGIST (*Hand over mouth, surprised. So are other customers.*)

PROF: Oh, I must explain.

DRUGGIST: Well, I don't know exactly what you mean.

PROF: When I buy a new one, I give her my old one. She uses it to clean her shoes!

BLACKOUT

Sixty Dollars a Week

SCENE: Office. Employer and applicant.

EMPLOYER: So you want to work for us?

PROSPECT: Yessir, I saw your ad in the paper.

EMPLOYER: Well, this is fine. You just starting out?

PROSPECT: Yes.

EMPLOYER: Now, this is an excellent job, and there is a fine chance for advancement. It's in our foreign services division.

PROSPECT: Well, I don't care as long as it's good pay.

EMPLOYER: You need a working knowledge of French and Spanish. The pay is $25 a week.

PROSPECT: Gosh, mister, I ain't got no eddication. I want a job in the yards, or something like that!

EMPLOYER: Oh, the yards? Well, in that case, go right out and see the yard boss. He'll start you at $60 a week!

BLACKOUT

Lumbering Along

CHARACTERS: Two workers and the foreman.

PETE: Shore am glad to git this job, Ephram.

EPHRAM: Yeah, if you didn't have to work so hard.

PETE: Yeah, that's right. Look at all these boards we gotta move.

EPH: Let's get movin' 'em.

PETE: OK.

They pantomime moving boards, but don't actually have any.

FOREMAN: Well, boys, how are you getting along?

PETE: Fine.

EPH: Yeah, we're moving these boards over to that lumber pile.

FOREMAN: That's what we need to do. But where are the boards?

PETE *(looking down at his hands and over at Eph's hands)*: Fer gosh sakes, Eph, we fergot the boards!

BLACKOUT

Fire![8]

As the program is going on or song leading is taking place, a character keeps coming through with a glass of clear liquid. (He runs around behind or uses back stairs, so that he is always coming from the same direction with a full glass.)

Finally the leader stops and asks him what he is doing.

"_____ (mentioning the name of some unpopular local place) is on fire!"

"Well, don't you know that one glass of water won't do any good?"

"Water? This is not water—it's kerosene!"

[8] From Roger Burgess, Nashville, Tenn.

What Time Is It?[4]

Two persons enter from one side, one person from the other.

The one says to the others, "Can you tell me what time it is?" and they answer, "Why, sure!" and immediately pull out strings, sticks, rulers, and lay them on the ground in elaborate array.

They sight on the sun, the moon, etc., and finally tell him the time (accurately).

The lone person says, "Thanks. How can you tell?"

"By looking at our watch," is the reply.

Carbolic Acid[5]

Two fellows come front, opposite sides, and meet in the center of the stage or area. Talk about weather, family, etc. One indicates that he must be going.

"Well, so long!"

"*Au revoir!*"

"Wait a minute! What's this *au revoir?*"

"That's goodbye in French."

"It is, huh? Well, carbolic acid!"

"Carbolic acid? Where does that fit in?"

"You say *au revoir* is goodbye in French?"

"Sure."

"Well, carbolic acid is goodbye in anybody's language!"

Hot News!

SCENE: City newspaper desk. City editor talking with cub reporter.

EDITOR: I've been around this game a long time, son, and I want to see you get ahead.

REPORTER: Sure, boss. What do I do?

EDITOR: See that thing that sticks out on the front of your face?

REPORTER: My nose?

EDITOR: Sure. That's the secret. Develop a nose for news. Learn to spot it almost before it happens!

REPORTER: I'll try.

EDITOR: Now go out and get some hot news!

Reporter leaves, comes back soon.

[4] Cubby Whitehead, Bradenton, Fla.
[5] *Ibid.*

REPORTER: Got some hot news, boss! Train wreck last week!

EDITOR: I said *hot* news! That's no good. Go get some hot news.

Reporter leaves. Re-enters.

REPORTER: Boss! Got some really hot news. Boat sank yesterday. Four people drowned!

EDITOR: That's no good. If you don't get some hot news *this time*, you're fired!

Reporter leaves; rushes back in.

REPORTER: Boss! Boss! Hot news this time! Building across the street just blew up!

EDITOR *(skeptically)*: Yeah?

(Noise offstage) BO-O-O-MMM!

The Proof[6]

This is a stunt in which a fellow is made a "victim," but he is actually aware of the stunt.

It is organized by one person, and is supposedly directed at someone who is well-known by the group and popular with them.

The organizer acts as a bus driver or streetcar motorman, and the vehicle is filled with passengers. Every time he makes a stop, some of the customers hold their noses, look at this certain person, and get off.

Soon everybody has left, and the driver goes back to talk to this offensive customer.

DRIVER: Say, you're running all the people off my bus.

PASSENGER: Well, it isn't my fault. They can leave if they want to.

DRIVER: Yes, but they seem to detect a peculiar odor about you. Do you bathe regularly?

PASSENGER: Sure do.

DRIVER: Do you use a deodorant?

PASSENGER: Sure do.

DRIVER: Did you wash your feet today?

PASSENGER: Sure did.

DRIVER: Change your socks?

PASSENGER *(irritated)*: Sure I did. And what's more *(holds up pair of socks, taken from hip pocket)*, I've got my old ones here to prove it!

BLACKOUT

[6] From John Collier, Toledo, Ohio.

It's My Brother

CHARACTERS: The visitor, the nurse in a psychiatrist's office. (A sign, large enough to be read by the audience, might be used to identify the office.)

NURSE *comes into office, dusts, hums, etc.*

CLIENT *enters. He has a piece of stale bread on a string around his neck, a piece of bacon in each ear.*

CLIENT: Good morning. *(Raises hat, discloses fried egg on head.)*

NURSE: Good morning. Did you have an appointment?

CLIENT: No, but I want to see the doctor, bad. I'm so worried!

NURSE: I think I understand. He has a patient right now, but let me make a note. Now, what is your name?

CLIENT: My name is _____. *(Fill in the blank with name of someone who wouldn't be offended by the joshing.)* But . . .

NURSE: But, what?

CLIENT: But I don't need to see him about me. I want to see him about my brother!

I Gotta Cold

Group comes tiptoeing out very cautiously. First one on the line whispers, "That's where I saw the ghost!" and points. (This is passed down the line.) The end man says, "Where?" This is passed in whispers back up to the head. First one says, "About twenty feet away." (This passes down the line.) The one at the foot says, "How big was he?" (This is passed back up the line.) "About ten feet tall." . . . "How long ago?" . . . "Two weeks ago." . . . "Then why are we whispering?" . . . "I gotta cold."

Evesdropping[7]

SCENE: The garden of Eden.

CHARACTERS: Adam, Eve, and a serpent. Eve is up a tree.

Adam and the serpent walk across the stage, talking so softly that Eve cannot hear. She leans out on the limb. Adam and the serpent move farther away, Eve farther out on the limb. Finally Eve falls (be sure that it isn't far enough to hurt her), and Adam looks around, glaring.

SERPENT: What was that?

ADAM *(in some disgust):* Oh, Evesdropping!

[7] From Mr. and Mrs. George Propert, Washington, D. C.

Oshkosh

SCENE: A train.

SUSIE: Mama, I'm glad we're coming to see Aunt Bess.

MAMA: Yes, it is always good to get back to Oshkosh.

JIMMIE: Are we getting pretty close, mama?

MAMA: Yes, pretty close. Now you stay here while I go and powder my nose a little.

CHILDREN: All right, mama. *(She leaves.)*

CONDUCTOR: The next station is *(says Oshkosh but practically sneezes).*

MAMA *(coming back hurriedly):* What did the conductor say, Susie?

SUSIE: Nothing, mama. He just stuck his head in and sneezed.

MAMA: Quick! Get your things. This is Oshkosh!

Lula

SCENE: Mental hospital. A guide is showing a visitor around. There are two cells.

Man in cell is moaning, "Lula," "Lula," in a hopeless, romantic tone.

VISITOR: Who is that?

GUIDE: He's a man who was in love with a beautiful girl once. Her name was Lula. He wanted to marry her.

VISITOR: Lula!

GUIDE: Yes. He keeps calling it all the time. She turned him down, and he lost his mind.

They go on a little farther. Another man is yelling "Lula!" "Lula!"

VISITOR: What is his situation?

GUIDE: Well . . . he's the one that married Lula!

Chivalry Is Not Dead

SCENE: A crowded bus. All seats are taken. Crowd in aisle, including woman.

WOMAN: You know, in the old days it used to be that a man would get up and give a lady a seat.

SECOND WOMAN: Yes, I know. But chivalry is not yet dead.

WOMAN: How do you get it that way?

SECOND WOMAN: I fell down, getting on the bus the other day.

WOMAN: Well?

SECOND WOMAN: And the man behind me didn't step on me—he stepped over me, to get on.

WOMAN: Humph!

Man seated next to her starts to get up.

WOMAN: Never mind, sir, just keep your seat. (*Pushes him down.*) I've been standing long enough, but I can stand some more.

Man looks at her peculiarly, sits there a bit, then starts to get up again.

WOMAN: Just sit back down and enjoy your ride (*pushing him down again*). You must be tireder than I am.

Man begins to look alarmed and tries to get up again.

WOMAN: It's no use. I know you really don't mean to be chivalrous. You just heard me speaking. (*Pushes him down again.*)

MAN (*quietly, but with rage in his voice*): If you'll pardon me, madam, I would like to leave the bus. I was trying to get off two blocks ago.

                                                                BLACKOUT

I'll Bite!

SCENE: A college room. Two roommates talking.

JIM: Say, Bill, I was just wondering the other day. What happened to Pete? He was such a good ball player.

TOM: Yeah, he was. They kicked him outta school.

JIM: No soap! Why?

TOM: Caught him cheating. He was counting his ribs on a biology exam.

JIM: Well, that's too bad. He wanted to go to medical school.

TOM: You know, Jim, I was just thinking the other day, what I'd do if I had a deadly disease.

JIM: What would you do?

TOM: Oh, I don't know. I'd like to write a book or something. You know, leave something behind me, if I could.

JIM: Well, maybe so. I read about a fellow the other day. He had hydrophobia, or thought he had.

TOM: Well, that's not fatal, is it?

JIM: I don't know, but he called for a paper and pencil.

TOM: What for? To write his last will?

JIM: No. He said he wanted it so he could make a list of the people he wanted to bite!

                                                                BLACKOUT

The Wrong Cup

SCENE: An office. A visitor and the boss.

VISITOR (*returning from another room*): I've been looking around your office, here, Jim. Think you've got a nice setup.

JIM: We think so too. Like it a lot.

VISITOR: While I was outside there, I just got me a drink. What is it, well water?

JIM: We have some of the best deep-well water anywhere around these parts.

VISITOR: You've got a cute dog out there, too.

JIM: Isn't he, though? He's a good mascot, and a real watchdog.

VISITOR: Seems friendly enough, though.

JIM: Yeah, he wouldn't really hurt anybody.

VISITOR: But he did make a start toward me a couple of times.

JIM: He did?

VISITOR: Yes. Every time I put the cup to my lips and began to drink, he would start at me and growl.

JIM: Oh, well I know why that was. He didn't like your drinking from his cup!

BLACKOUT

What a Breath!

Two friends are talking.

FIRST FRIEND: You know, I found out something the other day.

SECOND: What's that?

FIRST: Well, I've been studying statistics, you know.

SECOND: Yes, I know.

FIRST: And I have just discovered something that amazed me. Nobody ever told me this before.

SECOND: Well, what is it?

FIRST: It's that every time I breathe, somebody dies.

SECOND: Good heavens, man! That's awful!

FIRST: It certainly is.

SECOND: All I want to know is . . . why don't you use a good mouth wash?

BLACKOUT

Fresh!

CHARACTERS: Trainman, traveling salesman, woman.

SCENE: On the train, which of course can be formed by chairs, placed in rows. The trainman and the salesman are chatting.

TRAINMAN: Yessir, we'll be in Buffalo in three hours.

SALESMAN: I think I'll sit over here by the other window and make out some of my sales reports.

TRAINMAN: Who are you with?

SALESMAN: The Peachy Produce Company. Say, we're stopping.

TRAINMAN: Yes, gotta passenger, too. Good-looking young woman.

Young woman comes in, walks down aisle, selects seat salesman had.

SALESMAN: Pardon me, miss, but. . . ."

GIRL: If you speak to me or annoy me in any way, I'll pull the cord.

SALESMAN: I'm sorry. (*Goes over to his new seat. After a while, he tries to speak again.*)

Girl starts to reach up for the cord.

They do this a couple of times.

SALESMAN (*as train nears a station*): We're stopping now, and I don't care whether you like it or not. I want that torn bag of strawberries you've been sitting on for the last ten miles!

Girl gasps as

CURTAIN FALLS, OR BLACKOUT

I Asked Her First!

SCENE: The courtroom.

CHARACTERS: The judge, the prosecuting attorney, the lawyer, the beautiful blonde witness.

The lawyer has the blonde in the witness chair.

LAWYER: I want you to tell this court . . . where were you on Monday night?

BLONDE: Automobile riding!

LAWYER: And where were you on Tuesday night?

BLONDE: Automobile riding!

LAWYER: Where were you on Wednesday night?

BLONDE: Automobile riding!

LAWYER: And what are you doing tomorrow night?

PROSECUTING ATTORNEY: Your honor, I object!

JUDGE: Why, that seems to be a reasonable question. Why do you object?

PROSECUTING ATTORNEY: Because . . . I asked her first!

BLACKOUT

Pure Water

VISITOR: So you say the water around here is not so good?

NATIVE: Yep. It's mighty poor.

VISITOR: Well, what do you do about it?

NATIVE: State said 'twasn't safe. So we boil it.

VISITOR: Is that all?

NATIVE: Then we filter it.

VISITOR: Yes?

NATIVE: Then we add certain chemicals to it that they told us about.

VISITOR: Yes?

NATIVE: Then we drink something else.

BLACKOUT

Divorce[8]

A person walks through, carrying a coffee pot. He is challenged.

LEADER: Hey, what you got there?

PERSON: Coffee pot.

LEADER: Where you going with that?

PERSON: To court.

LEADER: What are you taking a coffee pot to court for?

PERSON: To get a divorce.

LEADER: To get a divorce? What has a coffee pot to do with divorce?

PERSON: Here are the grounds! *(Leaves.)*

BLACKOUT

Niag'ra Falls

SCENE: Railroad station, small town. The agent is talking to a young girl.

AGENT: Morning, Mary.

MARY: Good morning, Mr. Crossties.

AGENT: What can I do fer ye this mornin', Mary?

MARY: I want to buy a ticket.

AGENT: Whurr're ye goin', Mary?

MARY: To Niag'ra Falls.

AGENT: Niag'ry Falls! Well, sir! I didn't think nobody went there 'cept on their honeymoon.

[8] From M. Leo Rippy, Jr., Columbia, S. C.

MARY: That's why I'm going.

AGENT: Well, Mary. I never knowed ye was married. Who did you marry?

MARY: Jim Culbertson.

AGENT: Well, do tell! My, but I hope you'll be happy.

MARY: I think so. Jim is so wonderful!

AGENT: Now, let's see. You said you wanted one ticket, but I think you made a mistake. You meant two, didn't you?

MARY: No, one is all I want.

AGENT: You mean to say you're going on your honeymoon to Niag'ry Falls alone?

MARY: Well, Jim has already been there, so we're saving money and I'm going by myself!

BLACKOUT

The New York Visitor

SCENE: New York or anywhere.

CHARACTERS: Diogenes and questioner.

QUESTIONER: My friend, you look odd for this city. Are you a figure of the past?

DIOGENES: Yes, I am Diogenes. Through the years I have been on a search.

QUESTIONER: I had to quit school early. Don't believe I've heard of you.

DIOGENES: Well, I started out centuries ago to find a truly honest man.

QUESTIONER: Oh, yes, I've seen pictures of you. Always have a lantern, don't you?

DIOGENES: That's right.

QUESTIONER: Well, I'd just like to know. How are you making out?

DIOGENES: Not bad. I've been throughout your city, and I can at least say this. I've still got my lantern. (Shows it.)

BLACKOUT

Don't Brush Them on Me!

SCENE: The psychiatrist's office.

DOCTOR: Let's see. . . . Last week we were talking about your past.

WRIGHT: Yes, I think we were.

DOCTOR: How much sleep do you get at night?

WRIGHT: Oh, I can't complain. Anywhere from six to nine hours.

DOCTOR: Well, that seems pretty normal. I'm beginning to wonder what we are going to find wrong with you. You seem to be just as sane as I am.

WRIGHT (horrified): But, doctor, it's these crawling bugs. I can't stand them! They're all over me. (Starts brushing wildly.)

DOCTOR (recoiling): Well, for goodness sakes . . . don't brush 'em on me!

BLACKOUT

Kittle for Sale[9]

SCENE: Roadside, with large sign, "Kittle for sale," displayed so that the audience can see it. (You can make a quick sign by using the dauber in a bottle of black shoe polish.) *Tourists drive up, in an automobile made by chairs placed like seats.*

JONES: Here's a place where we can buy a kettle. How do we find out?

JOHNSON: There comes the rancher now. (To rancher) Say, I saw your sign. What kind of kettle do you have for sale?

RANCHER: Ain't got no kettle.

JOHNSON: Oh, it's cattle you have for sale?

RANCHER: Nope. It's a buffalo. Jest couldn't spell it.

BLACKOUT

Cough Syrup

SCENE: A drugstore. The druggist is there, also a customer.

DRUGGIST: Good morning.

CUSTOMER: Morning.

DRUGGIST: What can I do for you this morning?

CUSTOMER: Got cough syrup?

DRUGGIST: Yes, I have several kinds.

CUSTOMER: Cherry?

DRUGGIST: Sure, I have a good stock of cherry cough syrup. Want a bottle?

CUSTOMER: Six bottles.

DRUGGIST: Six bottles! Someone sick over your way?

CUSTOMER: No.

DRUGGIST: Somebody have an awful cough?

[9] From Harold Hipps, Greensboro, N. C.

CUSTOMER: No.

DRUGGIST: Then what are you going to do with six bottles of cough syrup? Who *is* it for?

CUSTOMER: Me! I like it on *pancakes!*

BLACKOUT

Jest Too Tired to Move

The tired family are all draped around the stage. The setting could be mountain or western. All speak very slowly.

Coyote howls offstage.

PA: Ma, what's that noise out there?

MA: Don't know, pa!

PA: Will you see what it is, ma? I'm jest too tired to move!

MA: Willie?

WILLIE: Yes, ma?

MA: What's that noise out there?

WILLIE: Don't know, ma.

MA: Willie, see what it is. I'm jest too tired to move!

WILLIE: Nellie?

NELLIE: What?

WILLIE: What's that out there making that noise?

NELLIE: Don't know.

WILLIE: See what it is. I'm jest too tired to move!

NELLIE: Henry!

HENRY: What?

NELLIE: What's that noise out there?

HENRY: Don't know.

NELLIE: Go see what it is, Henry. I'm jest too tired to move.

Henry wearily gets up, goes out, comes back, lies down.

PA: Henry, what was it?

HENRY: Jest a coyote.

PA: What was he doin'?

HENRY: Settin' on a cactus. He was jest too tired to move!

BLACKOUT

Big Mystery

SCENE: The street. A newsboy is hawking his papers.

BOY: Extra! Extra! Extra paper!

SMART GUY: All right. If you have an extra one, I'll take it off your hands.

BOY: You will for a nickel.

SAME GUY: Anything new in the paper, then?

BOY: Oh, the same things happening to different people.

GUY: OK, I'll take one.

BOY: Extra! Extra! Read about the great mystery!

People pass by without buying.

BOY: Extra! Great mystery. Fifty victims! Paper, mister?

MAN: Yes, I'll take one. (*Pays boy.*)

BOY: Extra! Great mystery. Fifty-one victims!

MAN (*angrily*): Boy, I don't see anything here about this. Where is it in this paper?

BOY: That's the mystery, mister. You're the fifty-first victim!

BLACKOUT

"Some of Them Are!"[10]

CHARACTERS: Stupid boy, his uncle, and a traveler.

Uncle is working about store as boy enters.

UNCLE: Well, John, you came at the right minute. Do you think you could keep store for me for a while?

BOY: Ah—mebbe.

UNCLE: It won't be hard. If anyone comes in and asks how much these oranges are, you say, "Two for a nickel, four for a dime." Can you do that?

BOY: Ah—two for a nickel, four for a dime.

UNCLE: That's right. Now if they say, "Are they sweet?" you must say, "Some of them are and some of them aren't." Can you do that?

BOY: Some of them are and some of them aren't.

UNCLE: That's right. If they say, "I guess I won't buy any today, you say, "If you don't, somebody else will." Can you say that?

BOY: Ah—if you don't, somebody else will.

UNCLE: That's right. Now do a lot of business while I'm gone and don't take any wooden nickels.

Uncle exits. Boy mumbles a bit until a traveler rushes in.

TRAVELER: Hey, boy, which way do I go to the railroad station?

BOY: Ah—two for a nickel. Four for a dime.

TRAVELER: Say, boy, what's the matter with you? Are the members of your family crazy?

[10] By Ella Gardner and sent in by Bruce Tom, Columbus, Ohio.

BOY: Some of them are and some of them aren't.

TRAVELER: Look here, are you trying to make a monkey out of me? I'll knock your head off!

BOY: If you don't, somebody else will.

Traveler swings at him as

CURTAIN CLOSES

Listen at the Wall[11]

This is a stunt in which one person goes along a wall just listening, listening.

Others come along and see him.

"What are you hearing?" they say.

"Listen!" he says, dramatically. So they do. But they don't seem to hear anything.

"Don't hear anything," somebody tells him.

"Listen!" he says, even more dramatically. So they listen some more.

"I don't hear anything," somebody says in a disgusted voice.

"You know," says the starter, with a far-away look in his eye, "it's been that way *all day!*"

The Berrys

CHARACTERS: Mrs. Berry, her daughter, her friend, a sentry.

MRS. BERRY: Well, Sarah, it's been so good to visit with you. We'll have to be going now.

SARAH: Well, I'm glad to welcome you and Lieutenant Berry to the post. I hope you'll like it here.

MRS. BERRY *(calling to her daughter):* Come, Susie, and let's be walking on. We'll have to get to the side gate before it closes.

They walk over to the other side of the stage or room.

SENTRY: I'm sorry, but we don't allow anyone through this gate.

MRS. BERRY: It's awfully inconvenient to go to one of the others.

SENTRY: Well, I've got my orders. You've got to go to the main gate.

MRS. BERRY: But I don't believe you know who we are. We're the Berrys.

SENTRY: Lady, I don't care if you're the cat's meeyowl! You can't get through this gate!

BLACKOUT

[11] From Harold Hipps, Greensboro, N. C.

A Day in Dog Patch[12]

(This is a group of jokes combined in dialogue, using the characters of the "Little Abner" comic strip. Your four participants may dress as the characters do in the comic strip, or, sketch the bodies of the four characters and let the heads of the characters come above the cardboard on which they are drawn. If you don't have time to memorize, just write the dialogue in large letters, put it on the table in front of your sketch, and read from it.)

PA: Ma, I think our boy Abner ought to go to school. I took him to a teacher yesterday and asked what they could larn him. He said their CURRYCULUM was GEEORGRAPHY, ARITH-MERTICK and TRIGGERNOMITERRY.

MA: That's what he'd better take, fix him up with Triggernomi-terry, cause he's the wust shot in the whole dern fambly. And speakin' of shootin', we got an awful passel of rats here in Dog Patch. Lil Abner, you'd better go down to the store and get us some rat biscuit.

LIL ABNER: Aw, Ma, if they don't like what we eat, let 'em starve. Ennyhow you caint beat that thar rabbit stew we had today. Honist, Daisy Mae, it was sure swell, and if it is your fondest dream to remain my happy and lovin' married wife, you'd best learn how to make it.

DAISY MAE: Tell me, Mammy Yocum, how does you make that DEE-lishous rabbit stew? I've got to know or I'm a daid duck.

MA: Well, you make it out of horse meat and rabbit meat, half and half, one horse and one rabbit. Ole Man Mose et some but he thinks it made him sick. Shucks! He only thinks he's sick.

PA: Now Ma, I wouldn't say that. I jest came past his cave and now he jest lies quiet and still there. Maybe he thinks he's daid.

ABNER: Sometimes I hanker to leave Dog Patch and go off to the other side of the mountings and see some of them lovely PANORAMAS they got in other places.

DAISY MAE: Jest let me catch you making eyes at one of them furrin women and you'll wish you was back in Dog Patch. I got a yen fer one of yer kisses right now, Lil Abner. Jest one more kiss.

[12] J. Neal Griffith, Indiana, Pa.

ABNER: On an empty stomach?

DAISY MAE: Course not, right where the last one was. Pa, the neighbors say you got to quit throwing Ma out of the winder. Think how dangerous it might be fer annyone that was passin by.

PA: Well, I treat yer Ma pretty good. Ain't I always buying purty things fer her? Tother day I went into Jake Tolliver's store and asked fer a corset fer her. "What bust?" sez the clerk. "Nothin," sez I, "The old one jest wore out."

DAISY MAE: Lil Abner, all my life I been saving my kisses fer you.

LIL ABNER: Then prepare to lose yer life's savin's. Pa, what do you do when yer in doubt about kissing a gal?

PA: I mostly give her the benefit of the doubt. But keep yer eye on Daisy Mae. Tother day in town they had a sign at the movies, "Service Men 25c." Well, she walked up and asked the ticket seller, "How many can I get fer a dollar and a bucket of elderberries?" Ma, I ain't been feelin so chipper lately. I think come Sunday I'll ask Parson _____ at meeting, to pray fer my floatin' kidneys.

MA: I don't think he'll do it.

PA: Course he will. Last Sunday he prayed for the loose livers, didn't he?

BLACKOUT

The Lying Hunter

CHARACTERS: He and She.

HE: Why, Doris, I'm glad to see you.

SHE: Glad to see you, Moffat. How are you?

HE: Fine! How do you find yourself these cold mornings?

SHE: I throw back the covers and there I am!

HE: Hasn't it been beastly weather lately?

SHE: What do you mean?

HE: Well, it's been raining cats and dogs, you know.

SHE: Say, you know Art?

HE: Art who?

SHE: Artesian.

HE: Artesian? Why, I know him *well*.

SHE: I saw him the other day. He has a new cedar chest, he says.

HE: Is that so? Last time he only had a wooden leg. He's got a good sense of humor.

SHE: How's that?

HE: Why, the other day he split the leg accidentally. Do you think he complained? No, he simply said, "Hi, ho, sliver!" and fixed it.

SHE: My uncle complained the other day about his wooden leg and how it pained him.

HE: Was it too tight?

SHE: No, he was hit over the head with it. Did you know that a lion got out of the circus yesterday?

HE: Yes, I heard about that. Boy, but that was funny!

SHE: Funny? I don't see how it's funny.

HE: Well, he had everybody he met in stitches! I came face to face with a lion once.

SHE (admiringly): You did?

HE: I certainly did. To make matters worse, I was alone and didn't have the sign of a weapon. . . .

SHE: What did you do?

HE: Well, I had heard of hypnotism, so I started looking straight into his eyeballs, but he kept crawling up on me.

SHE: My, how terrible!

HE: Then I thought of plunging my arm down his throat and grabbing him by the tail and turning him inside out, but I decided that would be too dangerous.

SHE: Yes, it would!

HE: He kept creeping up on me, so I had to think fast. . . .

SHE (excited): Tell me, how did you get away?

HE: Well, I just left him and passed on to the other cages!

BLACKOUT

Carrot Topped

SCENE I: A restaurant. There are several tables with chairs around them, and possibly a counter, and anything else that could be set up to make it look realistic. Joe is the owner.

TIME: Today.

JOE: Hi, there, Pete. What can I do for you?

PETE: Just gimme a coke.

JOE: Comin' up. (Gives him the coke.) Say, Pete!

PETE: Yeah?

JOE: You've known me for a long time, haven't you?

PETE: Sure. Why?

JOE: I think I'm going nuts . . . or somebody else is!

PETE: How's that?

JOE: Every day a guy comes in this place to get a cup of coffee and he has carrots sticking out of each of his ears.

PETE: You don't say?

JOE: Positively. Just about this time of day. There he is now.

Strange(r) enters. Has carrots sticking out of his ears.

STRANGE(R): Gimme a cuppa coffee! *(Sits at table by himself.)*

JOE: Sure. *(Gets it for him. Says to Pete in stage whisper)* Didn't I tell you?

PETE *(also whispering):* As I live and breathe. Did you ever ask him about them?

JOE *(whispering):* Never had the nerve . . . at least so far.

PETE *(whispering):* You say he comes in this way every day?

JOE: Every day.

PETE: I'll be here tomorrow, and we'll ask him.

JOE: OK!

SCENE II: Same as Scene I.

TIME: Tomorrow.

PETE: Well, I can't wait for that guy to come in today.

JOE: He'll be here, all right. Then we'll just ask him.

PETE: There he comes now!

Strange(r) comes in again, but this time he has bananas stuck out of his ears, fastened by wire frame behind or by strings.

STRANGE(R): Gimme a cuppa coffee!

JOE: Sure.

PETE *(whispering):* Ask him.

JOE *(whispering back):* OK. *(Aloud)* Say, sir.

STRANGE(R) *(a wild look in his eye):* Yes?

JOE: We are just wondering about something.

STRANGE(R): Yeeesssss?

JOE: Yes. Every day you've been coming in here with carrots in your ears.

STRANGE(R): Yessssss?

JOE: Today you come in with bananas. Frankly, we just can't

figure it out. Will you tell us why you have bananas in your ears?

STRANGE(R): That's easy! I didn't have any carrots!

Joe and Pete look at each other just before . . .

BLACKOUT

Down on the Farm

SCENE: A farm.

CHARACTERS: Two tourists, Mr. and Mrs. Nosey, and a farmer.

MRS. NOSEY: Well, Mr. Farmer, I'm so glad to get out to the country. I just love the air.

MR. NOSEY: In Chicago we can't keep dogs. You got any?

FARMER: You see that one over there? Genuine bloodhound!

MRS. NOSEY: Is that a bloodhound? It doesn't look like one to me.

FARMER: Here, Rover. Come over here and bleed for the lady.

MRS. NOSEY: Why don't you chain your dog?

FARMER: I would if he was a *watch* dog.

MR. NOSEY: By the way, what do you do with all your corn?

FARMER: Well, we eat what we can, and what we can't, we *can!*

MRS. N. *(to her husband):* How's that?

MR. N.: He said, they ate what they could, and what they couldn't, they could.

MRS. N.: Is hay a good crop?

FARMER: One of the best. Been makin' a heap, this year.

MR. N.: What's the hardest thing to learn about farming?

FARMER: How to get up at 5 A.M. My boy couldn't take it. Went to the city.

MRS. N.: What does he do there?

FARMER: He's bootblackin'.

MRS. N.: Well, what do you think of that?

FARMER: Oh, I guess it's all right. This way, I *make hay* while the *son shines!*

BLACKOUT

The Fountain of Youth

SCENE: Doctor's office where they will restore as much of your youth as you want.

PATIENT: Doctor, I want to get back some of my youth.

DOCTOR: Very good, madam. How much do you want back?

PATIENT: Oh, I want to take off about ten years of my life.

DOCTOR: Here, drink this and go into the next room and lie down five minutes. When you come out, your ten years will be gone.

PATIENT: Very well, doctor. (*Drinks medicine, leaves.*)

SECOND PATIENT (*entering*): Doctor, is this where you get your youth back? (*She is a young girl.*)

DOCTOR: Yes, it is.

PATIENT: Well, my youth has left me, and I want to get him back.

DOCTOR: Well, my dear, I don't have the answer here, but if you'll go down to the perfume counter at Gracey's, they may be able to help you.

THIRD PATIENT (*an old man*): Doctor, I want to get back my youth.

DOCTOR: We aim to please, sir.

PATIENT: I'd like to go back to my happy boyhood days.

DOCTOR: That can be done. We'll have to use some powerful stuff.

PATIENT: That's all right with me, doc. Anything to be a boy again.

DOCTOR (*mixing up a drink of stuff*): Here, drink this, and lie down, in the next room.

Patient drinks, lies down. Starts crying, offstage.

DOCTOR: Be patient, sir. It will hurt a little, but soon the pain goes.

Patient cries some more.

DOCTOR: Take your time. It won't be long now before we have the results.

PATIENT (*coming out in a little boy's costume, which he has had on under his other clothes*): I'm not crying because of pain . . . I'm afraid I'll be late for school!

BLACKOUT

How to Live Long

SCENE: Uncle Jim's 100th birthday celebration.

UNCLE JIM: Well, I'm shore enjoying this here celebration.

DOROTHY: We wanted you to, Uncle Jim. Did you know that some reporters are going to be here soon?

UNCLE JIM: No! You mean, from the papers?

SAM: Sure, Uncle Jim. They all want to know how you live to be 100. It isn't everybody who can do that, you know.

UNCLE JIM: Aw, 'tweren't nothin'.

DOROTHY: Here's the reporter now.

REPORTER: Howdy, Uncle Jim. I'm from the Chronicle. Just want to ask you a few questions.

UNCLE JIM: All right, son. Fire away.

REPORTER: They say that today is your 100th birthday.

UNCLE JIM: That's right.

REPORTER: How do you feel?

UNCLE JIM: Fit as a fiddle. Never felt better in my life.

REPORTER: Well, you've lived longer than your Uncle Lee, haven't you?

UNCLE JIM: Yes, son. He passed away at 80.

REPORTER: What do you think gave you this long life?

UNCLE JIM: Well, son, I never smoked, never drank, never over-ate, and always got up by 6 o'clock in the mornin'.

REPORTER: That certainly is interesting. You know, that's just what your Uncle Lee did, too. I was reading about it in an old Chronicle.

UNCLE JIM: Yes, he felt about the same as I did.

REPORTER: Then how do you figure it that he died at 80?

UNCLE JIM: That's easy. He jest didn't keep it up long enough!

BLACKOUT

The Ventriloquist[18]

CHARACTERS: The boy, the girl, his mother.

SCENE: The living room of an American home. Because the main property is an old album, or other large book, this stunt may be made as long as wished since its conversation may be typed and placed between the pages of the book. This skit offers a good chance for take-offs on local celebrities. This type of stunt makes for easy production, since memorizing is at a minimum.

THE BOY (*entering with his girl friend*): Hi, Mother, I want you to meet the woman in my life, Spectatia Goo. Spectatia, this is Mother. She's a gem, the mother of the finest boy a—What I mean is—the finest mother a boy ever had.

MOTHER: I'm very happy to meet you, my dear. Archibald has told me so many nice things of you. We all hope to get to know you better.

[18] J. Neal Griffith, Indiana, Pa.

SPECTATIA: Gee, thanks. (*Sits nervously on edge of chair.*)

ARCHIBALD (*after pause*): Wasn't it a nice day, Mother?

MOTHER: Yes, it was a nice day. Don't you think so, Miss Goo?

SPECTATIA: Yes, it was very nice.

ARCHIBALD: As Spectatia says, Mother, it sure was a nice day.

MOTHER (*after another pause*): Archibald, don't you think it would be nice to show Miss Goo our family album?

ARCHIBALD: Yes, that would be exciting. Would you like to see our family album, Spectatia?

SPECTATIA: Goodness, yes, that would be exciting.

ARCHIBALD: I'll just sit close to you so you can see it well. Now this is a picture of Mother when she was just a young girl. She isn't leaning against a horse; that's her bustle.

SPECTATIA: Oh, that's cute. Archibald told me you had a good background. And who is that?

ARCHIBALD: That's Uncle Ebenezer. He was in the Civil War but he could never remember which side he was on, so he just ran whenever someone started shooting.

SPECTATIA: And is that your own haystack he is standing before?

ARCHIBALD: Gracious no. He just needed a haircut. Now this picture was of Aunt Jessie, the one who had the five husbands. She always used the insurance from one to bait the trap for the next one.

SPECTATIA: But Archibald, aren't there any pictures of you?

ARCHIBALD: Yes! Now here is one that you'll like. (*Aside to Mother*) I'll show her this one of Daddy with me on his knee. Now, Spectatia, what do you think of this one?

SPECTATIA: Oh, Archibald, I'm disappointed, I thought it would be a picture of you. But just *who* is this ventriloquist with the awful dummy on his knee?

BLACKOUT

The First Date[14]

SCENE: A home. Mother, father, Dot, little brother.

SCENE I

DOT: I wonder what could be keeping Don?

FATHER: What's his last name?

---

[14] Suggested by Betty Pembridge, Endicott, N. Y.

DOT: I don't know, daddy. I met him at school and he asked me to go to the movies with him.

MOTHER: Dot, I think you're too young. I never went out when I was 13.

DOT: Yes, mother, but things are different these days. *(Doorbell rings.)* There he is, now.

Don comes in.

LITTLE BROTHER: You're not as good-lookin' as Dot said you were.

DOT: Jimmie! Come in, Don.

DON: We've got to hurry. The show is about to start.

FATHER: What is the show, Don?

DON: Frankenstein. It's almost six o'clock, time to start.

BOTH PARENTS: Have a good time. Be careful.

SCENE II

The kids come back from the show.

DOT: We had a wonderful time, mother. We went dutch on everything.

DON: I certainly did like Frankenstein. It's better than a murder mystery.

SCENE III

Two hours later. The kids are still talking.

Father parades through the living room with a box of corn flakes in his hand. Dot doesn't like it. Don leaves.

SCENE IV

Next Day

DOT: Daddy, why did you come through the living room with corn flakes last night?

FATHER: Just to let him know it was almost time for breakfast . . . time to go home!

BLACKOUT

Sixty Jokes for Stunts

The following jokes may give you ideas for stunts and may suggest the kind of material that can be collected and saved for "just that certain situation." Like much of the other material in this book, the jokes may be used by a single group to prepare a skit for almost any kind of audience. Or, if the guests at a social affair are participating actively, they may be subdivided into small groups, each of which is given a joke to act out.

1. PATIENT: Doctor, thank you so much. My pain is gone. What was my trouble? Rheumatism?

DOCTOR: No, your suspenders were twisted.

2. An old lady asks the ticket agent for detailed information about a trip to Kansas City, and then to Osowatomie. He digs it out for her laboriously. In a minute she is back at the window again for the same information.

"I just gave it to you a minute ago!" he says.

"Yes, but that was for me. This is for my sister over there. She wants to go too!"

3. PHOTOGRAPHER: Now, watch the birdie and smile real big!

MODERN KID: Aw, cut that "birdie" stuff. Check your light meter, and set the lens and shoot it!

(In taking a situation like this one, you need to see the many possibilities preceding the punch line. In this one, the fond mama could be bringing her child to get his picture taken. He is one of those modern "smart kids" who have lots of technical knowledge. Perhaps the photographer asks him what is the title of the book he is carrying, and the boy gives a long technical name. The photographer spends a lot of time adjusting his camera, to the disgust of the boy. Finally, the photographer is ready, and with an artificial smile, speaks to the boy, asking him to look at the birdie—and then comes the punch line.)

4. Several women appear in court, each accusing the other of the trouble in the flat where they lived. The judge, with Solomon-like wisdom, called for testimony. "I'll hear the oldest first," he said.

(The case was closed!)

5. Adam and Eve were walking through the Garden of Eden when they saw an animal. "That's a horse," said Eve.

"Why do you say that?" asked Adam.

"Because it looks more like a horse than anything else we've seen."

6. During the magic show, the magician says to his little assistant, called up from the audience:

"You never saw me before, did you, sonny?"

"No, daddy."

7. Young man appears at door, apparently making a survey. Asks the woman what kind of roach powder she uses. (None!) Does she like the new DDT? (Never has to use it.)

"Good!" says he, "May I see the room you have advertised for rent?"

8. The pilot put his plane down on a tiny island. He was the first white man who had ever touched that shore.

The folks were in color—red, white, and green, like a barber pole.

"He surely is a funny color, isn't he?" one of them remarks to the other.

9. He is sitting on the bank with a fishing pole in hand, a No Fishing sign nearby. Game warden appears.

"You the game warden?"

"Yep!"

"Jist teaching him how to swim," he says, pointing to minnow on the end of the pole.

10. "Look here, Sarah," says the housewife. "I can just write my name in the dust on this table."

"Land sakes," says the domestic help. "I think that's fine. There's nothin' like education!"

11. The dinner party is interrupted by a crash in the kitchen. (Madame has just been bragging about the new maid, but explaining that she has the fault of breaking dishes.)

"More dishes, Ada?" she calls to the kitchen.

"No, ma'am—less," is the reply.

12. The scene opens with the sound of clanking, obviously the garbage man collecting his material. (My business is picking up, he sometimes says.) Lady of the house appears in an old wrapper, hair flying, looking a wreck. Calls down to garbage man:

"Am I too late for the garbage?"

"No, ma'am," comes the cheery reply. "Jump right in!"

13. Symphony orchestras have pulled this musical stunt. A player comes in importantly, bringing some such instrument as

a triangle. He carefully takes off coat, hat, perhaps case around instrument, etc. Sits meticulously. Counts the beats, very carefully. At the proper moment he hits one sharp note on his instrument. Then with beaming smile, get up, puts on coat and hat, takes instrument, leaves. (Orchestra or other musicians continue playing the piece.)

14. He is the laziest man in the county, but keeps turning his rocking chair different ways.

WIFE: Bill, I never seen you so fidgety. What's the matter?

BILL: Jest tryin' to see whether it's easier to rock north and south with the grain, or east and west against it!

15. A kid is practicing at the piano. Someone knocks at the door.

"Is your mother home, little man?" says the visitor.

Kid glares balefully. "What do you think, mister?" he says.

16. Two old friends meet; one is a bachelor, one used to be.

"Glad to be married?" asks the bachelor.

"I married my dream girl. She is as beautiful as the day we were wed. Her complexion is beautiful, and her hands soft and white. She always looks as if she just stepped from a bandbox. Her clothes are always the most attractive, and the latest style!"

"You're glad you married her, then?"

"Yes. But I do get a little bit tired of eating in restaurants!"

17. FARMER (to banker): I'd like to borrow $5.

BANKER: All right. I'll fill out the papers. (Does so.) The interest is 30 cents for a year at 6 per cent.

FARMER: Could I give you some collateral?

BANKER: Certainly.

FARMER: Well, here's an envelope with $20,000 worth of bonds. They wanted $10 at the other bank jest to rent a safety deposit box to keep 'em in.

18. The scene is a deserted island except for one shipwrecked man. One day a boat comes into sight. A sailor tosses a bundle of newspapers to the man and says, "Captain wants you to read these and see if you still want to be rescued!"

19. Boxer *(to his second):* Am I doing him any harm?

Second: No, but keep swinging, kid. The draft might give him a cold!

20. Student: Yes, sir, we modern young men are more advanced than you might think. Do you know that I can tell exactly what another person is thinking?

Professor: In that case, I humbly beg your pardon!

21. Well-known figure gets on train. When conductor comes by, he cannot find ticket.

"That's all right, Dr. Chapel, you'll find it," says the conductor. "And if you can't find it, we can trust you to mail it to us."

"All right?" says the famous one. "No, it's *not* all right. I've got to find my ticket before I know where I'm going!"

(This actually happened to an absent-minded executive!)

22. Peculiar phenomenon. A man awakes to find a tulip growing out of the top of his head. He is advised to go see Ripley (Believe-It-or-Not).

When he arrives and takes off his hat, the receptionist says: "What do you want to see him about, please?"

23. "What would you like to drink?"

"Oh, ginger ale, I guess."

"Pale?"

"Oh, no, a glass will be plenty!"

24. A couple, just married, got among their wedding presents two tickets to a very fine show, with the notation, "Guess who" on the tickets. They went to the play. When they returned, all of their wedding presents were gone, and a note was left also:

"Now you know!"

25. Cannibal king: What was your occupation before we took you?

Reporter: I was a newspaper man.

Cannibal: An editor?

Reporter: No, only a subeditor.

Cannibal: Well, you can look forward now to being an editor-in-chief.

26. It was an ultra-exclusive restaurant, and the customer put a napkin around his neck. All the staff were shocked. One, under instructions, went around to the offender and said diplomatically: "Shave or haircut, sir?"

27. A bachelor eating breakfast in a restaurant found a note on the shell of his egg: "I am a farmer's daughter of 19. If anyone would like to marry, get in touch with Susie Jane Forbush." "Ah, my chance!" said the bachelor. He hastily wrote a letter. After a short time his answer came, "Too late. I am now married and have two children!"

28. CUSTOMER: "Waiter, I want you to know that there's a needle in my soup."

OWNER (who used to be a printer): Typographical error, sir. Should have been noodle!

29. "We think we're so good these days, but think of the old days! Those Spaniards used to go 3,000 miles on a galleon!"

"I really doubt that. You just can't believe everything you hear about them foreign cars and what they'll do!"

30. "How far is it to Oyster Bay?"

"Well, the way you're headed, it's 24,995 miles, but if you'll jest turn around, it's about 5 miles."

31. The man went into a very small western hotel, and sat down in the dining room. The waiter brought his water and asked:

"Will you have sausage and eggs?"

"Never eat the stuff."

"Well, in that case," said the waiter, "breakfast is over."

32. He was riding a mule. A passerby said:

"What'll you take for your mule?"

"One hundred dollars."

"I'll give you $10."

He dismounted. "Stranger, you've made yourself a deal. I'm not gonna let $90 stand between you and me on this deal."

33. They are discussing different neighborhood personalities.

"Now, take Mrs. Smithson. There's a woman who suffers for her beliefs," says the shoe salesman.

"How's that?"

"She believes she can wear a No. 5 shoe on a No. 7 foot!"

34. She was very rich, but he was very poor. One night he said so, and she replied that she was worth a million dollars. He said he was not worth anything. He proposed; she refused. He said, "I thought you would."

"Why did you propose?" she asked.

"To see what it's like to lose a million dollars."

35. She refused his proposal. He was dejected. To encourage him she assured him that her refusal would not mean that all girls would refuse him. "Yes, it does!" he said. "If you won't marry me, who will?"

36. He proposed to the college girl.

"Your pecuniary condition compels me to say that I would have to decline a marital arrangement with such a man as you."

"I don't get you," he says.

"That's what I'm telling you," is her reply.

37. Her team was losing the football game. Her boy friend said, as tears streamed down her cheeks, "I'll kiss those tears away!"

He kisses her cheek, but the tears continue. "Will nothing stop them?"

"It's hay fever," says the girl, "but go ahead with the treatment."

38. She tried on shoes. Some were too . . . . . and others too . . . . . She raised an objection to the current pair: "The soles are too thick."

SALESMAN: "If that is your only objection, Madam, then I should like to assure you that your objections will gradually wear away!"

39. WITNESS: I can't answer "yes" or "no." There are some questions that cannot be answered "yes" or "no."

LAWYER: All right, if that's true, you give us one.

WITNESS: Very well, sir. Are you still beating your wife?

40. He had laryngitis, and his friends urged him to go to see the doctor. The doctor's wife answered the doorbell.

"Is the doctor in?" he asks in a hoarse whisper.

"No," replies the wife, "come right on in!"

41. The young lady tries to make conversation with the distinguished old gentleman at a banquet.

"Do you like bananas?" she asks a couple of times. He can't hear very well, and finally replies, "To tell the truth, I prefer the old-fashioned nightshirt!"

42. She fell overboard into the shark-infested waters. All the people crowded around the rail, shouting. The crew rescued her, but before they did, they noticed that the sharks would start for her, get very close and turn away. Someone asked the captain why. "They were man-eating sharks!" said the captain.

43. Quite a number of people mistake the beginner on the links for a very famous golfer. As they stand watching him he takes a healthy swing at the ball, misses. Takes another swing, misses. (Audience begins to get embarrassed for him.) He takes a third swing, misses. (They are really embarrassed for him.) Not he. He looks up and says, "Tough course, isn't it?" and starts swinging again.

44. The boys are out hunting. You hear a big "pow" of a shot. Then a voice. "Bob?" He answers. "Bill?" He answers. "Pete?" He answers. "Sam?" He answers. "Dick?" He answers. They collect together. "Bob, are all the boys there?" "Yes." "All safe?" "Yes!" "Then I've shot a deer!"

45. The three girls were talking about their dates, and agreed to tell the next morning in the boarding house when they came to breakfast how many times they had been kissed the night before by using the word "morning" in their sentences. The first two use it frequently. The third one comes down and says, "Howdy!"

46. Mama returns to question the baby sitter about how she and junior got along.

"Fine, ma'am. He swallowed a bug, but don't worry. I had him swallow some insect powder."

47. The art lovers are visiting the studio of a famous artist, whose work is on canvas. They are O-o-ohing and Ah-h-hing. One lady says, "Here is a true work of art! What form! What soul! What expression! What true, true genius. You must spend much time here!"

"Yes," replies the artist, "that's where I clean off my brushes."

48. He bought a new shirt and found inside a request from a girl to have the picture of the man that bought the shirt. Thrilled, he sent her his picture. Her answer was that she just wanted to see what kind of a fellow would wear a shirt that looked like that!

49. His car was stalled at a traffic light. The lights went to red, to yellow, to green, to yellow, to red, to yellow, to green. Finally a cop comes up and says, "Pardon me, sir, but don't we have any color you like?"

50. Filling station scene. The customer gets ten gallons of gas. "Check your water?" "Yes." After checking, attendant asks about checking oil. "Yes." Then he asks about checking tires. "Yes." "Anything else?" asks the attendant. "Would you mind sticking out your tongue so I can seal this letter?" asks the customer.

51. The cyclone lifted the bed containing farmer and wife and gently set it down in the pasture. Woman cries. Man says not to be scared.

"I'm not scared," she says. "It's the first time we've been out together in twenty years, and I'm so happy!"

52. Two little microbes were swimming around in the blood stream of a horse. One heard that life was easier near the heart. Now they had already lived thirty seconds, and only had a minute to live, but they both asked to be transferred to the territory closer to the heart. They died before they got there!

The moral of this story is, "Don't change streams in the middle of the horse!"

53. A man was sitting in his cabin, when all of a sudden there was a knock on the door.

When he opened the door, he found a fully-armored knight

outside, accompanied by a St. Bernard dog, which he was riding at the time.

Now, it was a beastly night, as you could see, and so he invited the man in, gave him food, and warmed him. Soon the knight prepared to leave. The man opened the door, looked at the dog, and exclaimed,

"You must stay here. I couldn't send a knight out on a dog like this!"

54. Some people lived in a glass house. They had a hobby of collecting old thrones. Anywhere there was a kingdom that went out of business, they would show up and buy the throne, and stow it away in their home.

Now, the people outside could see inside, of course, because the house was glass, and of course they knew all about it.

One vacation time, when these people were gone, some thieves broke in and stole every throne in the house and left not hide nor hair for clues.

Moral: Those who live in glass houses shouldn't stow thrones.

55. Fellow comes in at the rear (perhaps while a meeting is going on, if the person in charge or leading the singing knows about it) shouting, "Woman the lifeboats! Woman the lifeboats!"

He continues in dramatic fashion to yell this out. Soon the leader interrupts him.

"You don't 'woman' the lifeboats. That's silly. You *man* the lifeboats!"

The herald stops and thinks a minute and then says, "You fill your lifeboats, and I'll fill mine!"

He starts away with his cry again, "Woman the lifeboats!"[15]

56. This is a song-leading stunt.[16] While the song is going on, a person comes in to the song leader and says: "Here, —————, hold this a minute," handing him a raw egg. The song leader says, "Sure," and continues leading the song.

Before long another individual comes in, looking vacant, dumb, and bored. He slowly walks around, spoon in hand, then walks

15 From Jack Frey, Texas A & M, College Station, Texas.
16 *Ibid.*

up to the song leader and pops the egg with the spoon, walking out in the same detached manner.

(A punch line is not necessary, but he could lean over and sniff before he leaves and say, "Good egg.")

57. Here's an oldtimer that people have been having fun with for years.

While something else is going on, a person wanders around with a case of soft drink bottles.

Finally the leader, or some other designated individual, says: "What are you doing, running around here with that case?"

"I'm taking my case to court," is the answer, and the person goes off stage.

Later he comes through, carrying a stepladder and his case.

"What are you doing now?"

"Taking my case to a higher court."

58. Another variation is to have someone accused of stealing some bottles of soft drinks. A trial may even be held right there in front of everybody.

The decision of the court is finally made known.

"He may have taken three bottles," says the judge, "but three bottles, as everybody knows, do not make a case."

59. This is another oldtimer from vaudeville days, and perhaps earlier.

A person dressed comedian style comes forward, backing and pulling a long rope. He keeps pulling and pulling until he leaves. Then he runs around behind the stage, catches onto the other end of the rope, and comes in, being pulled by the rope, holding onto it tightly, for a very amusing illusion.

This trick, of course, calls for at least two assistants, and for the possibility of crossing over behind the stage unseen by the audience. The rope needs to be only a little longer than the width of the stage.

60. The chaplain was passing through the prison garment factory.

"Sewing?" he said to a prisoner who was at work.

"No, chaplain," replied the prisoner grimly, "reaping!"[17]

[17] Chaplain Arthur C. DeVries, quoted in *Fun Fare*, published by Reader's Digest Association. Used with permission.

B. STUNTS THAT DEPEND ON ACTION

Then there are stunts that depend on action rather than on funny lines for their appeal. Actually some of them are much like the "blackouts" in the preceding section. Some of them are almost like "party games," and can be used thus. They involve improvising and "acting out" and for that reason have been included here.

Twelve Well-Known Stunts

Although these stunts may not be familiar to you, they will be to many others. It might be well to see how many know about them before you use them. However, they are always funny—sometimes because they *are* so old.

1. THE CAUTIOUS FAMILY. They want to cross the railroad tracks, so they ask the railroad ticket agent if there are any trains north today (no) south (no) east (no) west (no). Then the speaker delivers the punch line, "I guess it's safe for us to cross the tracks."

2. THE OPERATION STUNT. (Described on page 25.) A shadow play in which an operation is conducted, aided by cardboard instruments.

3. THE FAMILY CAR. One person becomes the spare tire, four the wheels (you become a tire by grabbing your ankles) and the family gets into its car (formed by chairs) and away they go. A tire goes flat. Father rolls it into the spare position and rolls the spare into place. The adventures are up to the family.

4. THE LIGHTHOUSE STUNT. The action is performed around a chair, each person running around it several times as if ascending a lighthouse tower. The keeper goes up and lights the light. The villain comes behind him, hits him over head and robs him, runs down stairs. Keeper's daughter comes up, gasps, goes down to get hero. Both come up, gasp, go down again, bring up a cop. All three go down, get the villain, bring him up and confront him with the crime, then take him off to jail. In some versions, the keeper comes to.

5. THE AH! STUNT. The whole stunt is played with different characters saying "AH!" in different tones.

6. CRYING STUNT. When called upon to do a stunt, one group usually comes out with this one. They all are crying. Someone asks why. They say because they do not have a stunt.

7. THE CONSCIENCE STUNT. While the actors are doing their lines, there are two others on the stage in symbolic costumes (robes, etc.) representing good and bad conscience. Frequently one or the other will get the ear of an actor and give him good advice (or bad advice).

8. INSTINCT. A family had two little pet skunks named Out and In. It was hard to tell when In was out and Out was in, etc. One day In became lost. The family looked for him, couldn't find him. Sent Out to look for him; he brought In back immediately. Out explained it: In-stinct, so he could tell where he was!

9. THE BEACH SCENE. A group of people are asked to be trees, lighthouses, etc., for a beach scene, then there are others representing the shore, and others the waves. The narrator tells the story, and ends when the waves beat on the shore.

10. ROMANCE IN SCENES. This was a very simple romance, in three scenes. He seen her. She seen him. They went to the beach and both seen a lot of each other. (Idea might be combined with No. 9.)

11. THE KNIGHTLY REPAIR SHOP. There are several shopkeepers who repair the armor of knights. There are fine opportunities for puns here, such as: sleepless night, bad night, still of the night, fortnight, suit of mail, black night, night fell, long knight, "It'll be a long day before you work on another knight"; come in, good knight . . . good morning, good knight; good day, good knight!

12. TELEPHONE DESCRIPTION. An actor tries to describe over the telephone (he is unseen at first) how to do something, make something. Tells the listener (who is of the audience) to wait a minute. Then he comes in out of breath and says, "Now, maybe I can tell you better!"

Magic Writing

This stunt is also called Chinese Writing, The Magic Cane, Mysterious Writing, and possibly other names. It is a confederate

game in which someone goes out of the room, and when he returns, the performer writes to him the secret word selected by
the group.

The writing may take place on the floor, using a cane or yard-
stick or poker; in an auditorium, it might take place on the wall,
on a blackboard, or against a backdrop on the stage.

If the group picks the word "basket," the writing will take
place in this manner, perhaps. The confederate comes in and the
performer makes mysterious motions with the cane and says, "Be
careful, O friend." The performer taps once on the floor and rubs
stick around wildly a few times, then says, "Stick to it and you'll
have the answer." After some other mysterious motions the performer says, "Keep your mind on this writing," then taps twice
on the floor, and says, "That's all." This completes the word, and
the confederate says immediately, "Basket."

The key is to use the first letter of each sentence to get the
consonants, and to count the taps on the floor for the vowels.
One tap is A, two is E, three is I, four is O, and five is U.

This has been done effectively by having the confederate costumed, sitting like a stoic Buddha. While the crowd looks on, the
performer writes the secret word to him.

Embarrassing Moments

Divide the larger group into several smaller ones, and have
each person tell in some detail of an embarrassing moment
in his life. (This is a good get-acquainted stunt.) Then each
group selects one of them and acts it out for the amusement of
the larger group. They need not tell who told of the embarrass-
ment in the first place, but sometimes it would add enjoyment
to the occasion if all knew *who* was embarrassed, as well as something about the situation.

A la Spike Jones

Divide the larger group into two or more smaller ones, and
give each of them the assignment of taking a song and arranging
it in the novelty manner of Spike Jones, with sudden pauses,
unusual noises, nursery rhymes inserted in the middle, men singing in falsetto voices.

After a lapse of say fifteen minutes, all come back together, and one at a time the groups perform for the others. The fun of performance is enough—prizes are not necessary.

Stocking Faces

Nylon stockings pulled over the head, covering the face, give a very interesting and unusual appearance.

Twist the toe and the rest of the stocking, and let it hang down the back of the person's neck. People garbed in this manner can get the desired fun by just walking through the crowd and greeting people, but they could also recite something like a nursery rhyme, or a humorous poem, or some Shakespeare. What they do is not important because people will have lots of fun just watching, and seeing the strange, distorted features.

Gopher Girls[18]

Some boys, dressed like girls, do a little chorus girl routine. They do it rather well (having practiced a good bit before) and probably get some applause. At the end of the stunt, the announcer or master of ceremonies says:

"I really liked that act."

"You really liked our act," says one of the boys.

"Certainly I did. And I'd like to know why you call yourselves the Gopher Girls."

The boys then take off their wigs (or do something quickly to identify themselves as boys) and say, "'Cause the girls go-for us."

Whereupon some girls come running across the stage after them, and all leave quickly.

The Greek Dance

This is built up by the master of ceremonies or announcer to be thought of as something very special—an authentic dance, used in connection with the famous Greek plays. Then the music begins (something very dignified, like Elgar's "Pomp and Circumstance," played with pomp and circumstance!), and the actors come from opposite sides of the stage, dressed in "togas"

[18] Gopher Girls, The Greek Dance, The Three Wits, and The Gesticulator were suggested by Martha Jane Koestline, Hammond, Ind.

(draped sheets) with bathing suits underneath. Each one is holding a pitcher of water on his shoulder.

To the music they walk slowly and seriously. As they pass each other, they tip their pitchers backward and fill each other's pitchers (*always splashing a little in the other person's face*). As they come and go, they step backstage and exchange their pitchers for others containing confetti (torn-up newspapers would do) or ice. Then they form a line across the front of the stage (or walk through the audience) and at a signal all lower their pitchers and toss contents over the audience.

The screams turn to laughter when the audience realizes that instead of being drenched, they are covered with confetti.

The Three Wits

To do this stunt, have three persons standing up at the front side by side.

The first persons tells a lively story (like one of the Mother Goose tales, or a melodramatic narrative); the second one does the facial expressions only, and the third one makes the gestures only. The first and third persons must be absolutely deadpan to make this effective.

The Gesticulator

Two actors are needed for this stunt, one standing directly behind the other. An oversized raincoat is buttoned around both of them, only the person standing in back uses the sleeves and does the gestures. The person in front tells the story. If the raincoat has a hood to cover the head of the person in back, so much the better.

The hands of the person in back, if larger than natural for the person telling the story (or smaller, for that matter) add to the fun. Sometimes they stroke the storyteller's chin, pat him on the head, wipe his mouth with a handkerchief, etc.

Mixed Props

"Props," you know, are "properties" used in a play or skit Here's an idea that would produce lots of fun.

Divide the larger group into two or more groups, and give each of them several unrelated properties. (If you do not have the objects at hand, tell them that they are to work up a skit, using all the items in the list you hand them.)

Such a list might include things like these: a 1928 newspaper; a wedding cake; a copy of the Boy Scout handbook; a Pepsi-Cola bottle; a toothbrush with red stain on it; a copy of Gray's "Elegy Written in a Country Churchyard."

Give each group time enough to work up a good skit and to refine it somewhat. This may mean twenty minutes to an hour. Then call all groups back to put on their stunts.

How Did You Get Back?[19]

Divide the larger group into several smaller ones, and give each one a slip, noting some famous place in the world, like The Great Wall of China, or Honolulu, Samoa, Sahara Desert, Mount Everest.

Each of the groups is to take some time and devise some unusual and clever way (to be acted out) to return to the spot where they are now. They may use props, and may speak. This idea was used once with the introduction that the group's jet plane had crashed at this destination handed them, and they were to work out a return. Seven groups brought back seven very clever ideas.

Giving[20]

This group stunt is like The Greek Dance. Get three or four people to do the singing. They will need peanuts, candy kisses, chewing gum, and eggs which have had a hole punched in the ends and the egg blown out, leaving only the empty shell (though of course the audience does not know the shell is empty).

The characters sing, to the tune of "Did You Ever See a Lassie?" or any other which will fit:

I. Martha has some peanuts, some peanuts, some peanuts,
    Oh, Martha has some peanuts; she'll give them to you.
        She'll give them for nothing,
        They're free and they're lovely,
    Oh, Martha has some peanuts; she'll give them to you.
Martha throws peanuts in the shell to the audience as they sing.

[19] Used by Ruth Norris, New York, N. Y.
[20] Thanks to Martha Stewart, First Methodist Church, Chattanooga, Tenn.

II. Helen has some kisses, some kisses, some kisses,
Oh, Helen has some kisses; she'll give them to you.
    She'll give them for nothing,
    They're free and they're lovely,
Oh, Helen has some kisses; she'll give them to you.

Helen distributes the candy kisses; the others help her.

III. Oh, John, he has some chewing gum, chewing gum, chew-
ing gum,
John, he has some chewing gum; he'll give it to you.
    He'll give it for nothing,
    It's free and it's chewy,
Oh, John, he has some chewing gum; he'll give it to you.

John tosses chewing gum to different people.

IV. Larry has some rotten eggs, rotten eggs, rotten eggs,
Larry has some rotten eggs; he'll give them to you.
    He'll give them for nothing,
    They're free and they're smelly,
Oh, Larry has some rotten eggs; he'll give them to you!

*They all co-operate, throwing the eggs—shells, that is—at the spec-
tators, who dodge until they find out what they are.*

(If the group is in old clothes, it might be fun to fill some of
the eggs with water.)

Driven Speechless

This stunt could be used anywhere, but with particular fun at
the table. The rule is that, for a specified length of time—3 to 10
minutes—no one may speak a word. All may conduct conversation in pantomime, if they like, or they may eat, but nobody may
speak until the signal is given.

The larger the crowd, the more fun. There probably won't be
complete silence, for somebody will have to laugh.

Yes and No Taboo

During the entire meal no one may use the words "yes" or "no."
Each person is given ten units of some kind—beans, peas, or
something—and each time he commits an offense, the person
catching him may call for a bean. At the end of the event, see
who has the most, and the fewest, beans.

Collection Stunt

Pass a glass around a table, as the music plays. When it stops, you ask the person holding it to drop in a penny. Continue, changing the amount to nickel, dime, quarter, if you like. Then, when people are getting a little skittish about it, let the one who is caught with the glass take out a quarter (or whatever you suggest). Continue until the money is gone.

After the fun, you could have the coins returned to their rightful owners. Sometimes if a collection is needed to complete the expenses of a meeting, the money is kept in the treasury. Do not call for a coin or for an amount of money that would be beyond the ability of persons in the group to pay. It would be better to keep it pennies, nickels, and dimes than to embarrass someone.

Hat Stunt[21]

This stunt is enjoyed by participants as well as the audience.

The only equipment needed is a collection of old hats—men's and women's. The funnier they appear, the better. About eight people take part, alternately boys and girls, and preferably with the taller standing next to the shorter. They stand in a circle, shoulder to shoulder, facing the inside of the circle.

Give these instructions: "When I say 'right,' use your right hand. When I say 'left,' use your left hand. When I count 'one' place your hat on your own head. When I say 'two' place your hat on the head of the person next to you in the direction of the hand used. If you move your hat on the wrong count or with the wrong hand, or in the wrong direction, you are eliminated."

At first go fairly slowly until they get the idea, then increase your speed of calling the numbers, and change hands more often. You can let others take the place of those who were eliminated, particularly in a small group.

Four Animal Cracker Ideas

These little confections can be used in several ways for stunts:

1. Hide them around; let the group try to find them, individually.

[21] Thanks to Maury Ostrander, Minneapolis, Minn. See a somewhat similar stunt on page 54, Hat Rhythm.

2. Hide them. Each group has a captain, and each group has an animal name and noise. When he finds an animal cracker hidden, he must give the noise, and only the captain may come and pick up the cracker.

3. Zoo. Hide the crackers or give them out. The first six to eight finders must arrange themselves in cages (made of chairs, perhaps) and make noises suitable to the animal while the rest of the group take a trip to the zoo and look at them to see what they are.

4. Give animal crackers to the boys or men only. Assign the names of flowers to each of the women or girls. Then do a Mexican stunt: Each girl or woman, one at a time, asks some man if she reminds him of (then gives the name of the flower she was assigned). He replies, "No, you remind me of a _____" (then holds up his animal and calls its name).

The Lie Detector

It is easy to rig up a lie detector, with electric dials, bells, buttons, horns, etc. In college student groups, the engineering crowd have a lot of fun.

The one to be tested sits, and the examiners put a cap on him which may be a real cap, or made from a bathroom plunger, connected to a garden hose, or some other ridiculous device.

He is asked a number of questions, and the machine responds with bells, buzzes, razzberries, or even signs held up by an operator behind the machine. Care ought to be used so as not to ask questions that would be unnecessarily embarrassing.

What's Wrong with This?

In this stunt you act out something that is unlike the human race, or unlike the person who is doing it, and the group tells the answer. Those who are actually going to put on the stunt would have fun thinking up what they are to act out. Here are some sample ideas:

1. A little boy washing carefully behind his ears, his neck.
2. A husband offering his wife some money. She refuses, saying that she has a lot left over from last week.
3. A dog being friendly with a cat.

4. A baseball player, turning to the umpire and saying, "You're right. That was a strike. I just let it go by."

Advertising Slogans

One of the best ways to get the timid to loosen up a bit is to have everybody, in turn, do something such as acting out advertising slogans.

Give the less creative ones the better slogans.

Another way to use this idea, of course, is to ask groups (perhaps tables, if at a meal) to act out a slogan for the others to guess. It really should be done in pantomime.

The Baby Sitters

This actually happened, but you could use it for a stunt.

The girls at college have no dates, and they are sitting around at their residence, disconsolate. Finally one has an idea, whispers it to the others, and is gone for a minute to telephone.

Soon there is a knock at the door, and three young men come in. One says that they were told by the "baby sitting bureau" of the college to come over.

The girls indicate that this is the right place, and that they are the "babes," and that the boys will get their money. Then the girls give the boys instructions about how to take care of them.

The boys indicate that this is the easiest baby sitting they have ever done, and set to work to amuse their new charges.

The Lost Sheep

This is an oldtimer, with a little embellishment. The person presiding builds up the idea of a wonderful song to be sung, and the marvelous singer who is going to sing, and the good fortune all have in being in the presence of such a great accompanist.

The singer comes out, amid applause, greatly encouraged by the master of ceremonies. The accompanist sits on the piano bench. It is not right. They bring out a book for him to sit on. It is not right. He tries another book. It is not right. Finally he tears one leaf from a book and puts it by itself on the piano bench. It is just right, and he sighs contentedly.

He starts on an elaborate introduction. The singer signals that he or she is ready to begin. Then he or she says or sings, simply, "Baa-a-a-a-a!"

Under the Hanging Mistletoe

This one could be used in a number of situations. It would be funniest, however, if a boy or man (especially one well-known by the group) took the part of the girl.

The hanging of the mistletoe can be an important part of the ceremony. The man (made up as a girl) takes great pains in selecting the proper location for the mistletoe.

Others could appear in the scene, set as if it were a party. But the central figure is in the center. "She" strikes a pose as the jingle is read:

> Under the hanging mistletoe,
> The homely co-ed stands . . .
> And stands and stands and stands and stands,
> And stands and stands and stands!

At the end she can shake her head hopelessly, take her mistletoe, and walk off with it (or you can figure out your own ending).

Klaud's Klimbing Kit[22]

The composers recommend the use of this during intermissions, or at times when the audience is highly tolerant of anything.

PERSONNEL NEEDED: 1. The Chief Salesman for Klaud's Klimbing Kit.
2. Some henchmen and stooges who will
help demonstrate.
3. Someone to help lead in the laughter and
applause.

PROPERTIES: Whatever is handy. A big suitcase is very helpful,
plus a shovel, sacks of rocks, etc.

At the outset the Chief Salesman comes out, followed by his aides, who stagger under the load of the kit. They come to the center of the group or the stage and begin the task "and privilege" of selling.

[22] Compound nonsense compounded by Clifford Zirkel, George Walker, Tommy Brown, and the 1952 Kerrville Senior Assembly.

CHIEF SALESMAN (*makes the opening speech, pointing out to the audience the help that Klaud's Klimbing Kit will be, or for getting up a nearby mountain or hill*): Climbing kids clamor for Klaud's Klimbing Kit! And now let us tell you about the wondrous, marvelous contents of this kit. (*He might play a bit with the words, "this kit" and "this skit."*)

The first item in Klaud's Kit is the all-important and necessary "Sack of Rocks," in 50, 75 and 100-pound sizes, depending on the intensity of your desire to throw rocks off of high places.

The second item in the kit is a "Gravel Replacement Shovel." Every climber has his ups and downs. Whenever you slip and fall you dislodge rocks, thereby adding to erosion. We ask you to be considerate of future climbers. Love your fellow men. Leave the mountain in as good *or better* shape than you found it. Replace the rocks and gravel with Klaud's Replacement Shovel and preserve the scenery.

By special arrangement with another company we are able to include in Klaud's Klimbing Kit an item for your comfort and relief. Blisters on the feet are a sign of the true climber, but to protect you against undue discomfort we offer "Baker's Blister Breaker." (*Hold up an axe, a sledge hammer, or something equally appropriate.*) This item will blast any blister out of exister—existence!

Climbing mountains demands quick thinking, ability to make prompt decisions—for after all, there are several trails wandering over mountains! When in doubt about the fork in the trail, when uncertain as to which to follow, you need not worry. Use Klaud's exclusive "Pathfinder"—a two-headed coin, pocketsize. All you do is to flip it for a quick decision. (Not to be used in choosing a life vocation or a lifemate.)

Here is an important inclusion in the kit—a "Flock of Sheep with Collapsible Fence." (*With vivid imaginations the producers here help to produce the sheep.*) Many climbers are so exhausted that they are unable to go to sleep at nights. For quick sleep, count sheep! Klaud's specially-trained fencejumping sheep. As a special added feature we include with the collapsible fence and the sheep, a handy pocket-size bottle of air wick. This will enable you to have your sheep AND endure them!

Klaud likes to foresee every possible emergency. For that reason, we have included an "Alteration Sewing Kit" for any situation. For instance, you might wish to use it to make any needed changes when your breath starts coming in short pants.

We take special pride in the next item. In the event that you become lost, we have the answer. You may be rescued by any one of our famous St. Bernard dogs. And to protect you against any possible discomfort after being saved and dragged by the St. Bernard, we offer a package of "Flea-X." After all, you never know about any old St. Bernard!

Actually, friends, with Klaud's Klimbing Kit it is practically impossible to get lost, or at least to stay lost. You see, we include one of Klaud's famous "Homing Pigeons." When you are lost, just write (ah, yes, we think of everything) with this midget ball-point pen made for writing, under pigeons, a note saying that you are lost. Simply scribble this on the handy slate under the pigeon, giving the location of the place where you are lost, and then release the pigeon. Immediately he will fly to his home in our central office in St. Louis, and the rescue party will be dispatched immediately.

Chief Salesman may ask an assistant where the pigeon is now. "Headed home below the Mexican Border" or some such answer may come from the assistant.

Now, here is another prize piece. This is a "Combination Telescope and Ear Trumpet." While climbing _____ (name of local hill or mountain) you can view the drive-in movies, occasionally using the ear trumpet feature to hear the sound.

Here, friends, you will find special protection from the natural-born hazards of climbing. Included in Klaud's Kit is a "Bee Hive," containing some of the fastest bees in the beesness! Yes, at the sight or smell of a bear, Klaud's bees whip up a batch of honey immediately, and this turns the bear's attentions from *you* to something sweet! Friends, don't get stung with other climbing kits. Remember that only Klaud's gives you bees, to save you from the bears. And as an added service, we include an informative little booklet entitled, "Bare Facts."

Be a real mountain climber—be authentic—learn to yodel! Here is a "Book of Yodeling Lessons with Guitar." Be a Swiss yodeler! *(The Chief or an assistant plunks out a few chords and*

yodels *"Song of the Islands"* or some other Hawaiian tune.)
This guitar is heavy enough to be used in weight-lifting exercises too, thus doing double duty.

Lastly we include Klaud's "Mountain Top Experience Diary," for recording your mountain top experiences.

Yes, friends, all you do is rip the box off any old top and mail to Klaud's Klimbing Kits, _____ (give a local address).

C. MUSICAL STUNTS

And finally, here are several musical stunts in this chapter. Because it is so easy to act out songs, we have not made detailed suggestions, but you will have much fun if you pick songs that are related to the theme of the occasion.

A good general collection of songs is *357 Songs We Love to Sing* (Hall-McCreary Company, 434 South Wabash Avenue, Chicago, Illinois). A clever collection of stunt songs is *Camp Songs 'n' Things* (1925 Addison Street, Berkeley, California). Also, *Paradology* contains several stunt songs; though it is out of print now, some libraries will have the book.

Band Music

Almost any occasion calling for stunts could use some of these trick band ideas:

1. For a stunt night, you might have a real band, using real instruments, named some tricky name.

2. COMB BAND. An interesting band can be formed quickly by getting participants to get out their combs and by putting a piece of tissue paper across, and humming. Kitchen pots and pans when added make good percussion background.

3. KITCHEN BAND. In this arrangement you may use anything available in any kitchen. What you can find for music and rhythm in a kitchen is amazing!

4. RHYTHM BAND. The children in many communities will be accustomed to this idea. Usually the music is played on the piano or sung, and those in the band add their noises by pecking on bottles, clicking scissors together, rattling boxes with coke caps in them, etc.

5. PICNIC BAND. On outings, divide the larger group into small-

er ones and let each one devise a band. Usually some combs will make their appearance, but many other interesting instruments can spring up.

6. FAMILY BAND. Using combinations of the ideas above, get either single families, or families in twos and threes grouped together, to join in the parade. Children love to parade with their elders!

Singing Commercials

Now that singing commercials seem to be here to stay you might as well have some stunt fun with them, too! Here are some ideas:

1. For a banquet where the group is seated at several tables, let each table make up a singing commercial about the organization sponsoring the banquet, and give it.

2. Instead, select a theme idea for them, such as a local football team, chapel, the school lunchroom, some fictitious product.

3. "Our camp is going to need some more campers next year. Will each cabin please make up a singing commercial, so that we can get campers with it?"

4. For stunt nights, a preselected theme is chosen, and each group must do not only a stunt, but also a singing commercial. The whole program might be centered around radio or TV.

5. Let each of several groups take the same familiar tune, like "My Bonnie," or "Jingle Bells," and see what it can work out.

6. Seasonal singing commercials. Divide the group into several smaller ones, the groupings based on the seasons. Each person joins the group of the season in which he was born. Then they do a singing commercial on that season.

7. Historical commercials. Do a commercial appropriate for the time of Julius Caesar, Columbus, Shakespeare, the Gay Nineties, etc.

Eleven Ideas for Quartet Singing

Quartets are "naturals" when it comes to musical stunts. Whatever your theme, you can usually get up a special quartet costumed appropriately. Here are some ideas:

1. MOUNTAIN MEN QUARTET. Have them garbed like U. S. or Swiss mountain dwellers, sing mountain songs.

2. COWBOY QUARTET. Dressed in cowboy costumes, they could sing western songs, do a little roping act.

3. FARMERS' QUARTET. Dressed like farmers, either sing humorous songs or some of the lovely folk songs having to do with tilling the soil. (Co-operative Recreation Service, Delaware, Ohio, publishes several fine collections.)

4. FIREMEN'S QUARTET. Dressed in firemen's equipment, these boys sing (perhaps of fire, water, etc.). They might say that after due consideration they want to sing "Scotland's Burning" followed by "The Old Oaken Bucket." Clang of fire alarm calls them away at the end.

5. POLICEMEN'S QUARTET. Dressed as policemen, they sing, "Hail, Hail, the Gang's All Here," and other songs appropriate for policemen. At the end there might be a strong blast on the whistle from offstage, and they rush off to help.

6. STRING QUARTET. After they are in place, they pass a ball of string around each other (one member holding one end) several times until they are surrounded with string, several strands of it.

7. THE BRASS QUARTET. In presenting them, the introducer points out that they have easily the most brass of anyone around these parts.

8. THE MUSIC DEPRECIATION QUARTET. Produce their music in the zany style of Spike Jones and his City Slickers.

9. THE SOCIETY FOR THE PRESERVATION AND ENCOURAGEMENT OF BARBERSHOP SINGING IN AMERICA QUARTET. There is such an organization, and you might have one in your town. If so and they can come over, you will doubtless have a treat, for those fellows can sing!

10. RELIGIOUS QUARTET. This could be a truly good quartet, singing good religious music in straightforward style.

11. TOPSY-TURVY QUARTET. This stunt is performed behind a sheet or blanket. The quartet have their shoes on their hands, sox on their arms, and their feet back out of sight. The shoes are arranged so that they just show under the sheet or blanket or curtain. Then, at the appropriate time, they suddenly withdraw the shoes from under the blanket and lift them up and expose them over the top of the blanket in such a way that they seem to be singing upside down! If the song is appropriate, so much the better.

Keep the Song Going

On songs that the entire group know, divide them into several smaller groups, easily identified by pointing. As they sing along, point to one group and have it immediately carry on the song by itself. If you are sure of your people and if they will co-operate, do it with individuals too, and let them "carry the tune."

Spot the Song

1. On the stage, or at least in front of the group, some persons perform the action of the song, in pantomime and speech, such as "Home on the Range," "Clementine," "Deep River." As soon as someone in the viewing audience thinks he knows, he holds up his hand, and is given a chance to guess.

2. *Variation:* Divide a larger crowd into smaller groups, and have each of them act a song for the others to guess. This is different from acting the *title* of a song.

Carmen

This is a song title stunt. The one who presents the stunt builds up the idea that the group loves good music very much. Carmen is one of its special-favorite pieces. As they go to school or to work, everybody just sings it.

Today (tonight) we want to give you a demonstration of this piece by acting it out for you. So here is our production of Carmen—"She'll be Carmen 'round the mountain when she comes."

(From here the group acts it out while some sing, "She'll Be Comin' 'Round the Mountain." It might be done with the motions.)

1. She'll be comin' 'round the mountain when she comes
   (TOOT! TOOT!) *(For this, yank like blowing a train whistle.)*
2. She'll be drivin' six white horses when she comes
   ("WHOA BACK!") *(Act as if pulling reins on horses.)*
3. Oh, we'll kill the old red rooster when she comes
   ("HACK, HACK!") *(Act as if hacking his head off.)*
4. And we'll have chicken and dumplin's when she comes
   ("YUM, YUM!") *(Rub tummy.)*
5. She will have to sleep with Gran'ma when she comes
   (SNORE, SNORE!) *(Act as if snoring.)*

6. She'll be wearing red pajamas when she comes
   (SCRATCH! SCRATCH!) *(Act as if scratching.)*
   *(Note: The sounds and motions are cumulative. When you sing
   verse 6, you do the actions and sounds of 6, 5, 4, 3, 2, and 1.)*

Romantic Notes

Someone sits at the piano and spins a yarn about the songs he
is playing. He uses songs that the people know, of course. If any
of the following songs are likely to be unfamiliar to your group,
be sure to make substitutions. The stunt might go somewhat
like this:

I once knew a young man whose name was "Captain Jinks."
As he sat there in his home one night, listening to "Grandfather's
Clock" ticking away, he was thinking of the time "Long, Long
Ago" when he was out west, and when he felt so much at "Home
on the Range," where he was in love with "Juanita." They were
going to the "Quilting Party" one day. He said they would walk,
but she said they might as well "Wait for the Wagon." When
the wagon came along, who should be driving it but "Clementine." They had a contest to see which couple could quilt the
best. Guess who won? It was "Reuben and Rachel." By the way,
this contest was held on "Old MacDonald's Farm." On the way
back, he sang to her "Sweet and Low." He liked "Juanita," and
she was always saying that she liked him so much "For He's a
Jolly Good Fellow."

Once he got his call to go "Sailing." She sang "My Bonnie Lies
Over the Ocean." She made a home recording for him of "Love's
Old Sweet Song." When he returned they were married in "The
Church in the Wildwood," and when he asked her what she
wanted to do for a wedding trip, she said, "Carry Me Back to
Old Virginny," and they settled down to live in "Dixie."

You can improvise your own. Every one of these songs is in
357 Songs We Love to Sing (Hall-McCreary, Chicago).

The Disappearing Quartet[28]

A quartet comes out to sing. It has a girl accompanist.
One member hits a sour note, and the leader pushes him off

[28] From Cubby Whitehead, Bradenton, Fla.

stage. There are lots of noises of beating, etc., behind scenes. Leader comes back and announces that he regrets they must continue with a trio.

The same happens, one at a time, to each member of the quartet, until only the leader and pianist are left. She hits a sour note. He leads her off. Loud cries heard, sounds of beating.

This time *she* comes back, dusting off her hands.

The Fake Musicians

This stunt has been done at least once before, but it is always funny.

As the record plays offstage, or as instruments play, there are actors on the stage who make the motions of playing such instruments. The climax comes when the offstage instruments continue to play after the actors have stopped.

Human Calliope and Xylophone

1. Have several individuals lined up, each assigned a tone. When the musician comes along, he grasps the outstretched hand of the one note he wants to play, and that person makes his sound. In other words, the hands stretched out become his keyboard.

2. A variation of this is to have them be notes on a xylophone, instead. When hit on the head (lightly) with a special mallet, they make their sounds.

Pantomiming a Record

Increasing in popularity is the idea of taking a phonograph record which is performed rather dramatically (song or story) and acting it out in pantomime for an audience, while the music plays, or the story is told on the record.

Oftentimes this is done by one person, but sometimes a group can work it well, too. In order to make it effective, you need to practice a lot for smoothness—also to memorize the record perfectly.

Singing Waiters

For a good table stunt, always have singing waiters—male or female. Customarily singing waiters are men.

This is good whether done at a banquet, or in a home, or at a summer camp or conference. Oftentimes they can pull little gags as a part of their performance.

For instance, the waiters at one conference grounds once advertised in this way the hamburgers to be bought there. One waiter came up to the other and said:

"Sir, we are making a test to see how the people like our hamburgers, and we would like to have you participate."

"All right," said the willing one.

"Now, we have here one of our conference grounds hamburgers. Do you have your own brand?"

"Yes, I do," said the willing one. "I'll try mine first." So he reached into his pocket and pulled out a hamburger, completely equipped with lettuce and tomato, and tasted a bite of it, then a bite of the other hamburger. He naturally liked the conference grounds hamburger much better. It was rounder, firmer, milder. And, they sold ten times as many hamburgers that night as the night before!

While the Organ Peeled

The description here is that of a group who took a spontaneous situation and, using an old song, worked out a stunt, adding their own twist and flavor. This is always the best way of doing a stunt.

The situation that tipped it off was that some grease caught on fire in the kitchen during the meeting, and the fire department had to come and put out the fire! So that started minds to working, and they came up with this old song.

They used signs to designate the people. The necessary signs are capitalized below. Eight persons each sang one line, then acted it out if possible.

TUNE: Silver Threads Among the Gold

1. "While the ORGAN peeled POTATOES,"
   (*A person labeled "organ" worked off the "peeling" from another person labeled "potatoes." The "peeling" was made of wrapping paper.*)
2. "Lard was rendered by the choir,"
3. "While the SEXTON tolled the CHURCH BELL,"

*(Here an actor labeled "sexton" told off the "church bell"
with nonsense syllables, said very fast.)*

4. "SOMEONE set the CHURCH on FIRE!"
   *(A person labeled "someone" took another actor labeled
   "church" and sat him on another—already seated—labeled
   "fire.")*

5. " 'Holy Smoke!' the preacher shouted,"

6. "In the rush he lost his hair . . ."
   (A mop wig was used for him. He lost it.)

7. "Now his head resembles heaven,"

8. "For there is no parting there!"
   (All bowed. Audience applauded.)

But it was not the end.

Another actor said, "I think this is a pretty low sort of stunt
for a group of this caliber to be pulling. Using that old song, and
the poor taste, and all. I just think this program should end on
a *higher plane*.

"OK," yelled a volunteer, who seized a carpenter's large-size
plane, stood on a chair, and held it high. "How's this?"

BLACKOUT

chapter 5

GROUP
STUNTS
and
"DRAMAS"

requiring a narrator

GROUP STUNTS AND "DRAMAS"

THE KIND of stunt that requires a narrator is popular because it usually needs relatively little rehearsal and advance preparation. The narrator not only reads the script but also can direct the stunt from his vantage point.

Sometimes the actors make use of signs to indicate who they are, or what their role is.

If you like this kind of stunt, you may want to get *Handy Stunts* (Co-operative Recreation Service, Delaware, Ohio) which contains "Columbus Discovers America," "The Mellerdrammer," "Pokey Huntus," and "Two Marionettes," or *Skit Hits* (Fun Books, 5847 Gregory, Hollywood, California) for "The Wild West Weakling" and "The Legend of Instant Postum."

THE ECLIPSE[1]

By MARGERIE G. STEPHENS

A Pantomime

Twenty players   Time: Fifteen minutes

CHARACTERS

Reader	Lengthening Shadows (two)	Mercury
Earth	Minutes of Totality	Jupiter
Sky	Snow	Altair
Sun	Great Fear	Vega
Moon	Period of Totality	Stars
Eclipse	Venus	Gusts of Wind

PROPERTIES

Table, three benches, jackknife, paper plate, five quarters, pair of scissors, blotter, postage stamp, string of beads, hatpin, dark cover for table, Corona typewriter and cover, curling irons, shoe

[1] From Katherine Rohrbough's *Successful Stunts* (Harper and Brothers). Used by permission.

brushes, toy wrist watch, two large sticks of wood, brush and crumb tray, dust brush, two brooms, two long strips of black cheesecloth, signs for each character, sign for "Eclipse" with "History" on reverse side.

PROCEDURE

As the story is read, the characters perform the action as given in parentheses.

INTRODUCTION

READER: Those in the audience who had the privilege of witnessing the eclipse of the sun on January 24, 1985, in the path of totality, were no doubt deeply impressed by the grandeur and wonder of the spectacle. If any were not so fortunate, they doubtless have heard much about it. We were told by astronomers at that time that another eclipse would not take place across the same path for a hundred years. However, it has just been discovered that the marvel is about to happen once more this evening. It promises to be more mysterious than the one in 1985.

This eclipse has two peculiarities: two solar eclipses have never been known to occur so close together, and in all history, known or unwritten, this is the first time a solar eclipse has ever been witnessed *after the sun has set*. Are you ready to witness this great phenomenon?

ACTION

You will first observe the position of the earth as it lies before you (*Earth comes in, lies in front of bench at center of stage*), with the sky above it (*Sky sits on the table behind bench*). The majestic sun sweeps across the sky (*Sun enters with brush which she sweeps across face of Sky*). It is time for the sun to set (*Sun and Earth sit on bench*).

The silvery moon trips across the sky and comes between the sun and earth (*Moon trips over Sky and sits between Sun and Earth*). Observe closely the motion of these three—the sun, the moon, and the earth—and notice their relative positions, and you will be better able to understand the theory of this eclipse. See the earth as it turns around the sun. (*Earth turns Sun around several times vigorously.*) Notice the moon as it turns around the earth. *(Earth continues turning the Sun while Moon, at the same time, tries to turn Earth around. Of course a general mix-up ensues.)* You can easily see how an eclipse would result.

The eclipse is now starting. *(Eclipse steps onto the stage slowly.)* The moon has begun to nick the sun's rim. *(Moon takes small bits from rim of paper plate with jackknife.)* In a few moments you will see the moon pass over the first quarter. *(Moon hands one quarter to Sun.)* It has passed over the first quarter. Silently it cuts off a part of the sun's light. *(Moon takes scissors and cuts off a lock of the Sun's hair);* now it has crossed the halfway mark *(Moon puts a chalk mark between Moon and Sun on floor);* it is slowly but surely blotting out the sun *(Moon takes blotting paper and pretends to blot Sun's face).* As it passes over three quarters *(Moon hands Sun three quarters)* you will notice other strange occurrences. Observe the lengthening shadows *(Lengthening Shadows slowly cross the platform, raising their brooms higher as they do so; strips of black cheesecloth are draped over the brooms for the shadows, which lengthen as the brooms are raised),* and now the moon is fast stamping its impression on the sun *(Moon sticks postage stamp on Sun's forehead).*

Ah! The moon is passing over the last quarter! *(Moon hands Sun another quarter.)* Things will happen quickly now. You will notice how very green the people around you look. Great gusts of wind are blowing *(Gusts of Wind cross the stage, loudly blowing their noses);* I can see that a great fear is shaking some of you *(Great Fear goes into the audience and shakes some of them gently).* Do not be alarmed, there is nothing to fear.

Bailey's Beads are now visible to those who have brought their telescopes. *(Moon places string of beads on Sun's left ear.)*

Now the period of totality has come *(Period of Totality enters),* the eclipse is on *(Eclipse moves nearer the center of stage),* and you may view this marvelous spectacle without dark glasses. The moon entirely covers the sun *(Moon removes dark cover from table and completely covers Sun. A typewriter is revealed on the table),* and for the first time the corona is visible. Since this corona is seen only during the period of totality most people do not even know of its existence.

Now observe the nearby planets—Venus, Mercury, and Jupiter keeping their silent watch *(Venus, Mercury, and Jupiter enter, sit on the bench at right of Sun, and pass a toy wrist watch back and forth);* notice Altair and Vega shedding their beams on the earth. *(Enter Altair and Vega, with large sticks of wood which they place at Earth's feet. They seat themselves on bench to left of Sun.)* Other stars are shining here and there *(others enter with shoe brushes and shine shoes).*

The period of totality is gone *(Period of Totality leaves stage after passing in front of Sun).* The sun begins to emerge from its covering *(Sun extends one hand);* the corona fades out of sight *(Moon partly covers typewriter),* the stars and planets disappear *(Altair, Vega, Venus, Mercury, and Jupiter leave stage);* now we see the spectacle in reverse order *(everyone on stage turns back to audience);* the sun pierces the dark shadow and it leaves the earth *(Sun pricks Shadows with hatpin, and Shadows leave stage).*

The sun slowly emerges *(Sun slowly removes covering, hands it to Moon, who then covers typewriter completely);* the sky returns to normal *(Sky leaves);* the sun, moon, and earth journey on their way *(Sun, Moon, and Earth skip out of room);* the eclipse becomes history *(Eclipse comes forward and reverses sign so that it reads, "History").*

LILY OF THE ALLEY[2]

By FLOYD S. FIELD

Five Men   Time: Ten minutes

CHARACTERS

Lily of the Alley, the winsome darling of Pigeon's Canyon, Arizona

Desperate Desmond, a wealthy ostrich grower of Kalamazoo, but at heart a bold, bad man

Homely Hiram, one of Nature's Noblemen, though he totes a face that only a mother could love

Vesuvius, Desperate Desmond's white mule (two boys covered by sheets)

A Rattlesnake (The double-barreled, sliding action variety)

DIRECTIONS

This story is read while action goes on in pantomime. Make the action snappily exaggerated.

[2] From Katherine Rohrbough's *Successful Stunts* (Harper and Brothers). Used by permission.

SCENE I

Pigeon's Canyon, Arizona, on a sweltering afternoon in February. Lily of the Alley is digging clams.

Desperate Desmond gallops up on Vesuvius, sees the beautiful maiden, and starts a flirtation.

Horrors! A rattle—and not a baby in sight. (Snake appears.)

Desperate Desmond escapes on Vesuvius, leaving poor Lily shaking hands with the undertaker.

Homely Hiram appears, looking for fourleaf clovers. He sees the snake and, after a desperate struggle, draws a saltcellar from his pocket and sprinkles salt on the snake's tail. The snake dies. Homely Hiram clasps Lily of the Alley to his heart.

SCENE II

Thirty seconds later, on Broadway, New York. Between Scene I and Scene II much has happened. Lily's father has died of sleeping sickness (he went to sleep on a railroad track). Desperate Desmond, unbeknown to Lily, has taken her father's papers to the blacksmith shop and had them forged. He now seeks to marry her and get the rest of the property.

The scene opens with Lily in the parlor of the fourteenth floor of the Hotel Ashcanderbilt. Desperate Desmond comes a-wooing.

Fire! Desperate Desmond escapes with the only parachute on the fourteenth floor. Will Lily of the Alley perish in the flames?

Homely Hiram appears from Arizona to do his Christmas shopping. He sees Lily on the fourteenth floor, reaches in his watch pocket for his trusty lasso, and yanks her from the fourteenth floor out of the window to safety.

They go off hunting a minister.

Desperate Desmond, foiled, blows out his brains with a bicycle pump.

COUNT TWENTY'S REVENGE[3]

(A thrilling story of the medieval days—very evil!)

STAGING NOTES

COUNT TWENTY, the noble sire, dressed in corduroy bathrobe with rope around waist, gray hair, big gray mustache, slippers.

[3] By Wilma Mintier, Pittsburgh, Pa.

LADY ISADUMBELLA, his fair daughter, is dressed in long house-coat. High conical headdress of cardboard, with veil fastened at peak. Face made up unattractively.

MARK TYME, her lover. Pail on head for helmet, washboiler cover for shield, spatula for broadsword, overshoes. Broad leather belt with tinware hanging from it, such as egg beater, spoons, etc.

PUNKO POLO, the great Asiatic sportsman. He has riding breeches, black mustache, sash around waist.

CHIN DEEP, his accomplice. He has kimono, bedroom slippers, drooping black mustache.

CAPTAIN OF THE MUDGUARDS, with a strange combination of uniforms—such as overalls, policeman's coat, army officer's hat.

The scene is laid in the castle of Count Twenty. Scenery is represented by two boys, one of whom stands at the rear to the left, and has a piece of printed cloth or patchwork quilt hanging in front of him, labeled TAPESTRY. The other stands at the rear, right, with a sign labeled DRAFT. On the other side of the TAPESTRY sign is the word IVY VINE, and on the reverse of DRAFT is RAZZBERRIES. Later they use signs, "DARK AGES" and "DAWN."

NARRATOR: In the dear old days of drafty castles and half-ton suits of mail, there lived the noble Count Twenty at Mustard-on-Frankfort.

Enter Count. Strides about, twisting mustache, looks fiercely at audience. Captain follows him fearfully.

NARRATOR: His constant attendant is the valiant Captain of the Mudguards. "I have a little shadow that goes in and out with me," says the jovial Count Twenty.

Count apparently recites the line, then laughs and shakes himself. Captain bows out. Count also leaves, laughing.

NARRATOR: The flower of the castle is the fair Lady Isadumbella, whose suitors need not be counted. There is only one.

Lady enters. She touches the "Draft" boy, shivers.

NARRATOR: She feels a draft.

Lady gazes out window which is apparently between the boys; sighs, clasps her hands. Peers beneath her hands, sees nothing; turns around, registers sorrow.

NARRATOR: Her heart is torn and twisted because she has not heard from her lover since last mail.

Enter Mark Tyme, pail over his face.

NARRATOR: Her lover, Mark Tyme, arrives at last after a cold trip across the Sahara. But the Lady Isadumbella mistakes him for a deep sea diver and swoons.

Lady faints and is about to fall. Keeps on being about to fall until Mark gets his visor up. Then he dashes to catch her. Enter Count, sees Mark, is enraged!

NARRATOR *(as if speaking for Count)*: "Gadsooks! Thou hast made my daughter faint, and the plumbers have turned off the water! Egad! Forsooth! Gadsooks!"

Count pantomimes this, storming around while Mark supports the lady.

NARRATOR: The noble knight trembles before the wrath of the Count.

Mark trembles, tinware rattles. Count snatches lady from him.

NARRATOR: "And now—out of my sight! Never darken my portcullis again!"

Count points to door. Mark pleads.

NARRATOR: The fair Isadumbella revives in time to plead for her lover.

Lady revives, and she and Mark kneel before the Count, lifting up their clasped hands.

NARRATOR: But the sire is firm. "Leave before I call the police!"

Mark rises, so does lady.

NARRATOR: The fair lady, seeing that her dear father is really only an obstinate old fool, faints again!

Lady faints, is caught by Count, who points to door with one hand, telling Mark to go. Captain enters with cards on large tin tray. Presents card to Count. Lady revives.

NARRATOR: Punko Polo, the great Asiatic Sportsman and his caddy, Chin Deep, arrive from Omaha.

Enter Punko and Chin. Much ceremony of meeting. Mark hides behind "tapestry."

NARRATOR: All unseen, Mark Tyme conceals himself behind the tapestry.

Punko kisses lady's hand, gazes at her rapturously. Mark registers jealousy. Punko beckons to Chin, who holds large box in his hands.

NARRATOR: Punko Polo brings with him the gem of the Orient,

the Hope Diamond, saying, "It is all too little for a big hand like thine!"

Opens box, takes out "ring" which has a picture of Bob Hope on it. They all leave except Mark, who shakes fist in their direction.

NARRATOR: It is well for the Lady that the noble Mark Tyme is on guard . . . well for the house of Mustard-on-Frankfort!

Mark leaves stealthily.

NARRATOR: The scene changes.

"Tapestry" sign is now turned over to read "Ivy Vine." Other sign is turned over to read "Razzberries."

NARRATOR: Behind the old castle at midnight, when the moon has risen, the brave but gentle knight comes to serenade his lady love.

Mark enters with ukulele or banjo; pantomimes singing.

NARRATOR: He had hardly knocked out three notes before he sees a sinister shadow slinking along the castle wall. It is Chin Deep with a raspberry bomb!

Chin enters stealthily, looking about like a stage detective. Plants bomb with alarm clock by raspberry bush, leaves.

NARRATOR: Mark Tyme heroically dashes to the bomb!

Mark does so, looks at his watch, then at the clock, then at his watch, then at the clock. Registers horror!

NARRATOR: The clock is slow!

Mark continues to register terror.

NARRATOR: There is not a moment to lose. He enters the castle and climbs to the room of Lady Isadumbella!

He starts at center and goes around and around the stage, as if climbing stairs. Stops at last at the right by the door. Puts hand to head and staggers as if dizzy. Dashes out door and returns immediately with the lady. They hurry down the stairs. When they are down, Mark explains what the trouble is.

NARRATOR: The fair lady saved, Mark Tyme explains to her the cause of his hasty action. The lady swoons.

Lady faints and falls to ground. Mark runs to look at the clock. Clasps his hand to his head. Rushes back to lady to support her. She revives. They listen for the explosion.

NARRATOR: They listened, dumb and breathless, for the explosion. Would it never come? Would nothing end this awful suspense? Then the Lady thinks of her old man. "My father!" she cries.

Lady holds hand to mouth.

NARRATOR: "Don't make so much noise or we can't hear the explosion," says Mark.

Punko and Chin enter.

NARRATOR: "Aha!" says Punko. "You have saved me the trouble of bringing the fair lady down!"

Mark advances and they meet at the center. Mark pulls out his sword. Lady swoons.

NARRATOR: "Advance!" cries the noble knight. "But do not fire until you see the whites of my eyes."

Mark pulls pail down over his face. Fights with Punko and Chin, wielding his shield vigorously. Others fall. Mark pulls up visor. Lifts up his sword.

NARRATOR: "Excelsior! Sawdust! Victory is mine!" quoth the brave knight.

Lady revives, rises, rushes to Mark. Explosion: bursting of a paper bag. They cling to each other in terror.

NARRATOR: Like an eruption of Vesuvius, the bomb explodes, tearing off three shingles.

Mark and lady look upward.

NARRATOR: The brave Captain of the Mudguards rescues his kind old master.

Captain drags Count out, and they go around and around until they reach the bottom. Count sees Chin, Polo, the clock, asks how it happened. Lady tells him. Points to Mark, who is embarrassed. Count rushes to him, but misses and rushes to arms of Captain. Mark misses and rushes to arms of lady.

NARRATOR: A miss is as good as a mile!

Count speaks to Mark.

NARRATOR: "Take her, my boy, you've earned her!"

He pantomimes this.

NARRATOR: And so the dark ages passed away—and then came the dawn.

One sign boy moves away with sign "Dark Ages" and the other sign boy comes on with a sign "The Dawn." Mark and the lady embrace for

CURTAIN

THE WEEK BEFORE CHRISTMAS[4]

'Twas a week before Christmas, and all through the school
Not a creature was stirring from desk, chair or stool.
Late papers were shoved under doorways with care
In hopes that professors would soon find them there.
Ardent prayers had ascended to God up above,
"Lord, help in these finals if you really do love."

'Tis said that some students, when finals they take
No more preparation than this ever make.
And I under Whitchurch—that course is a snap—
Had just settled myself for a brief classroom nap.
When out in the lobby there arose such a clatter
I jumped from my chair to see what was the matter.

When lo, in my sleep-laden sight there appeared
A vision of grandeur, one not to be feared.
'Twas a man clothed in raiment of clerical hue,
His suit a dark gray and his tie a dark blue.
A man who enjoyed good food to indulge
As was shown by his large equatorial bulge.
From the gleam on his pate which he polished forthwith
I knew in a moment it was Dr. Smith.

He paused in the lobby and chose a soft seat,
Then summoned his cohorts, the very elite,
"Here Nagler, Here Soper, Here Ramsey and Rall,
Come out for a moment, out in the hall,
Come Harkness, McKibben, Baab and Minear,
McSloy, Mead, Abbey, Whitchurch and Blair.
Now gather round closely and heed what I say
For soon comes to Garrett a reckoning day.
Let's surprise all the children, each student so dear,
And bring to each one some real Christmas cheer.

"We'll forget about finals through these next few days,
Burn all the term papers, give everyone A's.
You know that for knowledge these people so crave
That to higher learning each one is a slave.

"Why, Sherring and Lallement, roommates so true,
Do twice as much work as most students do.
And Hugh White, the student, I'm glad to relate
Has turned in Whit's paper just twenty weeks late,
But poor Larry Eisenberg hasn't a chance

[4] This version is given only as a sample of what you might do to adapt the
poem to your needs. It was done just before the holidays at Garrett Seminary,
Evanston, Ill., written by Dick Haley.

To pass an exam, he's so tired from the dance.
Hughes Morris, Jim Ferris, the Koerner lad too
All passed comprehensives as Garrett men do.
They're tired from their labors, poor lads one and all
What do you think of my plan, Dr. Rall?"

And then Dr. Rall drew himself to full height,
(I stood on a chair just to keep him in sight)
"My thought," he began, "is not a negation,
For this plan will set up a right relation,
And students and faculty, long at odd ends,
Will find in a moment that they are good friends,
However, I think, lest their studies they shirk,
Next quarter we'd best give to each, extra work!"

And so 'twas decided on that fateful day.
The meeting broke up and they all went away.
And each as he passed me gave such a nod,
As one might expect from the passing of God.
And Prexy called down from his place on the stair,
"Merry Christmas to all, and a Happy New Year."

And after they'd gone my spirits did raise,
With visions of grade cards, and nothing but A's,
No papers to worry, no books to be read,
No extensions of courses to bother my head.
Why, this is like Heaven, the city so fair,
No sorrows, no parting, no darkness up there!

Then my ear was disturbed by a voice soft and low,
Its ring was familiar, "Come on now, let's go!"
And back to this world of things as they are
My slumbering conscience was brought with a jar.
So now I'm convinced, things are what they seem.
My city called Heaven was only a dream.

"LADY CLARE"[5]

Only three characters are needed for dramatization of Tenny-
son's ballad of Lady Clare. These are Lady Clare, Lord Ronald,
and Alice, the old nurse.

The players impersonating Lord Ronald and Lady Clare enter
hand in hand as the reading of the first stanza is coming to an
end. Lord Ronald bids Lady Clare a slow and lingering farewell,
then goes out. Lady Clare watches him and waves goodbye. She

[5] As suggested by Ella Gardner in Handbook for Recreation Leaders, U. S.
Children's Bureau, 1936.

turns about, stretches her arms back and looks up. She stands there dreaming until Alice enters (on fourth stanza) and pantomimes her question. Lady Clare's gestures indicate a delighted answer. Alice smiles and nods. Then she spreads her hands wide in gratitude and appears to make the announcement given in the fifth stanza. Lady Clare shows her excitement, moves over and touches Alice's arm, then drops her head. The dialog continues. On the ninth stanza Alice pats Lady Clare's shoulder and nods consolingly. Lady Clare takes off the bright-colored robe that she is wearing and removes her jewelry while the nurse tries to restrain her. Lady Clare repulses this and pantomimes her determination to give up her rights. Finally when Alice asks her for a kiss she moves over and kisses her. Alice bestows her blessing, and they go out together.

The stage is empty when the fifteenth stanza is begun. Then Lady Clare comes slowly in. Lord Ronald comes to meet her from the opposite side. He questions her concerning her change of dress. She explains in pantomime. He shakes his head and laughs. While the last few lines are being given he puts his arm about her and leads her off the stage.

A suitable accompaniment for this poem is Schumann's Traümerei.

Lady Clare

By ALFRED TENNYSON

It was the time when lilies blow
    And clouds are highest up in the air,
Lord Ronald bought a lily white doe
    To give his cousin, Lady Clare.

I trow they did not part in scorn;
    Lovers long betrothed were they;
They two will wed the morrow morn—
    God's blessings on the day!

"He does not love me for my birth,
    Nor for my lands so broad and fair;
He loves me for my own true worth,
    And that is well," said Lady Clare.

In there came old Alice the nurse,
    Said, "Who was this that went from thee?"
"It was my cousin," said Lady Clare;
    "Tomorrow he weds with me."

"O God be thanked!" said Alice the nurse,
  "That all comes around so just and fair!
Lord Ronald is heir of all your lands,
  And you are not the Lady Clare."

"Are ye out of your mind, my nurse,"
  Said Lady Clare, "that ye speak so wild?"
"As God's above," said Alice the nurse,
  "I speak the truth; you are my child.

"The old Earl's daughter died at my breast;
  I speak the truth, as I live by bread!
I buried her like my own sweet child,
  And put my child in her stead."

"Falsely, falsely have ye done,
  O Mother," she said, "if this be true,
To keep the best man under the sun
  So many years from his due."

"Nay now, my child," said Alice the nurse.
  "But keep the secret for your life,
And all you have will be Lord Ronald's
  When you are man and wife."

"If I'm a beggar born," she said,
  "I will speak out, for I dare not lie.
Pull off, pull off, the brooch of gold,
  And fling the diamond necklace by."

"Nay now, my child," said Alice the nurse,
  "But keep the secret all you can."
She said, "Not so; but I will know
  If there be any faith in man."

"Nay now, what faith?" said Alice the nurse;
  "The man will cleave unto his right."
"And he shall have it," the lady replied,
  "Tho' I should die to-night."

"Yet give one kiss to your mother dear!
  Alas, my child, I sinned for thee!"
"O Mother, Mother, Mother," she said,
  "So strange it seems to me.

"Yet here's a kiss for my mother dear,
  My mother dear, if this be so,
And lay your hand upon my head,
  And bless me, Mother, ere I go."

She clad herself in a russet gown,
  She was no longer Lady Clare;
She went by dale, and she went by down,
  With a single rose in her hair.

Down stept Lord Ronald from his tower;
  "O Lady Clare, you shame your worth!
Why come you drest like a village maid,
  That are the flower of the earth?"

"If I come drest like a village maid,
  I am but as my fortunes are;
I am a beggar born," she said,
  "And not the Lady Clare."

"Play me no tricks," said Lord Ronald,
  "For I am yours in word and in deed.
"Play me no tricks," said Lord Ronald,
  "Your riddle is hard to read."

O, and proudly stood she up!
  Her heart within her did not fail;
She looked into Lord Ronald's eyes,
  And told him all her nurse's tale.

He laughed a laugh of merry scorn;
  He turned, and kissed her where she stood;
"If you are not the heiress born,
  And I," said he, "the next in blood—

"If you are not the heiress born,
  And I," said he, "the lawful heir,
We two will wed to-morrow morn,
  And you shall still be Lady Clare."

"HE AIN'T DONE RIGHT BY LITTLE NELL"[6]

Here is an old favorite, a burlesque on the old plays of the
1900's. It has been done extensively, and is included here not
because it is new, but because you might not have the script
handy.

It is done in rhythm, all the way through. The actors stand in

[6] Cubby Whitehead suggests the one-man version of "He Ain't Done Right
by Little Nell," in which the person doing it changes hats with each change
of character, and of course changes voice. The rhythm is still the same. The
audience then waits in anticipation of the missing of a change of voice or
dropping a hat (he does it deliberately). The length and rhythm are just
about right for you to end up entirely out of breath, while the group rolls
in the aisles with laughter.

a line, rather mechanically, and go up and down with half-knee bends (like exercises in school) or with a rocking motion, going forward on one foot for the strong beats, and backward on the other foot on the weak beats. The words are capitalized for extra help in reading.

Very often in using this stunt, I have had the parts ready and have passed them out to the group. (Sometimes I let the group choose the actors who are to play the parts, by such questions as "Who'll we have for the farmer?".) Then while the actors are off in another room (or in a corner of the room) practicing, I get started on the barnyard animals, which we bring forward for background.

"What kind of animals do we need in a well-regulated barn-yard?" I ask, and get the audience to answer. Someone says, "A duck," whereupon I ask that person to come forward and be a duck. Continuing, I get fifteen to twenty-five animals up front and have them practice the rhythm, too. After spending about 10 minutes in this choosing and practicing, I have the other actors come back. The animals stand in a semicircle behind, keeping the rhythm but not making noise. (Previous to the coming of the actors, though, they have practiced their noises, one at a time and then together.) This gets much more participation than if only four actors were used.

To help point up the ending, explain that at the end of plays, the little stock companies touring small towns used to announce tomorrow's show at the end. East Lynne is a famous old play of the same era.

"He Ain't Done Right by Little Nell"

FARMER: 'Twas a DARK and stormy NIGHT when my NELlie went aWAY.
i NEVer shall ferGIT it till my DYin' DAY!
she was JIST sixTEEN, the VILlage QUEEN,
the PURTiest little GAL i EVER have SEEN!
the FARM ain't the SAME since NELlie went aWAY,
the HENS all DIED and the ROOSTERS won't LAY.
THERE in my WINdow HANGS a LIGHT!
FORTY below ZEro! GOSH, whatta NIGHT!

NELLIE: K-nock, k-nock, k-nock, k-nock! *(Enters carrying bundle.)*

FARMER: WHO's that KNOCKin' at my DOOR?

NELLIE: it's yer LITtle NELlie, don't ye KNOW me any MORE?

FARMER: WHERE'S that ACTER feller that CALLED yew HONEY?

did he SEND yew HOME 'cause ye AST fer MONEY?

NELLIE: he's a GREAT big BUM, and he LIED with EASE,

he HAD more WIMmen than a DOG has FLEAS!

he LEFT me the NIGHT I was MOST ferLORN,

the VERY same NIGHT little DUMMY wuz BORN!

FARMER: Is THAT there, DUMMY?

NELLIE: 'tain't no OTHER!

FARMER: she's the SPITtin' IMage of yer DEAR old MOTHER,

but ye CAIN'T stay HERE with THAT there CHEEILD . . .

LIStenin' to hit HOLler would jest DRIVE me WILD!

VILLAIN: HOIty, TOIty, ME proud BEAUTY! (*He wears mustache, of course.*)

GIMme DUMMy, or I'll DO mah DUTY!

GIMme the CHEEILD or I'll DO yew HARM,

'cause i GOT the MORTgage on the DARGgonned FARM!

CONSTABULE: K-nock, K-nock, K-nock, K-nock! (*He wears a huge badge, of course.*)

FARMER: Who's that KNOCKin'? SOUNDS like a MULE!

CONSTABULE: i AIN't no MULE, yew DADburned FULE,

cain't ye SEE by my BADGE I'm the CONstaBULE?

WHAT's goin' ON here, COME an' TELL!

FARMER: He AIN'T done RIGHT by my LITtle NELL!

VILLAIN: O, YES I HAVE. . . .

FARMER: O, NO YE AIN'T. . . .

VILLAIN: O, YES I HAVE. . . .

FARMER: O, NO YE AIN'T. . . .

CONSTABULE: yew STOLE his FARM and ye LEFT his DAUGHTER,

that OUGHT to COST ye 'bout a DOLlar and a QUARter!

ALL (*speaking together*): Which GOES to SHOW the PRICE of SIN,

come BACK tomorrow NIGHT and we'll PLAY *East Lynne!*

(ALL BOW LOW)

THE JAIL BOWL GAME[7]

This could take the form of a simple "broadcast," and as such requires only an additional voice or two. It could be dramatized in more elaborate fashion, having an actual "Jail" and "Harved" team, and having them act out, to a great degree, what the announcer says, including the crowning of the queen, etc. In a similar situation, an ingenious "announcer" once had a pair of glass tumblers, which he held up to his eyes like binoculars in order to "see" the game. The illusion is interesting.

Material can be added or subtracted, as in any skit or stunt, of course. Local gags and names often make such a "broadcast" much more interesting. Care should be taken not to hurt feelings with gags, of course.

NARRATOR: Ladies and gentlemen, we are about to broadcast one of the most thrilling games of the day, over the facilities of station WMFM and WMFM-FM. Yes, here we are at the Jail Bowl, and the great annual classic between Jail and Harved is about to begin. It is a beautiful day for this sport, and the spectators are awaiting what they know is going to be the game worth watching.

The Harved Reds are already on the field, warming up, and ready to go. And here come the Jail Birds. My, what a big team these Birds are. Every one of them has had *plenty* of experience! Every man in the Jail team is now doing his stretch. Some of them have quite a stretch.

Jail has just won the toss. They elect to receive. And now they are lining up (say, don't those birds look natural in the line-up!) and the game is on with the kick-off!

Butch McGootch takes the ball and drives it out to the 25-yard stripe. Yes, friends, there are plenty of stripes all over, today. Now it's the Jail Birds' ball, first down and ten years— pardon me, yards, to go.

The ball goes to the fullback on an end-around play. The whole Harved team rose up to meet him and he did not quite get his end around. Second and 11. Now the Birds are trying again. This time it's a quarterback sneak. These boys are good

[7] From *Skit Hits*. Inspired by some material that Bob Mathews, Parkersburg, W. Va., sent in. It appeared in the *Parkersburg News* a few years ago.

at that! It puts the ball all the way down on the midfield stripe for a good gain. The Jail team asks for time out. The parole board won't allow it, so play is resumed.

The Birds have the ball, and it looks like they are about ready to take up the assault again. There goes Bull Malone with the pigskin. My, just watch that fellow drive! He's going 10 yards—20 yards—30 yards . . . it looks like he's going all the way! No, he was stopped by a guard! That was a great play. The guards have had the key to the situation out here this afternoon. But the ball is on the 2-yard line. Now, here is the crucial play of the game. Slug McThug takes the ball, and breaks through the Harved Reds for a marker! Jail scores!

Now, here's the kick!

JAILBIRD-LIKE VOICE: "Cheese it, Warden, de food around here is rotten."

The investigating committee rules:

ANOTHER VOICE, MORE "CULTURED": "The kick is no good."

NARRATOR: With the score 6-0 it is time for Harved to receive. And now the ball is sailing through the air, received by Hugh McFoo. He runs it out to the 10 . . . to the 20 . . . to the 30 . . . to the 40 . . . to the 50-yard stripe before he hits a stone wall. (There are stone walls on all 4 sides of the field, too!) But wait a minute. The Birds are penalized 15 yards for felonious assault, putting the ball down on the 35-yard line.

Now it looks like Harved is going to take to the air. (Jail would like to do that, but they lack a good passer. The last good one got out last week.) Here goes a long Red pass down into the end zone . . . for a TOUCHDOWN! And here is the try for the extra point—blocked, by the Jail team.

And there goes the gun for the half. The players file slowly out, as is their custom. And now for the most colorful ceremony of all . . . the crowning of the homecoming queen. The procession is getting ready, and is moving across the field. The band is playing a few bars of the alma mater, "Jail, Bail, Hail!" And now we are ready for the impressive crowning of Miss Siren.

(*Sound effect:* WHAM! or B-O-N-G!)

Ladies and gentlemen, that was the most impressive crown·ing since 1899!

And now for a little athletic chatter between halves. We have here in the booth the head line backer of the Jail team, Warden Smith. He is important to the team. They cannot go anywhere without him! Warden, we welcome you to our booth today!

WARDEN: I'm glad to be here.

ANNOUNCER: Your boy Butch McGootch is a great player. How did he happen to join your squad?

WARDEN: Well, he didn't really intend to come. We surprised him.

ANNOUNCER: Did he join you because of the need of money?

WARDEN: Well, I couldn't say that. As a matter of fact, he was simply coining money right and left before he came here. The F.B.I. scouted his work for us. He is their greatest find in years.

ANNOUNCER: Has plenty of beef, too, doesn't he?

WARDEN: Yes . . . you might say he was our leading beefer!

ANNOUNCER: Thank you so much, warden, for coming up today. Now, let's go down on the field and see if we can pick up a few strains of the pep song, "Battle Cry of Freedom." It's almost time for the second half, and the players are coming back onto the field.

Now they are lining up, and Jail kicks off to Harved, and a Red starts back up the field. The Jail Birds tackled the ball carrier so hard that they jarred his pigskin loose and Jail recovers. Now Jail takes the ball, and they give it to Light Fingers Harry. He twists and turns like the knob on a safe, right in the center of Harved. He's gaining 5 yards, 10 yards. That boy is deceptive. But the score is tied, and the seconds are ticking away.

What is Coach McGoon doing? The Jail Birds are trying to hang on, hoping for a win, but they have not made the progress expected. Ah, I see the coach's strategy now—he's putting a little lifer into the game. Yes, Pee Wee Stiletto is coming in for the Birds. That's what McGoon does—when he wants to change the play, he sends in a player with a new sentence!

Stiletto takes the oval and stabs his way through to the 45-

yard stripe before he is arrested. First and 10. Now he tries to knife his way with a line buck. No gain. Really, Stiletto is not as good as McGootch in making bucks. Stiletto slits the Red line again, but what's this? Harved stole the ball. Yes, it looks like Jail might be beaten at its own game. Cabbot Loddge took the pigskin and raced all the way over the Jail goal line for another TOUCHDOWN. The kick is . . . good! These Harved boys can execute their plays! Jail execution has not been too good this afternoon.

Jail receives again, and an unidentified player races up the field, where there is a big pileup. This game is becoming rough. It's murder! The referee recovers the pigskin and it looks like a first down. They are bringing in the chain. (What are all the Jail Birds running for?) Ah, it's a first down. A reprieve for Jail. Can they make it?

Now Jail tries it again. They are attempting to blast their way out into the open to give their broken field runners a chance. But there's a handkerchief on the play! (Now the referee has blown his nose, and the game continues.)

Fifteen seconds to play. Jail's ball. Will they make it? McGootch now has the ball. He tries a buck right through the line. He goes to the 40—to the 30—to the 20—to the 10 . . . he's out in the open.

(Sound effect: RAT-TAT-TAT-TAT-TAT combined with siren sound)

No, they got him. Got him on the 1-yard line!

Now five seconds remain—4–3–2–1. The timekeeper has just raised the gun. What's this? All the Jail players have their hands up. Now there goes the gun, and it's curtains for this contest.

HARVED BEETS! This is the Miracle Broadcasting System. If it's a good broadcast, it's a miracle!

chapter 6

LONGER
STUNTS

HUMOROUS and SERIOUS

requiring scripts and rehearsals

LONGER STUNTS—HUMOROUS AND SERIOUS

I N THIS CHAPTER of longer stunts there is a variety of selections—"opera," melodrama, a discussion on religion, a folk festival script, and other types. When time permits, it is worthwhile to stage these longer skits, particularly for stunt nights, which call usually for more elaborate performances than "quickies."

HUMOROUS SKITS

For most of the humorous sketches in this section it is quite satisfactory for the actors to carry their scripts. Some have done it in ingenious fashion. One group, doing "Othello," had written their lines on little pads. As an actor came to the end of a page, he would tear off the sheet and throw it nonchalantly over his shoulder, to the glee of the audience. Sometimes the mistakes that actors make add to the humor of the situation, but it is also true that smoothness in such a skit as "The Farmer's Daughter" helps to give it an air of its being worthy of presentation.

These longer playlets are for the most part as lighthearted as the shorter skits in other parts of the book, and should be played for fun. Be sure to caution the actors to hold their lines for laughs.

If you wish to get others of this type of skit, you can find them in the following references: *Skit Hits* (Fun Books, 5847 Gregory, Hollywood, California), containing "This Man's Family—a TV soap opera"; "It Pays to Be Snickering"; and the opera "Two Gentlemen of Verona." In *Handy Stunts* (Co-operative Recreation Service, Delaware, Ohio) is "The Fatal Quest"; in *The End of Your Stunt Hunt* (Fun Books, above) are "Romance in the Park," "The Bored King and the Bandit," "The Romance from Pif Pif Land." In *The Fun Encyclopedia* (Abingdon-Cokesbury, New York and Nashville) is "Bluebeard."

CORN BUT NOT FORGOTTEN

Том (*meeting Bill*): Hello there, Bill!

BILL (*meeting him*): Hi, Tom. Say, I heard your uncle died.

Том: Sure did. I was fond of him.

BILL: Leave much?

Том: Only his old clock.

BILL: Well, it won't be much trouble to wind up his estate.
Girl walks by, smiles at Tom.

Том: Say, did you see that good-looking girl smile at me?

BILL: Well, I can understand that. When I first saw you I had to break out into a broad grin.

Том: Say, I saw Joe the other day. Did you know he had a glass eye?

BILL: No! Did he tell you that?

Том: No, it just came out in the conversation. He's a smart man, though. He's making a living with his pen these days.

BILL: I didn't know that. So he's a writer now!

Том: No, he's raising pigs!

BILL: Say, you know old Osborne? He's just about the most pious fellow I know.

Том: I never thought that about him. Always thought of him the other way.

BILL: Well, for instance, I just know that he never kisses his girl without saying grace!

Том: He must be pious. What does he say that for?

BILL: That's her name! (HAW!! HAW!!)

Том: Did you hear the story about the peacock?

BILL: No, I don't think I did.

Том: Oh, it's a beautiful tale!

BILL: Say, I strained my arm the other day and put on some liniment. I want to tell you, it made it smart.

Том: Why don't you rub some on your head?

BILL: You think you're so smart. All right, tell me how you get down off an elephant, and I'll give you five bucks.

Том: You jump down.

BILL: Wrong.

Том: You grease his sides and slide down.

BILL: Nope.

Том: You take a ladder and climb down.

BILL: Not at all.

TOM: Well, you take the trunk line down.

BILL: Nope.

TOM: All right, then, I give up.

BILL: Well, you don't get down off an elephant. You get it off a goose!

Tom chases Bill off stage for

BLACKOUT OR CURTAIN

SOFAPILLIO[1]

A Tragic Triangle

Two men and three girls

CHARACTERS

Rudebagio ⎫
Spaghettio ⎬ In love with Sofapillio

Sweep Uppio ⎫
Sapolio ⎬ Maids of Sofapillio

Sofapillio, the heroine

PROPERTIES

Broom, brush, bushes, pillows, stilettos (rubber or paper)

NOTE: The following announcement should be made for the greatest effectiveness of this production: "Kindly refrain from applauding until the last person has died!"

INTRODUCTION

SPAGHETTIO: I am Spaghettio, I love Sofapillio,
  But me she'll not havio, for she loves Rudebagio.

RUDEBAGIO: I am Rudebagio, I love Sofapillio
  And her I will marrio to spite old Spaghettio.

SWEEP UPPIO (*carries broom*): I am Sweep Uppio, the maid of Sofapillio;
  The friend of Spaghettio, the foe of Rudebagio.

SAPOLIO (*carries brush*): I am Sapolio, the maid of Sofapillio;
  But I do not likio the way she does actio!

SOFAPILLIO (*surrounded by pillows*): I am Sofapillio, I don't know what to doio,
  For two men do fightio to win my lovio.

[1] From *Successful Stunts,* by Katherine Rohrbough (Harper and Brothers). Used by permission.

SCENE I

SAPOLIO: Ho there, Sweep Uppio! What is the last reportio of the
love affairio of Sofapillio?

SWEEP UPPIO: Oh, it is worse than everio! It's enough to make
one sweario.

The way she keeps Spaghettio on the jumpio.

SAPOLIO: Oh, but she is a flirtio (winks), but I know what I'll doio!
I'll go and help Spaghettio, for I hate Rudebagio,

Because he got my floor dirtio which I had just washed upio.

SWEEP UPPIO: Good for you, Sapolio, and I too will helpio

Every bit I canio to stop that Rudebagio from winning Sofapillio,

For I just cannot standio the way she does actio.

SAPOLIO: Look, here comes Rudebagio. Let's get behind this
bushio

And see what she doesio, then go and tell Spaghettio!

Enter Sofapillio and Rudebagio.

SOFAPILLIO: Oh, is it you, Rudebagio? My heart it went thumpio
For fear it was Spaghettio. You know not how I feario
To tell him that my lovio has gone from him to youio.

RUDEBAGIO: O my sweet Sofapillio! Be it ever my endeavorio
To spare you any painio, but why not this avoidio,
And with me elopio in my little Fordio
And to some preacher goio?
And we will wedio this very nightio;
Then we'll take a tripio and to our home we'll goio—
You as my wifio, my dear Sofapillio.

SOFAPILLIO: My clever Rudebagio! Of all the rash thingsio
I ever heardio, this is the worstio!
But it does temptio my spirit of adventurio
And I will sure be readio to go with youio
This very same nightio when the moon comes upio.

RUDEBAGIO: My brave Sofapillio! You have saved my lifio
For I was getting desperatio in my love for youio,
My dear Sofapillio. But I must awayio
And get the Ford readio for our grand flightio.
Farewell, my sweet girlio!

Kisses her hand and waves farewell. As Rudebagio leaves,
Sofapillio goes into house, and maids come out.

SWEEP UPPIO: I'm sure it was worthio the cramp in my legio
For sitting so stiffio behind that old bushio
To hear that grand plotio for that wild escapio.

SAPOLIO: And I, too, agreeio, that it was worthio—
But we must awayio to tell Spaghettio.

SWEEP UPPIO: Oh, there's no needio, for here he does comeio.
They pull Spaghettio down on bench.
Say, do you knowio that old Rudebagio
And sweet Sofapillio are going to elopio
In the little Fordio this very same nightio—
And they're going to wedio?

SPAGHETTIO: This is not truio, for sweet Sofapillio
Is my betrothedio. How came you by this newsio?

SAPOLIO: We heard it just nowio from behind this bushio,
And saw as they plannedio that they would elopio.

SPAGHETTIO: That blankety-blank Rudebagio! I'll get his goatio,
I'll make him payio! I'll spoil his schemeio—
I'll make him deadio!
But thanks for the newsio. And now I must goio.
All go out.

SCENE II

Spaghettio and maids come in looking for a hiding place.

SPAGHETTIO: We'll hide hereio. Hist, here he comesio.
They hide and Rudebagio comes in.

RUDEBAGIO: Come, Sofapillio. The time is now hereio for us to
elopio.
Sofapillio comes in, if possible as through a window.

SOFAPILLIO: Oh, Rudebagio, I cannot goio! I am so scaredio!

RUDEBAGIO: Hark, what is thatio? Ah, it's Spaghettio!
Spaghettio and maids come from their hiding place.

SPAGHETTIO: I've got you, Rudebagio! I'll make you deadio.
We'll have a duelio with our stilettio.
They fight while Sofapillio runs around screaming.
Finally both men fall dead.

SOFAPILLIO *(on knees to Rudebagio)*: My heart is brokeio, I, too,
shall dieio.
For one of my griefio cannot liveio.
Alas, I am deadio! *(Falls dead over Rudebagio.)*

SAPOLIO *(hitting herself on the head with a spoon, falls dead):* Alas, I am deadio!

SWEEP UPPIO *(falls dead):* Alas, I, too, am deadio!

THE NERVOUS FATHER[2]

The scene is laid in the living room of the Williams home. Penny, their daughter has gone out on a date. Mr. Williams had retired to bed, but not seeing Mrs. Williams in bed, he gets up to look for her.

MR. WILLIAMS: Cora! Cora! Where in the blazes . . . *(Mr. Williams enters the living room, sees Mrs. Williams, looks her over.)* What! Waiting for your daughter again? She's been out twice this week already.

MRS. WILLIAMS *(trying to get a word in edgewise and in a very restrained voice):* Now, father! This is the first time this week.

MR. WILLIAMS: Well! *(muttering under his breath)* Always galavanting around. Just like your sister.

MRS. WILLIAMS: Anyway, I hope that our daughter won't have to spend the rest of her life knitting stockings for her friends' babies, like your sister Sue.

MR. WILLIAMS: Errrr . . . where'd you say she went? Who did she go with? What does he . . . *(Telephone rings, mother answers.)*

MRS. WILLIAMS: Hello . . . yes . . . yes, I understand . . . G'bye . . . *(hanging up the receiver)* You see, George, everything is all right. They have a flat tire on the way back from the Garden of Allah. *(Father sputtered during phone conversation, trying to get in word. At her remarks he explodes.)*

MR. WILLIAMS: All right. Garden of Allah. Just a flat tire. Hmm . . . Cora, you have absolutely no discretion. If I had been home, this would never have happened. The Garden of Allah. Of all places. Just a cheap honky tonk. That's what it is.

MRS. WILLIAMS *(very sweetly):* Oh! Have you been there?

MR. WILLIAMS: Of course not, but the Garden of Allah. Humph . . . And a flat tire. The boy's idea, no doubt. In my days we always brought the girls in before nine o'clock. The liberties the young people take these days!

[2] From Harry D. Edgren, George Williams College, Chicago, Ill. Done by some of his students.

MRS. WILLIAMS: Why, George! Don't you remember the night when the wheel came off the buggy while we were out on a date?

MR. WILLIAMS: But that was different. We were almost engaged. Besides, there was no question about my reputation. Who's this young upstart?

MRS. WILLIAMS: Well! He has a very nice voice over the telephone.

MR. WILLIAMS: Must be one of those smooth-talking hep cats, all brawn and no brains, with nothing to do but to whistle at girls. And your daughter, no doubt, whistled back at him. If he forced my daughter to go to that place, I'll wring his neck.

MRS. WILLIAMS: Now, now, George, calm down. Keep away from that window. The neighbors will think that you are having the jitters.

MR. WILLIAMS: Let them talk! I want that simple daughter of yours home and accounted for . . . (Door bell rings—enter Harry followed by Penny) Well! (sarcastically) Home so early?

PENNY: Oh! daddy, we had such a ravishing evening. Oh! mother and daddy, this is Harry. And look, he bought a bar of candy for me (showing them the candy she was eating). And he bought one for you too (pulling a bar from her pocket book).

HARRY: Mr. Williams, I want to offer you my most sincere apologies. I hope that we didn't cause the family too much concern.

MR. WILLIAMS (grumpily): Humph . . . Well! did you have a wonderful time at the Garden of Allah?

PENNY: Oh yes! The weavings were just gorgeous.

MR. WILLIAMS: Weavings! What weavings?

HARRY: Yes, of course. We went to the Historical Museum of Mohammedan Art Treasures.

MR. AND MRS. WILLIAMS: Museum?

PENNY: Yes, why? The Garden of Allah.

Mother smiles knowingly—father looks flabbergasted.

PUSH BUTTON TUNING[3]

A radio listener is seated at a table with an imaginary radio before him. A group of people stand to the side of the stage.

[3] Thanks to Harry Edgren, George Williams College, Chicago, Ill. Done by some of his students. See also a similar stunt, "Radio Jumble," on page 62.

They read their parts from the script as indicated. The radio listener "clicks" the push button as indicated on his script by the asterisk (*).

RADIO LISTENER: "Gee, it is time for the Lone Stranger. Wonder which station it is on. I'll try these buttons and see if I can find the right station." *(Pushes a button in pantomime.)

VOICE NO. 1: And here we are, ladies and gentlemen, ready to bring your way another Man in the Alley program. Here is where radio interviews Mr. Average Man in his daily trip down the alley. Would you like to win a ticket for a short .... at Kearney's? Then you too should take a walk down a dark alley and find your Man in the Alley. This program is a special presentation of Kearney's—the store with the professional attitude. And now, here is our first man in the alley. Would you mind telling us your name, destination, number of children, number of days until your birthday, size of shoestrings, kind of productive labor you do, favorite dish, and any other pertinent information you would like to tell us.

VOICE NO. 2: Yeah.

VOICE NO. 1: Thank you, and now we'll see if we can find someone else in the alley. Ahh, here is a . . .
*Radio listener pushes a button. Sound-effects man makes clicking noise for push button.

VOICE NO. 3: . . . shady lady. Yes, don't be a shady lady, ladies. Don't be half-safe. (In a whisper) Mrs. Hush recommends Hush deodorant. Shhhhhhhh—Hush!! Use Hush hush hush hush hush . . .
*Radio listener pushes a button. Sound-effects man makes clicking noise.

RADIO LISTENER: Where is that Lone Stranger program?

VOICE NO. 4: Are you weak and undernourished? Do you feel run down when hit by a truck? Do you have that "all out" feeling just before payday? Have you frequently experienced that grrrrrinding grrrrroaning sensation in your inner self? Then you too need to try Marter's Little Fliver Pills. Remember, they do the work of Kalamazoo, but have no Kalamazoo in them. They wake up the flow of that vital digestive juice that flows at the astounding rate of 3¼ miles per hour. To speed up this flow in your subterranean subways situated in the stomach, use Marter's Little Fliver Pills. Reach for the bottle with the little red pills, take one as directed and wait for . . .

Button clicks again.

VOICE No. 5: . . . the report. Yes, this is the latest news report reaching you through the courtesy of Rig R. Mortis, the gay mortician. Now a word from your friend and mine, Rig R. Mortis.

VOICE No. 6 (*fiendishly*): Hah hah hah! This is your lively host, the smiling mortician. Hah hah hah hah! If you don't know me, you soon will. Because we never let a friend down unless it is absolutely necessary. Hah hah hah! Your patronage is invited, and we extend a hearty welcome to all who wish a free tryout. Hah hah hah! Remember, our business is dead. Well, I'll be seeing more of you later. Take care of yourselves. I'll be shoveling off now . . .

VOICE No. 5: Thank you, Rig R., and now for the latest news. Ah yes, it's grave news tonight. The Rushans are Rushin', the Indians are Endin' it all, and the Belgians are . . .

Push button clicks.

VOICE No. 7: . . . suffering from indigestion. Now if you, friend, have acute sorehead, just forget about it. Mother-in-laws aren't really too bad. But if you suffer from indigestion, then take a new lease on life with "Nature's Nurture for Nagging Nuisances." "Nature's" is an entirely new remedy. It is so brand-new that it has never been tried. Here is the opportunity to get in on the surprise excitement that will await you. It is no telling just what this preparation is liable to do to you! But remember, Nature spelled sideways spells . . .

Push button clicks. Radio listener is becoming frustrated at not getting the Lone Stranger. He tears hair, etc.

VOICE No. 8: . . . and so we are bringing this program through the courtesy of Rucklesmeyer, Rucklesmeyer, and O'Connor, who make that world-famous soap "Soiled Suds." A box of Soiled Suds contains enough suds to fill Chicago's Soldiers' Field! Soiled soils everything! And now we take you to "The Half Moon Hideout"—or "John's Other Joe." Remember last week John seemed to be all washed up with "Clohoe." This week he has other plans to softsoap her into feeling the same way he does. How exciting! Will John clean up this time? Will Clohoe give him the old brush-off? But wait, we'll take a look into John's . . .

Push button clicks. Radio listener becomes more frustrated.

VOICE No. 9: . . . tall glass of _____. "Jibber" is the drink with the collegiate kick. Our motto is "A jigger of Jibber stops the jabber."

Push button clicks.

VOICE No. 10: Now get on your tummies and we'll read the funnies. I wonder what kind of a mess Pieface is in today? We'll soon see. Pieface turns with his gun and says . . .

Push button clicks.

VOICE No. 11: . . . Now lie down on your backs. That's it. Now raise your left leg. One two, one two, now lift yourself up with your elbows. Now drop, roll over and do two handstands. This is bound to take off excess pounds. Now throw your left leg over your right shoulder making sure your right heel does not get behind your toes. Isn't it simple to reduce? Now gracefully fall to the floor on your face, being careful to get the full rolling motion against your nose. Now . . .

Push button clicks.

VOICE No. 12: . . . they come galloping over the horizon. Here comes the Lone Stranger and his trusty steed Pronto. (*Radio listener leans back and sighs, looking very satisfied.*)
A man enters, picks up the radio in pantomime and starts to walk off.

RADIO LISTENER: Hey, you, who are you?

VOICE No. 13: I'm the man from the credit agency, and you are behind on the payments. I'm taking the radio!

OTHELLO[4]

You will want not only to give this clever "opera," but also to use it as a model for what you can do. Shakespearean costumes (bathrobes, towels, scarves, and the like) will give it color. Singers sing in exaggerated opera style. Remember—to overdo the thing isn't funny.

[4] We're grateful to Wilma Mintier, Pittsburgh, Pa., for permission to use this script (which has been slightly modified). It was first presented by an English mission girls' school in Jerusalem. The tip for getting the opera was from Mary Hubbard, Orlando, Florida.

One group who presented Othello used a *Concert Master* who gave an elaborate introduction to the characters in presenting them to the audience. For instance, he said the role of Othello was sung by Lauritz Meelk-your-cow, etc. For the "orchestra" (actually a pianist) he presented the player over and over again, as "Ophelia Foot, first violin," "Ophelia Foot, first clarinet," and the pianist would feel his foot, each time.

The chorus could add other appearances. Also they could double as the fire department.

PROLOGUE

ALL (*Chorus singing to tune "Long, Long Ago"*):
Come now and look at our tragical show,
Of Othello and Desdemon.
This play will move e'en your hard heart of stone,
Poor Othello, poor Desdemon.
They loved each other clear to distraction,
He got so jealous he stopped her heart's action,
Then stabbed himself to his own satisfaction,
Poor Othello, poor Desdemon.

OTHELLO: I am the villain who lived long ago:
I'm Othello, I'm Othello.
My nasty temper caused my wife lots of woe,
I'm Othello, I'm Othello.
I wish I'd never seen that handkerchief,
It was the thing that caused us all the grief,
I had to kill my poor self for relief,
I'm Othello, I'm Othello.

DESDEMON: I am the heroine who died in disgrace,
I'm Desdemon! I'm Desdemon.
Died with a sofa pillow stuffed in my face,
I'm Desdemon! I'm Desdemon!
Othello thought I was playing with men,
Innocent was I, and quite free from that sin,
I loved him truly in spite of his din,
I'm Desdemon, I'm Desdemon.

IAGO: I am Iago, the villain, you know,
I'm Iago, I'm Iago.
Blackguard am I who has caused all the woe,

I'm Iago, I'm Iago.
Oh, how I tortured that man and his wife,
Until he snuffed out the poor lady's life,
Then turned on himself and inserted a knife,
I'm Iago, I'm Iago.

EMILIA: I am the lady-in-waiting, you see.
Emilia, Emilia.
I saw her this morn at her window,
I saw the red rose in her hair,
I wonder for whom she was watching,
She looked so adorably fair.
Take care, take care, she looked so adorably fair, fair, fair,
Take care, take care, she looked so adorably fair.

CHORUS (singing): "Take care" . . . etc. (Skips on and off stage.)
I think that I saw her give Cassio
A smile as she stood on the stair,
I think that she gave to him also,
The rose that she took from her hair.
Take care, take care, the rose that she took from her hair, hair, hair!
Take care, take care, the rose that she took from her hair.

CHORUS (singing): "Take care," etc. (Skips on and off stage.)
Exit Iago. Enter Desdemon.

DESDEMON (Tune—"Maryland, My Maryland"):
You find me waiting here for you; Othello, my Othello,
I've loyal been to you, and true; Othello, my Othello.
Since you've been gone, I've been so sad,
This handkerchief was all I had,
To cheer me up when I felt sad; Othello, my Othello.

OTHELLO (Tune—"My Bonnie Lies Over the Ocean"):
My head it is likely to bust, dear,
My head it is likely to break;
If ladies weren't present, I'd cuss, dear,
I have such a horrible ache.

DESDEMON (singing that chorus):
There, there, there, there,
We'll wrap it up tight in this handkerchief,
There, there, there, there,
Then maybe it won't cause you such grief.

OTHELLO *(speaking):* Take it away! *(Drops handkerchief.)*
Exeunt Desdemon and Othello. Enter Emilia who finds hand-
kerchief.

EMILIA *(Tune—"Juanita"):*
Down on the floor here, a nice handkerchief I see,
Sure, 'tis the same one, that he begged of me.
How oft old Iago bade me steal it when I could,
But I still refused him, I was quite too good.
Found it, yes, I've found it,
Finding's keeping, so they say,
Found it, yes, I've found it,
He'll have it today!
Iago can find it a cinch to use me.
Emilia, Emilia.
I found that kerchief that caused all the woe,
I found the villain and made him glad to the toe,
Little did I guess that my man was bad, tho,
Emilia, Emilia.

SCENE I

Enter Othello and Desdemon.

OTHELLO *(Tune—"Red River Valley"):*
Goodbye, darling, I must leave you,
Tho' it breaks my heart to go,
Something tells me I am needed,
If we're going to fight the foe.
Here's a token at the parting,
And to you I'll e'er be true,
See the ships are in the harbor,
Goodbye, darling, and adieu.

DESDEMON *(Tune—"Old Black Joe"):*
I thank you for this handkerchief, my dear,
'Twill serve to wipe away my grief and tears,
I'll cherish it with loving care, my dear,
And never lose it, that I promise, have no fear!
Exit Othello. Desdemon stands forsaken. Enter Emilia.

EMILIA *(Tune—"Yankee Doodle"):*
Othello has gone to sea, but do not feel so badly.
It won't bring him back to thee to look so glum and sadly,

Othello has gone away, Othello has gone away,
Othello will fight, they say,
Until they've conquered Turkey. (*Exeunt.*)

SCENE II

Enter Othello, Iago.

OTHELLO (*Tune—"Spanish Cavalier"*):
I'm home from the wars, from the wars I've returned.
To greet my dear wife, Desdemona,
And if I know wimmen, she's waiting, eyes brimming,
Attired in her nicest silk kimona.

IAGO (*Tune—"My Bonnie Lies Over the Ocean"*):
Othello, I'm glad you've come home, sir,
It's time you came back to your wife,
I'd hate for you longer to roam, sir,
Lest it should cause trouble and strife.
Take care, take care,
Lest it should cause trouble and strife, and strife,
Take care, take care, lest it should cause trouble and strife.
Enter Iago. Emilia gives him the handkerchief.

IAGO (*Tune—"I've Been Working on the Railroad"*):
I've been hunting for this handkerchief,
All the livelong day.
I've been wishing I could find it,
Just to prove the things I say.
Now I'll make Othello jealous,
Cause him grief and pain,
Now, I guess that I'll have fixed him,
When he meets his wife again. (*Exit, followed by Emilia.*)

SCENE III

Enter Othello and Desdemon.

OTHELLO (*Tune—"Oh Where, Oh Where Has My Little Dog Gone?"*):
Oh where, Oh where has my bandanna gone,
Oh where have you kept it hid?

DESDEMON: It's safely stored, and will treasured be,
You know I'm not one to kid.

OTHELLO: I believe, I think that you lie to me,
  I think you gave it away.
DESDEMON: Oh, why do you hurt me and cause me woe.
  I couldn't; that's all I can say.
  Exit Desdemon. Othello paces back and forth. Enter Iago.
IAGO (*Tune—"Did You Ever See a Lassie?"*):
  I have found the handkerchief, handkerchief, handkerchief,
  I have found the handkerchief that she gave away.
  She tossed it, she waved it, to Cassio she gave it,
  Oh, I've found the handkerchief that she gave away. (*Exit.*)
OTHELLO (*Tune—"How Dry I Am"*):
  How mad I am, how mad I am,
  Nobody knows how mad I am. (*Exit.*)

SCENE IV

Enter Desdemon.
DESDEMON (*Tune—"Old Black Joe"*):
  Gone are the days when my heart was young and gay,
  Gone are my joys, they have fled so far away,
  Sadly I sigh for the days of long ago,
  I hear his angry footsteps coming, OTHEL-LO!
  He's coming, he's coming, and my head is bending low,
  I hear his angry footsteps coming, O-THEL-LO!
  Falls asleep on couch. Enter Othello.
OTHELLO (*Tune—"Clementine"*):
  O my darling, O my darling,
  O my darling Desdemon,
  You'll be lost and gone forever,
  Dreadful sorry, Desdemon.
  Fair thou wert, and like a fairy,
  But you played me for a sucker,
  You have played upon my heart strings,
  Now, I'll make you a harp plucker! (*Smothers her with cushion.
  Enter Emilia.*)
EMILIA (*Tune—"Juanita," beginning with chorus*):
  'Thello, O, Othello, What in the world have you done?
  'Thello, O, Othello, she's an innocent one!
  Over that there kerchief,
  What an awful fuss you've made,

You got hydrophobia,
When 'twas just mislaid.
Desdemon dropped it, once when you were cross and mad,
Finding it I gave it, to my husband bad.
Iago, Iago, used it then with wicked art.
Iago, Iago (*He looks in from wings with wicked leer*),
What a wretch thou art!

OTHELLO (*Tune—"Hot Time in the Old Town"*):
I've killed you, I loved you best of all,
In my grief, I'll stab myself and fall,
When I'm gone, bring on the bearers-pall,
There'll be some funerals in Venice tonight. (*Stabs self.*)
Original ends here. One group added this epilogue for a "happy ending."

EPILOGUE

Enter friendly undertaker.

FRIENDLY UNDERTAKER (*Tune—"Old Gray Mare"*):
This old play it ain't what it used to be,
Ain't what it used to be, ain't what it used to be,
This old play it ain't what it used to be,
Many long years ago.
Fire department enters and revives the two.

FRIENDLY UNDERTAKER (*Tune—"Yankee Doodle"*):
For we called the fire department,
Gave first aid to 'thello,
On the maiden used pulmotor,
And the grease of elbow.
They were down, and now they're up,
Toast of all the nation,
Gratitude they give to arti-
Ficial respiration!
Representatives from the fire department march around singing, "Hail, Hail the Gang's All Here," or stand in a line, arms on each other's shoulders, singing.

"THE FARMER'S DAUGHTER"

In the early 1900's the plays were all pretty much on this pattern. This one is a take-off on that style of play.

The production can be fairly elaborate or simple. A narrator is needed and someone at the piano or organ (or orchestra) to play "atmosphere music."

There are many blanks in the script, deliberately put there so that you can fill in the names of local or well-known people. Even the years are left blank so that you can fill in appropriately there.

Except for the speeches themselves, indicated after the names of the characters, the narrator reads everything else, perhaps in a soupy radio or television voice.

If desired, the "play" could be broken at a couple of spots to insert commercials, radio style.

This one should have enough rehearsals to make it fairly smooth, although it would be all right to have the scripts read by the characters. It might be done as a radio play. (Actually it was done that way when first presented.)

If the lines don't fit, change them around. It is well to explain to the audience the nature of the play—and the fact that it is a take-off on the 1900 melodrama with its usual farmer, villain, farmer's daughter, mortgage, and hero.

_____ presents . . .

(Chord)

THE FARMER'S DAUGHTER

(Music: The Farmer in the Dell)

A play in __2__ scenes and several dastardly acts!

In seeing this play, remember that any resemblance to any person, living, dead or otherwise, is positively coincidental. The characters are 99 44/100 per cent fictitious.

SCENE I

As the play opens, we notice the setting. We find Farmer (Hiram?) _Hiram_ macDonald setting at a table which has a coal oil lamp on it. It is night. You can tell—because the lamp is lit, and Farmer _Hiram_ never bothers to light his lamp except at night. It is 19_70_ Farmer _Hiram_ is drinking buttermilk.

FARMER: Bills, bills, bills. *(Opens bills.)* Seeds, $95.49. And none of 'em ever come up! Dress for comin' out party, $100.00. The gals these days comes out of 'em too much anyway. And to-morry is Monday, the time fer that skunk _Dick J._ _Dastarly_ to foreclose the mortgage on the farm. *(Drinks buttermilk.)* Woe is me! And besides, I've got lumbago!

Farmer's wife (Matilda?) enters.

FARMER'S WIFE: Why, _Hiram_, yew scum of the earth, worm! Git yoreself right up from there and git out to th' milkin'. Ye're the laziest creat'r in the caounty of ___Cataby___

Farmer grunts.

FARMER'S WIFE: What's that ye're drinkin', buttermilk? There ye go. I wish I'd never married ye. Oh, if Mr. _Jones_, my first husband, had only lived!

Farmer gets up.

FARMER: Well, jist keep up yore yowlin' a few more months and I'll wish so too! By grab, I never seed sich a sour woman. Think I'll git out in th' fresh air t' where I can git a little body rest in peace.

Farmer _____ exits just anywhere he cares to go.

(Music: The Farmer in the Dell)

ANNOUNCER: *FARMER'S DAUGHTER (BESSIE?)* _Bessie_ *EN-TERS—IS THE PRIDE AND JOY OF HER MOTHER'S HEART. SHE IS JUST HOME FROM SCHOOL, WHERE SHE SHOULD HAVE GRADUATED, BUT DIDN'T.*

FARMER'S DAUGHTER: Good evening, Mothah deah!

FARMER'S WIFE: _Matilda,_ mah little gal. Here yew are home from school. Come ovah here and give yer ma a big juicy kiss. (_____ *does—with great gusto.*) And naow set right here and tell yore old ma everything.

DAUGHTER: Well, mothah, the ___Charm School___ *(School or College)* is chawming, simply chawming! I don't know when I ever had such a good time as during the six years I've been there!

FARMER'S WIFE: Did yew graddiate?

DAUGHER: Well, mothah, it's a long story. I never did graduate. The professors did me an injustice.

FARMER'S WIFE: Well, we'll jist git paw to go over and tell 'em a thing er two. What was it?

DAUGHTER: Oh, mothah, it was terrible. I was supposed to take a silly old comprehensive or something, and I didn't know any-thing about it.

FARMER'S WIFE: Yew didn't?

DAUGHTER: No, and neither did anybody else that I asked. I asked them all what a comprehensive was, and they couldn't even spell it!

FARMER'S WIFE: What did ye dew, chile?

DAUGHTER: Well, Prof. _Smith_, the old meanie, set the comprehensive for the same day we were supposed to have a picnic, so I didn't go.

FARMER'S WIFE: That's the spirit of ye father, chile. He never done nothin' he didn't want to. What did that there Prof. _Smith_ say?

DAUGHTER: He said it was just as well—I wouldn't have passed anyway.

FARMER'S WIFE: Never yew mind, honey. Daughter, yore ol' ma's heart is heavy tonight. Tomorry the mortgage is due on the farm, and that there villyan _Dasterly_ is goin' to foreclose.

DAUGHTER: Isn't there something we can do, mothah?

FARMER'S WIFE: No, child. He wants yore hand in marriage, and as I told yore paw, no, no, 1,000 times no!

DAUGHTER: But why, mothah?

FARMER'S WIFE: Because there ain't no _Dasterly_ good enough fer a _Macdonald_ _Jr. Dasterdly_

ANNOUNCER: _Dick_, _THE BIG VILLAIN, ENTERS. HE SMIRKS AND TWIRLS HIS MOUSTACHE WITH ONE HAND WHILE HE HOLDS IT ON WITH THE OTHER._

VILLAIN: Ah, me proud beauty, I have ye in me power!

FARMER'S DAUGHTER: Listen, mug, maybe you don't know what a wicked right I can swing!

VILLAIN: Ah, I hold the mortgage on the fahm. Either you marry me or else . . .

DAUGHTER: Or else what?

VILLAIN: Or else I'll foreclose and eevict ye!

FARMER'S WIFE: What does that mean?

VILLAIN: It means I'll put ye out in the cold.

FARMER'S WIFE: Very well. I'd rather die by freezin' than t' think of my daughter married to the likes of ye.

ANNOUNCER: _HIRAM ENTERS WEARILY. HE WAS BORN TIRED._

FARMER: What're ye doin' here, _Dasterly_?

VILLAIN: I come to give ye yuh last chance, Hiram.

FARMER: What do ye mean, scum?

VILLAIN (*leers and twitches his moustache*): I mean that ye'll pay the mortgage or git put out of this here house, bag and baggage!

FARMER: We ain't got no baggage. Hit's all in the pawn shop in Conover (name of a town).

VILLAIN: Then I'll put ye out of this here house . . . *period!* (*Glowers at the farmer*) Kin ye pay?

FARMER: No, I kaint, Dasterly Ye'll have to come back Tuesday. Ye kain't git blood out of a turnip.

VILLAIN (*aside*): Curses, my plan is foiled. (*Aloud*) Very well, I'll come back Tuesday. And I'll not come alone—there'll be the sheriff!

FARMER: Go, and never darken my door again!

VILLAIN: Blast you, _____. It won't be your door. By jiminy, it'll be my door next Tuesday. (*Villain storms out triumphantly.*)

SCENE II

ANNOUNCER: *THE SCENE CHANGES. AS THE SCENE OPENS, WE FIND* Bessie, *THE LOVELY FARMER'S DAUGHTER, READY TO GO OUT TO DO HER MILKING. BUT NOW WE MEET A NEW CHARACTER, OUR HERO HOMER* Noodleman. *IT IS LATE AFTERNOON. IT IS SPRING. THE BIRDS ARE SINGING. OUR HERO HAS COME OVER TO SEE* Bessie, *FULLY DETERMINED TO HOLD HER HAND TONIGHT IF THE OPPORTUNITY PRESENTS ITSELF.* (*Music: "Light Cavalry Overture" or something similar.*)

FARMER'S DAUGHTER: Homer! How wonderful it is that you've come over!

HOMER: Don't I come every Tuesday?

DAUGHTER: Yes, that is true. You can help me with the milking. Listen, don't the birds sing sweetly?

Sound of birds singing sweetly. Music: "Let's All Sing Like the Birdies."

HOMER: Yeah!

DAUGHTER: Ah, Homer, it is the springtime. "In the spring a young man's fancy . . ."

HOMER (*bashfully*): Uh-huh!

DAUGHTER: Yes, it seems that this very night was made for romance! (*There is a long pause.*) . . . That's enough!

HOMER: Bessie! (*Or whatever daughter's name is.*)

DAUGHTER (*tenderly*): Yes, Homer!

HOMER: Sumpin' I wanted to ask you for a long time!

DAUGHTER (*breathlessly. She uses Listerine*): What, Homer?

HOMER: Some night soon, I was wondering if . . . if . . .

DAUGHTER: What . . . Homer?

HOMER: I was wondering if . . . you'd let me hold your hand!

DAUGHTER: Homer, you darling! I knew you hadn't been coming over here for fourteen years without something on your mind.

HOMER (*encouraged*): Gorsh! Let's go out and do the milkin'.

Music: "Let Me Call You Sweetheart," or something like that.

DAUGHTER: Mothah, oh, mothah, come here!

FARMER'S WIFE: What is it, my child?

DAUGHTER: Mothah, you can stop calling me child now. I am grown up. Homer wants to hold my hand.

FARMER'S WIFE: Why, Homer, I didn't know. I'm so glad for both of yew.

Music: Mendelssohn's Wedding March.

DAUGHTER: Oh, Homer! My heart is filled to overflowing with romance!

FARMER'S WIFE: Bessie! You'd better go on out and milk Bossie!

DAUGHTER: All right. Come on, Homer, Love!

ANNOUNCER: *HOMER AND BESSIE LEAVE, HAND IN HAND, SWINGING A MILK PAIL . . . WELL, IT'S ABOUT TIME TO HAVE THE VILLAIN COME BACK. NO PLAY OUGHT TO GO LONG WITHOUT HAVING THE VILLAIN IN OCCASIONALLY TO KEEP THINGS IN SUSPENSE. HERE COMES THAT LOW-DOWN _____ TO COLLECT THE MORTGAGE AGAIN.*

FARMER'S WIFE: There ye are, _____ , again!

VILLAIN: Yes, here I am agin'. Some day my patience is going to git the better of me. Even a villain has his weak points.

FARMER'S WIFE: What do yew mean, yew blackguard?

VILLAIN: I mean that I am tired of coming over here every Tuesday for the last twenty years to collect the mortgage on the farm.

FARMER'S WIFE: That's what a villain is fer, ain't it?

VILLAIN: Maybe it is.

ANNOUNCER: *AH, HERE COMES FARMER HIRAM McDonald. HE IS TIRED AS USUAL. MAYBE HE CAN HELP KEEP THE CONVERSATION LIVELY. IT'S DRAGGING.*

VILLAIN: Ye're the man I want to see, Mc Donald. When are ye goin' to pay the mortgage on the farm?

FARMER: When I get good and derned ready. The sheriff is on my side.

VILLAIN: Yes, but yew forget the National Guard. I'll put ye off yet.

FARMER: Well . . . that'ud be fair enough. We've been puttin' *yew* off for the last twenty years.

VILLAIN: And furthermore, I'm either goin' to marry the gal . . . *(Tweaks mustache and growls and threatens)* . . . or else . . .

FARMER: Or else what . . .

VILLAIN: Or else she'll be so decrepit that even a villain wouldn't marry her. Just wait.

ANNOUNCER: *VILLAIN STORMS OUT AGAIN. IT IS A GOOD STAGE TECHNIQUE FOR A VILLAIN TO STORM.*

FARMER'S WIFE: Hiram, I've been wantin' to talk to yew about Bessie.

FARMER: Well . . . ?

WIFE: It's about that there Filler Bresh Man, Jim Drush.

FARMER: Well . . . ?

WIFE: He's been comin' over to see her too often.

FARMER: Well . . . ?

WIFE: Hit ain't right. And besides, Homer Noodleman is interested in her.

FARMER: Whut makes ye think so, Matildy?

WIFE: Why, I heered him, plain as day, ask her if he could hold her hand tonight.

FARMER: Glory be!

WIFE: And with a little encouragement he might be one of the family in a few years.

FARMER: Say, Matildy, that wouldn't be so bad. He's got a big red Cadillac, ain't he?

MATILDY: When that Filler Bresh man comes agin', we'll jist tell him!

ANNOUNCER: *AT THIS POINT THE FILLER BRUSH MAN COMES ALONG . . . READY TO SELL HIS WARES ONCE MORE TO THESE SIMPLE FOLK. (OF COURSE IT MAY BE A FEW MINUTES BEFORE HE GETS HERE . . . BECAUSE YOU CAN HEAR HIM A COUNTRY BLOCK AWAY, AND THE BLOCKS IN _____ COUNTY ARE LONG BLOCKS.)* Catawba

BRUSH MAN: Good evening, madam, how did you like the last brush I sold you?

MATILDY: Hit was turrible. All the bristles come out.

BRUSH MAN: I can't understand it. I sold one to _____'s wife, and she has been using it for the usual combination—hairbrush and shoebrush. I just can't understand it.

MATILDY: It wouldn't be fer the likes of ye to understand it. Comin' over here to act like you're selling breshes, and then making up to our Bessie!

HIRAM: Yes, young man, what are yore intentions?

BRUSH MAN: My intentions are perfectly honest. I'm an honest man!

MATILDY: If ye was honest, yew wouldn't be stretchin' the truth about yer breshes.

BRUSH MAN: Well, that's different—it's just business! Now, speaking of business, we have here a little brush that can be used for cleaning the finger nails, polishing the toenails, as a vegetable brush, and for cleaning the corners of the stairs. It is excellent for all these purposes, yet as a weekend special, we sell it for only 39 cents.

HIRAM: Son, if that bresh could do all you say, ye'd be rentin' it by the week. Bessie don't want nobody like you.

BRUSH MAN: You want a successful business man for your daughter, don't you, Mr. _____?

HIRAM: Well, let's see. What kind of a car have ye got, son?

BRUSH MAN: I drive a 19__ Chevrolet.

HIRAM: Well, son, you've just lost in the battle of the sixes. Homer _____ has a 19__ Packard! Goodbye.

BRUSH MAN: If you need one of those fingernail brushes, Mrs. . . .

HIRAM: Son, I said goodbye. That means git out!

ANNOUNCER: _____ *BRUSH MAN GOES OUT, WAGGING HIS BRUSHES BEHIND HIM. AND NOW WHO SHOULD*

BE LURKING IN THE CORNER BUT _____, *THE DAS-TARDLY VILLAIN!*

VILLAIN: Yew know what, Hiram _Noodleman_?

HIRAM: No, _____, what?

VILLAIN: The National Guard is comin' over to put yew off in ten minutes.

MATILDY: I told yew he'd git us out some day, Hiram!

VILLAIN: Ye'll rue the day ye told me to leave yore house, Hiram _Noodleman_

ANNOUNCER: *THIS IS THE OPPORTUNE TIME FOR THE HERO TO COME IN. TEN MINUTES IS A PRETTY SHORT TIME. HE COULD WAIT TILL IT WAS FIVE MINUTES AND MAKE IT MORE DRAMATIC, BUT HE TALKS KIND OF SLOW, SO TEN MINUTES IS BETTER. BESIDES, BESSIE IS WITH HIM.*

HOMER: Wait there, _____ (villain's name). I'd have a word with ye!

VILLAIN *(aside):* I wonder what this young sprout has up his sleeve?

HOMER: The ace card. *(Pulls out an ace.)* Also a diploma. *(Pulls out diploma.)*

MATILDY: Why, Homer, I never knowd ye had any schoolin'.

VILLAIN *(aside):* I smell a rat, methinks!

MATILDY: Bessie, go see if we caught a rat in the trap!

HOMER: _____ *(villain's name),* how much income tax did ye pay in 19__?

VILLAIN: I refuse to answer that question.

HOMER: I know—ye didn't pay none.

> "If for your evils you don't atone
> They'll put you where they put Al Capone!"

VILLAIN *(aside):* Curses! *(Music chord)* Foiled! *(Another one)* I might have known you couldn't beat a hero. *(To Hiram)* All right, Hiram, the farm is yours.

ANNOUNCER: _D.V.D_ *(Villain's name) SLINKS OUT THE BACK WAY TO THE OBLIVION THAT ALWAYS AWAITS GOOD VILLAINS. THEY ARE OF NO USE WHEN THE FINAL LOVE SCENE COMES AROUND.*

BESSIE *(softly):* Homer, how wonderful you were!

HOMER: Aw, it weren't much, Bessie.

BESSIE: You're simply wonderful, Homer. Simply!

MATILDY: Let's let it go at that.

HOMER: Bessie, there's somethin' I've been wantin' to ask you.

BESSIE: Anything, Homer, anything!

HOMER: Well . . . Bessie . . . you know our family lot over at the graveyard?

BESSIE: Why, I think so, Homer. Why?

HOMER: Well, I've jist been wondering . . . if you'd like . . . to be buried in it!

BESSIE: Homer, I'm just dying to!

HIRAM: Well, son, I've got to hand it to ye. That was great, the way ye handled that there villain, _____.

MATILDY: It shore was, Homer.

HIRAM: And it showed me if I'm goin' to have a good clear brain, I'll jist have to give up buttermilk.

MATILDY: Blessings on ye, Homer. Ye've cured Hiram. I knowed ye was a hero, way back in the play.

ANNOUNCER: *HOMER AND BESSIE TAKE THE MILK PAIL AND GO ONCE MORE TO DO THE CHORES. HIRAM AND MATILDY ARE AT PEACE.*

EPILOGUE

The moral, my friends,
　　Is to always be good,
If _____ (*name of villain*) had done
　　Everything that he should,

He'd not been the villain,
　　Blackhearted as Nero
He'd have won him a gal,
　　And perhaps been the hero.

To all who have heard it,
　　Let this be a lesson . . .
(*Slower*) If you've been asleep
　　You've received a great blessing.

THE RACE

With a little care, this one can be made clever. It will depend on the get-up of the characters. If you can think of other gags, by all means, use them.

A horse comes out and faces the audience. (This could be one of those improvised horses, composed of two persons with a blanket over them, and perhaps an improvised neck and head. Sometimes a broom is used to make a horsehead, with a paper sack over the straw part. The sack, of course, is painted like a horsehead. If in order to have the person heard he must have his head out from under the blanket, perhaps his own head could be made up, horselike.)

ANNOUNCER HORSE: Well, horses, it's a great day for the race! And what a race—the human race. Here we are out at the PEOPLE ARE FUNNY Race Track, ready to begin the big race for a purse of 100,000. (That's a lot of hay!) In a few minutes we are going to bring you some news of interest to our social set, but first a word from the sponsor.

COMMERCIAL: Horses, when you lie down in your stalls at night, does your back ache? Then try one of our new mattresses, filled with people hair, and you will find new comfort, new relief. Remember the spelling—P-E-O-P-L-E.

ANNOUNCER: And now back to the track where the people are already trotting. The day is clear and cold. Some of the racers are already down there—we see browns, and reds and whites and yellows and blacks. What a race! At first there was a little trouble in getting them all to run, but as we heard down at the stables (pardon me, bunkhouse) this morning, one of them said, "We are all of the same race—the human race."

Well, while we are waiting for the race, let's see what we can see of famous personages out here at the track, in their favorite stalls. Here is our social editor, Nellie, who has some remarks.

Another horse, obviously female, comes out.

ANNOUNCER HORSE: Hi, Nellie!

NELLIE: Hi, there, Nag!

ANNOUNCER: What about some social news, Nellie?

NELLIE: All right. There are lots of horses out here this afternoon for the PEOPLE ARE FUNNY race. All the stalls are filled with finery. I don't believe I have ever heard so many excited whinnies, and I'm sure that this track has never seen so many fine horsefeathers. Let's see who is here. Down in a front stall there is Whirlaway. Next to him looks like Butterfingers, and then Turnabout.

ANNOUNCER: Excuse me, Nellie, but that's not Turnabout, is it? It's Fairplay!

NELLIE: Oh well, *Turnabout* is *Fairplay*, eh? Don't get horsey with me!

ANNOUNCER: Do you know who that *dark horse* is down there?

NELLIE: Why, that's Brown Bomber. And look who is next to him!

ANNOUNCER: It's Silver, isn't it?

NELLIE: It surely is. Now that's a horse of a different color!

ANNOUNCER: Nellie, you must be getting thirsty. Have something to drink?

NELLIE: Sure, get me something.

ANNOUNCER: Straw?

NELLIE: No, but I'll take a little hay on the side.

COMMERCIAL: Here's a word from our sponsor. Horses of the feminine persuasion, are you longing for a new hat? When you see our new ones, you will find it hard to restrain yourselves. We mean the new—all new—Alfalfa-woven creations by Gum. There never was a chewier, more delicious hat than these new tenderized creations. And remember . . . they are round, firm, and above all, they are mild, with no unpleasant aftertaste. Try an Alfalfa hat *today!* And now back to the race.

ANNOUNCER: While our social columnist is munching on a little hayburger here, we have a guest from the human race. Will you send in I. M. Human, please?

I. M. HUMAN: Thank you for inviting me today. This morning I wasn't sure I could come up.

ANNOUNCER: What was the trouble?

HUMAN: I was a little horse. Had a little colt. (Hoarse, cold)

ANNOUNCER: Well, we're glad you're better. How are things coming down at the track?

HUMAN: In fine shape now.

ANNOUNCER: Yes, you've done a grand job. You had to work like a—shall I say, *person*—to get the job done, eh? Did you have trouble with the platform?

HUMAN: No, we had plenty of (excuse the expression) saw-horses, so we used them underneath.

ANNOUNCER: That's fine.

HUMAN: By the way, I'm just curious, being a member of the human race, about all these horses out here this afternoon. Are they betting on the race?

ANNOUNCER: Betting on the race? I should say not. Any horse would know better than to bet on *people*.

HUMAN: I'm curious to know why this is so true.

ANNOUNCER: That's simple, Mr. Human. We've got *horse sense!*

BLACKOUT

SERIOUS MATERIAL

In the informal drama field there seems to be a definite place for the serious sketch. This section includes the following examples:

1. "What Would You Do?" as an illustration of a dramatic sketch used to introduce discussion.
2. "A Folk Festival Script," showing how such a program may be tied together with a narrative.
3. "Seven Stages of Womanhood," an interesting setting for a mother-daughter banquet.
4. "Man's Eternal Quest for the Good Life," an effort to help bring additional understanding about the variety of man's expression of his religious faith.

It is likely that none of these serious skits would be used "as is" but would be adapted considerably—particularly the folk festival script. They are presented here only as stimulators.

WHAT WOULD YOU DO?[5]

CHARACTERS

George Burnam, Superintendent of Hospital
Margaret Sherman, Secretary and Receptionist

SCENE

Office, Wesley Memorial Hospital

TIME

1 a.m.

PROPERTIES

Two desks	Telephone	Stapler
Typewriter	Sheet of green paper	Two chairs
	Hatrack	

[5] Written by Adona R. Sick, Endicott, N. Y., and suggested by Betty Pembridge, Endicott, N. Y.

As scene opens Superintendent Burnam is folding papers, placing them in folio, clearing his desk, and preparing to leave the building.

Miss Sherman is finishing the final copy of the hospital budget for the next year. She pulls the last sheet from the typewriter, gives it a final check and hands it to Mr. Burnam.

Miss Sherman: Here it is at last, Mr. Burnam, right on the dot of one a.m. The final figures of your precious budget with not a single typographical error. Such a beautifully prepared manuscript should make a favorable impression upon the trustees of Wesley Memorial Hospital. (*Mr. Burnam reaches for it.*)

Mr. Burnam: I've worked on that thing for five weeks and I can hardly wait to get the final form into my hands.

Miss Sherman: Now just a minute, Mr. Burnam, first let me put on a nice green back sheet and staple it together. It will look so much more official. You know it is necessary to have your dream child dressed in her Sunday best. . . . There, how do you like it?

Mr. Burnam: Swell, elegant! Beautiful, perfect! It surely has the "Come hither" look. And Miss Sherman, I want you to know that I sincerely appreciate the extra time you have put on this project.

Miss S.: That's quite all right, Mr. Burnam. You know my heart is in this work and I'm glad to do anything I can, even to the point of giving up my beauty sleep from nine to twelve.

Mr. B.: You have shown a wonderful spirit, even if you are going to look tired tomorrow.

Miss S.: Tomorrow—did you say? You mean today! It's after 1 a.m. now, you know.

Mr. B.: So it is. But what I started to say was that even if your face does look tired tomorrow—you may console yourself with the fact that you have a pure heart, and Miss Sherman, God looks not upon the outward appearance; he looks into the heart.

Miss S.: I think you really believe that and I wish the world believed it too.

Mr. B.: Miss Sherman, they will in time. Now for just a minute, look at this budget.

Miss S.: You mean *proposed* budget.

Mr. B.: Yes! Yes! Of course, "proposed budget." When I present a nice crisp copy to each of the board members next week and they see this comfortable margin in the black instead of the usual deficit in red, I'm sure they will be so happily surprised that they will—

Miss S.: What! Raise your salary?

Mr. B.: No, no—I never think about myself—right now, all I think about day and night is that new wing we must have on this hospital—if we are to continue serving this community in an efficient way. You know, Miss Sherman this is really a superior section of the city and the people demand the best and the latest in hospital service and equipment.

Miss S.: How soon do you expect to start your big financial campaign for the $50,000 needed for the new wing?

Mr. B.: Just as soon as I get the approval of the hospital board. But you know those men—careful, scrutinizing, sophisticated business men. They are proud of this hospital and the prestige it enjoys in our community. As long as everything moves to their fancy, they will approve the architect's plan for the $50,000 wing, set up a high-powered financial campaign and in less than two years our ten-year's dream would be a reality. If I could see this wing constructed, and in service to suffering humanity, I should count it one of the high points in my life.

Miss S.: What do you mean by saying "if things move according to the board's fancy"?

Mr. B.: You know, Miss Sherman, just as well as I do—well, how the board feels about admitting Negroes to our hospital. Always I have the feeling that the color-line problem is an explosive issue with our hospital board. Just one little spark would set off a big flame, cut our financial support, split the hospital board, and harm the whole hospital cause.

Miss S.: Yes, I know all that, but surely the board knows the position the General Conference has taken on the question of racial discrimination.

Mr. B.: Yes, and it also knows the strength of community sentiment.

Miss S.: Of course, but do *they* know that in April, 1950, the

United States Supreme Court ruled against the segregation of Negroes in state universities, dining cars, etc.?

MR. B.: I suppose they know all that, and when it is in Oklahoma or somewhere else they would agree with the decision of the Supreme Court. But it's quite a different story at Wesley Memorial Hospital, you know.

MISS S.: Say! It's already 1:30 a.m., and you are tired out and a bit pessimistic. Tomorrow things will look brighter. (*Miss S. puts on her coat.*)

MR. B.: I guess it's time to go home all right.

Mr. B. puts on scarf and coat. Telephone rings and from force of habit Miss S. takes down receiver.

MISS S.: This is Margaret Sherman at Reception, Wesley Memorial Hospital. Who? Where? Just a minute, please. (*Miss S. turns to Mr. B.*) An ambulance has just driven up with a Negro taxi driver, critically injured in an accident down at Five Points a few minutes ago. Shall we admit him?

MR. B.: They had better take him over to Asbury. That's where we send all our colored patients, you know.

MISS S.: We're very sorry, but we usually send all our colored patients over to Asbury. (*Miss S. turns again to Mr. B.*) It's Dr. Bushley on the line and he insists that Asbury doesn't have equipment needed for the case.

MR. B.: Tell him we consider their equipment modern and up to date.

MISS S. (*over phone*): Really, Dr. Bushley we are very sorry, but the equipment at Asbury is considered modern by most medical men. (*Miss S. in desperation—turns to Mr. B. and says*): Mr. Burnam, you take the phone. It's Dr. Bushley, and I don't know how to deal with him.

MR. B.: You're doing fine. Go right ahead.

MISS S. (*back on line*): Yes, I know, we're sorry—you understand of course how it is—Oh! I see, just a minute, please! I'll clear again. (*Miss S. turns to Mr. Burnam.*) This is serious—Dr. Bushley won't be put off—it's a matter of life or death. He says, "Seconds count." What shall I tell him?

MR. B.: This is what I meant—the color line. If I admit him, the issue will again come to the headlines. The board will not allow Negro patients in this hospital. The financial drive will not be organized, and our new wing will be pushed into the future for at least ten long years—What shall I do? What shall I do?

Miss S.: Hurry up—Dr. Bushley is frantic—he is demanding. He says we daren't discriminate. Human life is precious—it is a matter of seconds with the patient. Now what shall I say?

Turns again to the phone.

Yes, Dr. Bushley—What did you say? Oh! yes, certainly, certainly; just a minute—

Turns again to Mr. Burnam.

Dr. Bushley is desperate—he says that at least a dozen times he has heard you close your dramatic financial campaign speeches, with the words—"Inasmuch as you have done it unto one of the least of these" . . . He says to tell you this taxi driver is "one of the least" and he *must* be admitted; it's only an emergency case. Mr. Burnam, what shall I say?

Mr. B.: Of course I know we should admit the taxi driver. I agree he is "one of the least," but what about the members of the hospital board? What will they say? What about the financial campaign? What about the community sentiment? What about *the new wing?*

Miss S.: What would you do? (*Miss S. hangs up receiver and turns to audience.*) It is true enough Asbury does not have the best equipment, but it is a first-rate good hospital. This is a typical question the church and its institutions face today. The question is too involved to be answered by two persons. The answer demands social action and so we turn it back to you, THE CHRISTIAN PUBLIC. *What would you do?*

The curtain now opens on Scene 2 with chairman in charge.

NOTE: The chairman then directs a general discussion.

DOING A FOLK FESTIVAL

This skit program was used on the platform of a large youth conference before 5,000 young people. You will need to adapt it to your *own* situation. You might want to use the accompanying script as a starter, but build it around your own performers. If you do not have a storyteller available, make use of some other angle. The poetry-song-game-story formula makes for good balance and change of pace, however. In a true festival, many different groups participate. Perhaps there are some displaced per-

sons, or others with backgrounds across the seas, who would
take part.

What about material for a festival? You might have a wonderful storyteller or someone from another land with a fine collection
of folk art material which could be used. A thorough search of
the community may produce just the person you need. Mr.
Richard Chase, of Big Stone Gap, Virginia, is famous for his
folk stories, oral and on paper. His book *Grandfather Tales*
(Houghton Mifflin, New York) contains a number of folk stories
suitable for presentation. Let someone read the stories several
times, then tell them. *Ol' Man Adam an' His Chillun* by Roark
Bradford is also popular as a source for stories for a festival.
These are folklike material, gathered by Bradford in the vicinity
of New Orleans. They are tales of the days when "de Lawd
walked on the earth like a natural man." You can get the pocket
edition from Fun Books, and you can get recordings of E. O.
Harbin's readings of three Roark Bradford stories.

Festival for Fun

Whatever is done in a folk festival, it ought to be for fun. To
offer prizes to the best group tends to put the affair on a different
basis from that of "just having fun." If various groups (e.g., sub-
districts, or various schools or scout groups) are to put on
performances, encourage them to be as authentic as possible.
Too many flourishes and frills can call attention to themselves
and not enough to the activity and the group fun.

Fun and Festival from the Other Americas is chock full of
ideas for presenting a festival, including table decoration ideas,
songs, games, and menus. Other books in the Fun and Festival
series would help, like *Fun and Festival . . . Among America's
Peoples . . . From India . . . From Japan . . . From China.*

Source Material for Folk Festival

1. Grace Creswell records
2. E. O. Harbin records ("Little David," "No Vacancy," "How
   Come Christmas"
3. Dean Faulkner records (six Negro folk tales)
4. "Ol' Man Adam an' His Chillun" from Fun Books, 5847 Gregory, Hollywood, California, only

5. *God's Trombones,* by James Weldon Johnson. Contains "The Creation," Viking Press, publishers. ("The Creation" may not be used if admission is charged, except by special arrangement with Viking Press.)
6. *Grandfather Tales,* by Richard Chase, Houghton Mifflin, publishers
7. Fun and Festival series, described above
8. World of Fun folk game records
9. *Lift Every Voice,* 125 folk songs, Service Department, Box 871, Nashville 2, Tennessee

FOLK FESTIVAL SCRIPT

Presented "Radio Style" at the Methodist Youth Conference, Purdue University

ANNOUNCER: The National Convocation of Methodist Youth presents. . . . The World of Fun Folk Festival *(organ music)* with 200 Merrymakers . . . the Illinois Wesleyan Choir . . . a mystery guest . . . Grace Creswell . . . Dick Chase . . . Lou Hilbert at the organ . . . and the Grand Chorus of 5,000 under the direction of Augustus Zanzig.

Costumes made by Mrs. D. C. Bowman, Barbara Eskew, and others.

This Festival was arranged by the committee: Bert Lyle, May Titus, E. O. Harbin, J. Lem Stokes, II, and the chairman, Larry Eisenberg, who is your host for the evening.

NARRATOR:

By the shores of Rio Wabash,
On the Boilermaker campus,
In this wigwam, "Hall of Music,"
Gather we for folkish festival,
Sharing game and song and story,
From across the world-wide parish.

Let there come forth merrymakers,
Bringing with them joy and laughter,
Give us wholesome merrymaking
And the joy that comes thereafter.

MERRYMAKERS *enter and do these three folk games:*
Helston Furry Processional (organ) using music "Cornish May Song" from *Lift Every Voice*

Cumberland Square Eight (Record M109)
Kalvelis (Record M101)

VERSE CHOIR and NARRATOR *are on for the next section.*
NARRATOR:

Long ago, near the beginning,
Ever since man was created,
He has looked aloft and wondered . . .
WHAT IS THERE BEYOND THE VASTNESS . . . ?
WHY THIS WORLD, ITS FAR-FLUNG BEAUTY . . . ?
WHO AM I . . . WHAT KIND OF CREATURE . . . ?

From within the heart of mankind
Face upturned to the eternal

Came expressions of these wonders
(FOLK ART OF THE HIGHEST ORDER)

VERSE CHOIR (*Quote Psalm 8, "When I consider . . ."*)
NARRATOR:

Turning from celestial wonder,
Then man paused to look about him;
Looked at others of his likeness,
Longed to be with them and *like* them.
Through this deep and wistful longing,
Understood the Great God's longing,
As he stopped this world's creation
Making mankind in His likeness,
Wanting man to come up to Him.
Listen to this great folk sermon,
Masterpiece by Weldon Johnson,
"*God's Trombones,*" the book contains it.

VERSE CHOIR (*Reads "The Creation" from* God's Trombones)
NARRATOR:

Just as God has longed for people,
So have they yearned for each other,
Deep within the souls of persons
Are the longings to be brothers.

Passing years brought men together,
Joining in the friendly circle,
First, perhaps, around a campfire
As they acted out their stories.
Then when man had learned a language,
Spun he yarns about adventures.

Thus it was when came the springtime,
Folks rejoiced at this new season,

Made a maypole in the village,
Gave their praises for the springtime.
Formed themselves in lovely patterns,
Put their poetry in motion,
Dramatized their daily labors;
Like "Kalvelis"—Lithuanian
Imitating village smithy.

So it was, in days of old-time,
In this very very country,
Even here in Indiana,
That our pioneer forebears,
Sang and played for joy of living,
All worked hard to get the crops in.
Then someone would have a party,
They would play some games with singing.
Out would go the glad announcement,
Everywhere the news was welcome.

So it was that the whole family,
Loaded up onto a wagon,
Rode for miles and miles to get there,
Eager, ready for the funtime.
(It might last from dusk to sunup)
Singing, playing, telling stories,
Joyful in association.

Long before the days of Burl Ives,
Since man first heard wind in treetops,
Listened to the flow of water;
Thrilled to sound of bird and insect,
Man has longed to make some music,
Through his music to find happiness,
Singing of his pain and sorrow,
Singing for the joy of living,
Singing praises to the Great One;
Harmony is his in music,
Music flowing out spontaneous,
Rhythmic sound to bring him pleasure.

Thus it was that came our folklore,
From the lives of simple people,
Song and story, game and poetry,
Like the wild flowers in rare beauty.
Ageless art, yet always timely,
Sincere, earthly and eternal.

Ringing stones charmed Chinese emperors,
Africans found some bones to rattle,

Hebrews blew their "Land-ram sheep horns,"
And the drum delighted Indians.

These and more man did at fun-time
Did them for the joy of doing,
Long before our Tin Pan Alley,
Long before the Grand Ole Opery.

Now that we have had this background,
Let us join the world in harmony.
Let us sing, from France and Danzig,
Guided by Augustus Zanzig.

*Zanzig takes over for group singing from center mike, using "Lift
Every Voice."*

Verse Choir off. Narrator off. Narrator on at end.

NARRATOR:

Were you ever in the mountains?
Did you ever stay or live there,
Way beyond the tourist cabins,
Where you couldn't buy a post card?

God made hills for many reasons,
Made them to preserve folk treasures,
Or, at least, hills give protection
To old customs, songs and stories.
There our folklore passes, living,
From the older to the younger.

Thus it was from an oasis,
Near the foothills of the mountains,
Young Grace Creswell learned from Granny
Many songs from "Way back yonder."

Listen, all within this wigwam
As she sings her songs of beauty.
(We've made records of her singing—
It was just our folklore duty.)

Grace Creswell sings with autoharp.

NARRATOR:

Let us have more games and music,
Let us look across the ocean,
Where the famous Danish Chicken,
"Crested Hen" is in full motion.
Come again, our merrymakers,
This game is a joy to tackle,
Start the music, let us hear her
Lay an egg, and hear her cackle.

The Merrymakers return to do "The Crested Hen." Record M108.

NARRATOR:

Let us go south of our border
For the Mexican "La Raspa."
It is done the country over
In each village, and each casa.

Dancers do "La Raspa," Record M106.

NARRATOR:

Finally we go to England
(This is where our costumes come from)
For the music of the Grand Square.

*Merrymakers do "Grand Square" to "Newcastle" music and leave.
Record M113.*

NARRATOR:

Let us go back to the mountains,
Up the hills and down the hollers.
If we're roaming in Virginia,
We might meet our next performer.
"Richard Chase" some people call him,
But to children through the hill-land
And to many others like them,
He is just "the man with stories."

Miles and miles he tramped to get them,
Talking, living with the people.
Full are they of folk tradition,
Stories of the cabin fireside.
(If you like his kind of folklore,
Check the Convocation bookstore.)

"Come, Sir Richard, can you tell us,
How a corn stalk grew to heaven?
Fill this wigwam with your stories,
Of the fabulous "Old Roany"
Far surpassing Hopalong's pony.

*Chase tells two folk stories, leads the group in singing "Garden
Hymn."*

NARRATOR:

Now our festival moves location,
To the wigwam called the Field House.
Follow flashlights to the field house
For good games, good songs, good humor.
(You can even buy refreshments
If you've got enough Mazuma.)

SEVEN STAGES OF WOMANHOOD[6]

PROLOGUE

GRANDMOTHER PIERSON (*knitting in chair at one end of the stage*): My, but my hands are tired. The fingers seem to be getting stiff as the years go by. I guess I'll just put this knitting down for a moment. (*Looks at picture on a nearby table.*) Isn't Linda a pretty child? She looks a great deal like our Barbara when she was four weeks old. I wonder if I can't find a picture of her in this album and compare the two.

SCENE I. MOTHER'S JOY

Mother with baby in her arms sings lullaby.

GRANDMOTHER: Ah, here's one. Yes, they do look very much alike. Same little nose and wide-set eyes. I remember the day David took this snapshot of us. It had been a beautiful day.

SCENE II. HER FIRST DEPARTURE

And Barbara is left at school with the teacher but refuses to let mother go home.

GRANDMOTHER: And here's Barbara when she was five years old. I believe this was taken on her first day of school. How she hated to have me leave! That was one of the hardest days in her life, hard for both of us.

SCENE III. PIGTAILS

Barbara recites for school program, forgets, and embarrasses her mother. Teacher tries to prompt her.

GRANDMOTHER: I remember another day I visited school. It was about three years later. Barbara was eight years old then, and it was her first assembly. She was performing in front of the whole school. And, oh, was she naughty!

SCENE IV. ADOLESCENT

Home alone; girl friends learn to smoke, put on make-up, talk about boys and other teen-age concerns.

GRANDMOTHER: It wasn't long after that when Barbara started to grow up—that difficult adolescent stage. What a problem that was! Make-up, boys, and cigarettes!

SCENE V. DATING

Preparation for first formal—got wrong color of flowers—waltz around—boy is waiting.

[6] Thanks to Harry D. Edgren, George Williams College, Chicago, Ill. Done by some of his students.

GRANDMOTHER: And then there was her first real ball. I'll never forget how she looked in her first "formal." What an exciting night that was! And it was so hard to realize she was no longer my baby, but a charming and poised young lady.

SCENE VI. BRIDAL SHOWER
Small surprise shower is being held for Barbara.

GRANDMOTHER: I thought I had her safe in college, but she wasn't there long before she met Jim. They had so much fun together and so many things in common—well, it's just obvious that they were meant for each other.

SCENE VII. BARBARA'S JOY
Mother with baby in her arms sings a lullaby.

GRANDMOTHER: And now there's a third generation. Who could ask for a prettier, more lovable grandchild than little Linda? Barbara is such a lovely mother!

H'm, I've certainly been daydreaming for a long time! I'd better get back to my knitting. Linda will be needing this sweater before long.

MAN'S ETERNAL QUEST FOR THE GOOD LIFE[7]

The lights go on for only one side of the stage. Here sits a priest behind a desk.

He is a kindly-looking young man with clerical collar and either black suit or black robe. He is busy with some papers. Books and papers are piled up on his desk.

A student walks in with books under his arm. He is in typical student dress, sport shirt, etc. He walks up to the desk. The priest recognizes him as he looks up.

The priest stands up, shakes his hand, and tells him to sit down.

PRIEST: Sit down, my boy. I'm so glad to see you. And how is school going these days? (*Sits down.*)

STUDENT: Thank you, Father. (*Sits down.*) School is going fine, but I am a little puzzled about a few things. I thought I'd like to talk them over with you.

---

[7] This was first done by the students of Dr. Harry D. Edgren, George Williams College, Chicago, to interpret the world's religions. Because of the obvious symbolism of the priest, he is used to draw the whole skit together. The person might just as well be pictured as a minister or a rabbi, if that seemed more appropriate for the occasion on which you are using this sketch.

PRIEST: Certainly. I think that would be splendid. What's on your mind?

STUDENT: Well, we've been studying different creeds and religions in a couple of my classes, and I'm all mixed up.

PRIEST: I can see why you would be. All of us are puzzled at the wide array of religions and faiths. But do go on.

STUDENT: First we learn about the good points of one faith, and I almost become convinced about it as the faith I want. . . . Then we skip to something else, and I get all confused about religion. Say, just what is religion, anyway?

PRIEST: I'm glad you asked that, son; it is a good place to start. Think about all the things different people of all times have attempted to get from their religion. Think about the American Indian, for instance. You've heard of his belief in a "Happy Hunting Ground."

Lights dim on the two as a light comes on the other side of stage where an Indian is standing. His arms are at his side and then are raised in the Indian fashion of praying. His face upward, he starts to chant the Omaha Tribal Prayer. Wagner's "Magic Fire Music" furnishes a musical background, coming on softly.

INDIAN: "Wa-don-da dhe-dhu, Wa-pa-dhin a-tan-he." *(Repeat.)*
Light fades out on scene as Indian lowers hands. Light goes on to light up the other two. The music lowers and fades out.

PRIEST: You get the picture?

STUDENT: Sure, the Indian wanted his Great Spirit's blessings on his crops, on his hunting, and on his daily living. And he wanted a place in the Happy Hunting Ground. I guess you might say he wanted success and happiness both here and later on. So he called on his belief in a supernatural power to provide these.

PRIEST: And don't we all feel that need? The Confucian is another we might think of. He wanted rain for his crops. He appealed to the rain god for help . . . *(Lights start dimming and coming into focus on the other side of stage. Some music in Far East style is played softly. "Orientale" by Lancers is one record that could be used. A Confucian is standing before a black altar as the lights go on. There might be some oriental trinkets on the altar. He is dressed in an oriental robe and is made up appropriately.)*

CONFUCIAN: *(Rings small bell)* Hear us now, rain god. *(Chanting)* *(Rings small bell)* Hear us now, and bring moisture to our soil. *(Rings small bell)* Know that it is rain for our crops we seek. *(Rings small bell)* Know that before you we are humble and weak.

(Rings small bell) Hear us now! *(With feeling and louder.)*
Light switches at ringing of last bell. Music fades.

PRIEST: Methods change, but rarely do the motives of mankind. Man realizes his insignificance in this universe. That is why religion has always been and always will be a searching out of man's needs—a searching for truth, for warmth, for a here-after. . . .
Lights switch and Negro man and woman dressed in work clothes lay down their gunny sacks full of cotton. Musical background comes up softly. This is either "Swing Low, Sweet Chariot" or "Gwine' to Lay Down My Burden." This fades as they start singing "I Got Shoes."

MAN: "I got-a-shoes," *(Singing or chanting)*

WOMAN: "You got-a-shoes,"

BOTH: "All God's children got shoes. When I go to Heab'n, gonna put on my shoes, Gonna walk all ober God's Heab'n, Heab'n, Heab'n; Everybody talk about Heab'n ain't goin' there, Heab'n, Heab'n: Gonna walk all ober God's Heab'n."
Lights fade out about the next to the last line of the song. Lights go on the priest and student.

STUDENT: I think I'm beginning to see what you mean . . . everyone finds he needs some kind of spiritual help in attaining the things he desires of life.

PRIEST: Right. It seems that all peoples of all times have wanted about the same things out of their lives. They all sought the very best life they could attain through the instrument of religion. Finding their religion, they worshiped. They worshiped their own God in their own particular way . . .
Lights dim on the scene and lights go up on the other side of the stage. Music starts softly and increases. Music backdrop is either "The Holy City" or "Open the Gates of the Temple." A minister is standing in a pulpit which is facing an imaginary

audience. It is standing at an angle with the stage, for effect. The minister is dressed in a black robe with a Bible in his hand. He starts reading and is answered by an unseen audience which consists of several people backstage.

MINISTER: "The Lord is my shepherd, I shall not want."

PEOPLE: "He maketh me to lie down in green pastures; he leadeth me beside the still waters."

MINISTER: "He restoreth my soul: he leadeth me in the paths of righteousness for his name's sake."

PEOPLE: "Yea, though I walk through the valley of the shadow of death, I will fear no evil: for thou art with me; thy rod and thy staff they comfort me."

MINISTER *(Lights start to fade):* "Thou preparest a table before me in the presence of *(Voice trails off to a whisper and the music dims down to almost nothing)* mine enemies, thou anointest *(Voice becomes unheard as lights go off and music quits. Lights switch to the priest-student scene.)*

A musical background comes up very softly to play while the priest talks—"Schubert's Symphony," "New World Symphony."

PRIEST: Well, I suppose you might say that all religions from the primitive to the present groups have sought some of the same things for themselves. They have desired warmth and beauty in life, friendship, love, and happiness. These they have sought and found through religion. Some have found that their religion called for worshiping and appealing to their God. An expression of the belief in the worth of these things in other people is a present-day expression of the possession of the good or the religious life. Some of us choose a certain road, others another. Some take an easy way and ride, others walk; some take the highway, others another way. We are all on this long road striving to get to the same place—a *good* life and to find what there is when we reach the end of that long road of life.

STUDENT: Then religion is recognizing not only the good in ourselves, but also in others. *(Enthusiastically)* It is appreciating the beauty and love of other peoples, no matter what their creed, race, or religion. . . .

Lights dim on this scene and switch to the other side of the stage. Music fades.

The scene is two boys walking across the stage in student's clothing. They carry books under their arms. One boy is white, the other Negro.

FIRST BOY: I voted for you, Bill. You will make a real chairman; you've really got the ability. And I'm a guy who likes to see the guy as chairman be one with plenty on the ball.

NEGRO BOY: Thanks, Jimmie, you're a real pal.

This conversation takes place as they walk to the stage exit. Lights switch to the student and priest.

STUDENT: And then the religious life is one in which we share with others those things that we have and they don't. Is that right?

PRIEST: You bet that's right, my boy. Sharing work, play, health, all those things which make life richer and fuller . . . that's what a religious life seeks to exemplify.

Music starts coming in very softly. This might be "Pilgrim's Chorus." Light to the other side of the stage. There is a table with four or five people sitting around it. One is reading a paper.

CHAIRMAN OF COMMITTEE: You all know what we are gathered here for. All of us are persons who can influence action and legislation bringing about the clearing of our city's slums. The things we need are better housing, playgrounds for underprivileged children, and more sanitary conditions in the area.

FIRST PERSON: Mr. Chairman, I'd like to move that this committee adopt a resolution which it will present to all the clubs here represented, that would provide for such action to be taken.

SECOND PERSON: I second Joe Marlow's motion and would like to say that it wouldn't hurt any of us to dig down and give money to such a cause, too. I think we too often take our neighbor's hardships for granted.

Lights switch to other side of stage. Music continues.

PRIEST: So you see this expression of the good life that is religion is observed in people who are willing to share what they have, even sacrifice, so that other people will have a chance to grow as they grow, and to enjoy their lives. We see it in action right now in our community when we are asked to contribute to bombed-out and destitute countries across the sea. . . .

Music fades out. Chopin's "Funeral March" plays very softly. Lights go on other side of stage. The scene is a girl, dirty and in ragged clothing, sitting on the floor crying. A man in good street dress walks up and speaks to her.

MAN: What is the matter? It is a cold day, you shouldn't be here on the street.

GIRL (*bitterly*): What do you expect when my home is bombed out, my parents dead, no relatives? I'm cold, I'm hungry, I'm numb in my hands and feet. (*Continues to weep.*)

MAN: And to think that in our country there is abundance of everything! I'm going to see to it that my people give until it hurts. . . .

Music completely fades.

Lights dim out and switch to the other scene.

STUDENT: I think I see it quite clearly now. What you are talking about is tolerance, love, the opposite of hate; the recognition that I am not as important as I think I am, that other people are important too. That other people need to have their sense of worth, their sense of belonging. Religion is the instrument to gain these ends.

PRIEST: That's it.

STUDENT: Oh, then what you're talking about is the "One World" idea.

PRIEST: No, not one world, a lot of different parts. This world has passed the stage of needing a colorless unity. What this old world needs is a *colorful harmony.* (*Lights on other side of stage go on. First they go on dimly. Music comes up softly. "Finlandia" is the selection. Music plays while Priest is talking. On stage is the entire cast of the different peoples that have been portrayed.*) Not a unity of one world, but an orchestration of people playing their own instruments in their own way, even with a difference in rhythm but working at the same theme; that is, of human beings enjoying a chance to live not only on the basis of continuing to live, and to live long, but continuing to live well.

Chorus of people sings "A Song of Peace" the words of which follow.

A SONG OF PEACE—*Tune: Finlandia*

This is my song; O God of all the nations,
A song of peace; for lands afar and mine;
This is my home; the country where my heart is,
This is my hope, my dream, my shrine;
But other hearts in other lands are beating
With hopes and dreams the same as mine.

My country's skies are bluer than the ocean,
And sunlight beams on clover-leaf and pine;
But other lands have sunlight too, and clover,
And skies are sometimes blue as mine.
Oh, hear my song, thou God of all the nations,
A song of Peace, for their land and mine.

At the end of the chorus the light goes out on the people and back to the Priest. The music is still playing, "Finlandia," very softly.

PRIEST *(at end of song):* You see, religion is a co-operative quest for the good life.

chapter 7

STUNTS

FROM

OTHER

LANDS

STUNTS FROM OTHER LANDS

THE SKITS in this chapter have been carefully worked out by their author from the folklore of the countries represented. Each has the flavor of a stunt, yet carries with it a ring of authenticity.

Catherine Miller Balm has become well-known the world around for her ability to make enjoyable stunt material from a country's folk tales and legends. All five examples in this book were written by her.

You may want to delve further into folklore sources, such as F. H. Lee's *Folk Tales of All Nations* (Tudor), B. A. Botkin's *Treasury of American Folklore* (Crown), Richard Chase's *Grandfather Tales* (Houghton Mifflin), and others in bookstores and public libraries, as sources of material from which you could produce somewhat similar stunts.

Dramatizing folksongs can help to make an international night successful. There are many fine collections available, some of the best of which are available from Co-operative Recreation Service, Delaware, Ohio.

THE AWFUL FATE OF A FIBBER[1]

A stunt from Japan

by CATHERINE MILLER BALM

CHARACTERS

The Judge	The Recorder
Black Devil, Red Devil	The Woman

COSTUMES

The Judge and the Recorder are in the usual Japanese men's

[1] From *Stunts of All Lands,* by Catherine Atkinson Miller (Richard R. Smith, Inc., N. Y., 1930). Used by permission of the author, Catherine Miller Balm. The playlet is based on the Japanese Kyogen pantomime "The River of Fate."

kimonos. That of the Judge is of bright color; the Recorder's is black.

The Devils may wear the usual costume of tights and close-fitting tunic with long, close sleeves and head covering with horns and an opening for the face. One should be black, the other red. Or they may wear grinning devil's heads.

SETTING

A background of screens or plain curtains. At the center, rear, is the cushion on which the Judge sits. At the right, rear, is a huge kettle with fire under it. The kettle must be large enough to hold the woman and may be cut out of black cardboard and so arranged that only one side shows, or it may be made of paper or muslin over a foundation, such as little chairs arranged in a semicircle. The flames are red paper.

ACTION

The Judge is seated on his cushion. He is sitting on his heels in Japanese fashion. The Devils crouch on each side of the kettle, blowing at the flames.

JUDGE: Is there none coming today across the river which separates life from death?

BLACK DEVIL *(jumping up and running to kneel before the Judge):* There is one, excellency. A woman only.

JUDGE: Bring her before me at once.

The Black Devil orders the Red Devil to fetch the Woman. The Red Devil goes out and returns, dragging the Woman by her wrists. She is terribly afraid, and falls on her knees before the Judge.

RED DEVIL: Here she is, Excellency!

JUDGE: Are you a sinner?

WOMAN *(trembling):* Oh, no, most gracious Judge.

JUDGE: Bring the Keeper of the Book!

The Red Devil goes out and returns with the Recorder who kneels before the Judge, opens his book, and reads.

RECORDER: This woman told fibs, Excellency. Black fibs, white fibs, and gray fibs.

The Devils rub their hands and jump about gleefully.

JUDGE: Pull out her tongue!

The Devils bring an enormous pair of tweezers. While the Red

Devil holds her the Black Devil pulls out her tongue. It is of flannel or paper, and is amazingly long.

JUDGE: Complete the punishment!

The Devils fan the flames beneath the kettle, test the water with their fingers, suck fingers to cool them. The water is very hot. They put Woman in kettle. She screams and screams, and then gradually the screams grow faint and cease. Black Devil peeps into kettle, beckons to Red Devil.

JUDGE: Is the punishment complete? Has she been boiled down?

BLACK DEVIL: Yes, Excellency.

JUDGE: Let me see.

Devils stand on tiptoe and reach into the kettle. Then they pull out a very small Japanese doll.

RED DEVIL: Here she is, Excellency.

JUDGE: She is yours to play with. So perish all who tell fibs—black fibs, white fibs, or gray fibs!

Each Devil takes a hand of the doll and they dance around for

CURTAIN OR BLACKOUT

THE GENEROUS FISHERMAN[2]

A stunt from Italy

by CATHERINE MILLER BALM

CHARACTERS

| The Nobleman | The Fisherman | The Steward |
| The Guests | The Porter | |

COSTUMES

THE NOBLEMAN. Long-sleeved doublet and two-colored hose, hair to shoulders or bobbed. Low-pointed shoes. (Bedroom slippers of the Romeo type are all right.) Jeweled neck chain.

THE GUESTS. Men dressed like the nobleman in various colors. Woman's costume, long gown fitted to the figure and with train from the shoulder. Hair held in place by a net of jewels.

THE STEWARD. Bright-colored smock belted in the waist, V neck edged with fur (absorbent cotton tacked on with yarn or thread). Wears long chain and has bunch of keys hanging from belt.

THE PORTER. Like steward in style, but with dull-colored smock turned in at neck—no fur.

[2] From *Stunts of All Lands* by Catherine Atkinson Miller (Richard R. Smith, Inc., New York, 1930). Used by permission of the author.

THE FISHERMAN. Straight, sleeveless belted tunic of rough cloth. No stockings. His fish may be cut from cardboard, and should be enormous in size, and a vivid color—pink, red, or blue.

As the curtain rises, the guests are seated around a long table on which appear bowls of fruit and glasses. It is the end of the feast. The guests may be laughing and talking merrily, or they may be listening to some musicians playing violins or mandolins.

Enter the Steward.

STEWARD *(bowing before the Nobleman):* Signor, there is at the gate a fisherman.

GUESTS: But the feast is ended, we need no fish.

STEWARD: Signor, it is the largest fish in the world!

WOMAN GUEST: I want to see the largest fish in the world!

NOBLEMAN: Bid the fisherman bring in his fish.

Steward goes out, returning with Fisherman and his fish. He bows once more before the company.

FISHERMAN: Signor, the most beautiful fish ever caught!

NOBLEMAN: A fine fish indeed. And you will sell it for. . . .

GUEST: He'll ask a fortune for so huge a fish!

FISHERMAN: I will not accept gold for it, nor jewels.

NOBLEMAN: Are you mad? What will you sell it for?

FISHERMAN: One hundred blows with a whip!

GUESTS: One hundred blows!

The man is mad!

Let us see him get paid!

NOBLEMAN: Steward, take the fish to the cook and bring back a whip.

Steward goes out, returns with the whip.

NOBLEMAN: Begin the payment!

Steward cracks the whip loudly but does not hit the Fisherman. The Guests count in chorus up to fifty.

FISHERMAN: Stop!

Steward stops, and Guests look on in astonishment.

FISHERMAN: The other fifty blows belong to the Porter at Signor's gate.

NOBLEMAN: What mean you?

FISHERMAN: The Porter, Signor, would not let me in to sell my fish until I agreed to give him half of what you paid me.

GUESTS: A noble Fisherman!

   To punish the wicked Porter he bore half the blows.

   Here is a gold coin, Fisherman, for your courage!

NOBLEMAN: Bring in the Porter.

The Steward goes out and returns with the Porter.

NOBLEMAN: You have been grafting from the tradesmen.

PORTER: Signor!

NOBLEMAN: But this generous fisherman insists that you get half of what I paid him.

The Porter grins happily.

GUESTS *(laughing):* The generous fisherman!

   The Porter gets his half!

   Pay him!

PORTER: Signor, what comes to me? Half of how much money?

FISHERMAN: Half of a hundred blows from the whip!

NOBLEMAN: Pay him his share!

Porter struggles, but Steward holds him fast. Whip descends and the Porter screams as the curtain falls.

THE OGRE OF RASHAMON[3]

A shadow play (Japanese)

by CATHERINE MILLER BALM

This play is based upon a Japanese legend. The action takes place behind a sheet or other translucent cloth. The characters move between the light and the screen. The audience must be in darkness. The storyteller's voice must come through clearly.

For the Ogre, prepare a huge head on a framework. When the Ogre appears as the Old Nurse, he can carry his head in his hand and hide it behind the skirt of his kimono. The Ogre needs an extra arm—a long stocking stuffed with a glove on the foot end.

For the soldiers' horses, cut the outline of a horse's head from cardboard or stiff paper and fasten to the end of a broomstick. It is not necessary to build the head of wire, for only the silhouette will appear. The helmet, shield, and sword can be made of paper.

[3] From *Joy from Japan,* by Catherine Atkinson Miller (Heidelberg Press, 1924). Used by permission of the author.

CHARACTERS

Raiko (pronounced rah-eke-o), the General
Watanabe (pronounced Wah-tah-nob-e), a Soldier
The Storyteller
Another soldier (or several, if possible)
The Ogre

STORYTELLER: In the days of old there were hideous ogres abroad in the land. They dined upon human flesh and had many evil habits.

(*The Ogre appears—makes threatening gestures.*)

But there were brave soldiers in those days, and at one time the great Raiko slew so many ogres that it was supposed there were no more ogres left in all the world.

(*Gen. Raiko rides in on his horse, waves his sword at Ogre, who flees in terror.*)

One night Raiko's soldiers were feasting in the Castle Guardroom.

(*Soldiers appear, raise glasses, and go through motions of eating.*)

Said one of the soldiers, "A terrible Ogre has been seen near the Gate of Rashamon."

"That cannot be true," said Watanabe, one of the soldiers. "Our brave General Raiko killed all of the ogres."

"It is true," protested the other soldier, "the Ogre has been seen by many witnesses."

"I don't believe it," insisted Watanabe.

"You can prove it yourself," said the other soldier, "if you are not afraid to go to the Gate of Rashamon. Take this paper with my name upon it and tack it to the gate, so that tomorrow I will know that you have really been there. If you do not do this, we will all be sure you are a coward."

(*Illustrate this discussion with most emphatic gestures.*)

Watanabe put on his helmet and shield and sword, called for his horse (*one of the soldiers brings in the horse*), mounted his fiery steed, and rode off to the gate of Rashamon.

(*He rides off. Soldiers exeunt in opposite direction. Watanabe must cross the stage behind the light and gallop in on the side opposite that from which he went out, to give the effect of a continuous journey. Halfway across the stage he will pause and appear to dismount, tack the paper on the wall and remount.)*

As he had expected, there was no one there, so he tacked the paper on the wall and was about to ride off when he heard a loud voice calling:

"Watanabe!" And a huge hairy arm was thrust at him.

(The Ogre has appeared behind Watanabe.)

Watanabe seized the arm and struck at it with his sword. To his horror the great hairy arm came off in his hands and the Ogre fled with a yell of terror.

(The Ogre flees and Watanabe rides off.)

Imagine the astonishment of the soldiers when Watanabe returned to the Castle, proudly carrying with him the arm of the Ogre. They crowded around to examine this frightful object and at last one of them warned Watanabe that he had better lock up the arm of the Ogre, for since the Ogre could not fight without his arm he might send someone to steal it and return it to him. So Watanabe got a huge box and carefully locked up the Ogre's arm.

(Action is indicated by text. After Watanabe puts arm in box, he sits on box; other soldiers go out.)

One day, while Watanabe was seated upon the box which contained the arm of the Ogre and was reflecting what a brave fellow he was to have so wounded the terrible creature, an old, old woman came into the Castle and bowed before him.

"I am your old, old nurse," she said. "Having heard that the child whom I cared for so long has grown to be a brave soldier, I decided to come visit you once more before I die."

Watanabe was very much flattered to hear the words of the old woman. Of course, he had not seen his nurse for so long that he had forgotten what she looked like. They talked together for a little while and then she asked him:

"Is it true that you have actually seen an Ogre, and that you managed to cut off his arm?"

Watanabe proudly related the story. Then the old woman bowed very low and said:

"Oh, honorable Watanabe, please let me see the Ogre's arm!"

"I dare not do that," said Watanabe, shaking his head, "be-

cause the Ogre might suddenly appear and steal his arm, and
then very dreadful things would happen."

"But," said the old woman, "you are very ungrateful to refuse
my request. Did I not care for you as a child? It is the greatest
wish of my life to see, before I die, the arm of an Ogre."

Finally Watanabe, persuaded by her pleading, opened the box.
Instantly there was a loud noise. In a twinkling of an eye the
old woman had seized the arm and was suddenly turned into
an Ogre before Watanabe's frightened eyes!

With one blow the Ogre struck Watanabe to the ground and
dashed away so fast that no one has ever seen an Ogre since!

THE PROUD PRINCESS[4]

A German folk tale in pantomime, with rhymes

by CATHERINE MILLER BALM

CHARACTERS

The good king most polite

The proud princess

The heralds

The pages

The suitors: Fat Prince, Thin, Pale, Blushing; The King with
the Beard

The priest

Country folk, courtiers, court ladies, musicians, singers

The cook

COSTUMES

The usual fairy-tale costumes. For the princess, a flowing robe,
a low crown over a thin, gauzy scarf, and many jewels in the
first scene. Her ragged dress can be made of large towels or
lengths of muslin.

The princes wear knee breeches and blouses with gay ribbons
around the knees, waist, or across the shoulder. They have short
cloaks and perhaps hats with long plumes.

The heralds may wear long hose over colored trunks (even
bathing trunks) or knickers, blouses (shirts with attached collars

---

[4] From *Stunts of All Lands*, by Catherine Atkinson Miller (Richard R.
Smith, Inc., New York, 1930). Used by permission of the author. Adapted from
the prose of King Grisly Beard by the Brothers Grimm.

turned back from the throat) short capes from one shoulder, long-plumed hats. (Plumes can be made of crepe paper or newspaper.)

Pages wear trunks or knickers, long hose, and over their blouses, straight panels hanging from shoulder to halfway between hip and knee. These panels could be made of newspaper with a play upon the word "page."

The priest has a black robe with white surplice.

The men of the country folk may wear knickers and blouses, the women short full skirts, white blouses with laced dark girdles over them, and short colored aprons.

The cook is in conventional garb. There may be kitchen maids in country dress.

The musicians will wear adaptations of the herald's costumes without cloak and hats. Courtiers and court ladies wear costumes similar to those of princes and the princess.

STORYTELLER:

> I'll tell you from this Story Book
> The terrible fate which overtook
> A Princess who was vain and proud
> And said ill-mannered things *out loud!*

STORYTELLER: Chapter One. The Palace of King Most Polite.

> The King was seated upon his throne,
> Nodding a bit, for he was alone,
> And a golden crown is an awful weight
> For one who must always appear in state.

> *Enter herald.*

> When all at once there came to the King,
> A herald who said, "My lord, I bring,
> Greetings from young Prince Puddinghead
> Who comes with hope your daughter to wed."
> The King replied, "Bid him enter, pray!"
> And ordered the pages without delay
> To bring the Princess there to decide
> If she wished to be this Prince's bride.

> The princess came in a silken gown,
> But her face was puckered up in a frown,
> "Why must I marry," the Princess pouted.

"I'll have no old-maid daughter!" her father shouted.
So the Princess sat by her father's side,
And, "Behold Prince Puddinghead!" the heralds cried.

Each suitor is announced by heralds with a flourish
of trumpets—silent, of course—and each suitor kneels
before the Princess with violent gestures of devotion.

The Princess took just a single look,
Then she laughed 'til the walls of the palace shook.
"He's as round as a tub," laughed she. "Enough!"
Prince Puddinghead cried and went off in a huff.

Then the King commanded, "Usher in
A suitor who is tall and thin!"
So a tall, thin Prince bowed low and sighed,
"Dear Princess, come and be my bride."
"Why, you'd make a good Maypole!" the Princess cried.
Which so grieved the Prince that he forthwith died.

Heralds carry him out.

Then the good King shouted in awful rage—
"You unmannerly miss, try to act your age!
This rudeness of yours will quite upset
All the rulings of royal etiquette."
The Princess merely stifled a yawn
And sighed, "Bring the rest of the suitors on!"

The next Prince in size was exactly right
But he wouldn't do, for he looked too white.
Quoth the Princess, "He's pale as a garden wall,
As a husband he just won't do at all!"
And the next Prince, too, she refused to wed,
"He's as red as a cockscomb," the Princess said.
At the next one she laughed 'til she couldn't stop,
"Why, King Kindly's beard's like a kitchen mop!"
Her father was angry through and through.
"You conceited Princess, I'll settle you.
I'll teach you to turn away in scorn
From Princes and Kings who are nobly born.
For wed you shall be ere this day is o'er,
To the first ragged beggar who comes to our door!"
And though the Princess wept and wept,
The angry King his promise kept.
And when a beggar man came that way,
He was wed to the Princess without delay.

STORYTELLER: Chapter Two. On the Road in King Kindly's country.

> *Country people are laughing and happy. The Princess and beggar are weary. The Princess listens to the happy chatter, leaves weeping. For color, the country people may carry eggs, vegetables; even lead a cow.*

And so, I am sorry to relate
The Princess fell from her high estate
And was doomed to beg for her daily bread
And sleep on a rock for a featherbed!
And wherever they begged, in village or town,
Was King Kindly held in high renown.
"A King," said the people, "So good and kind,
You can travel the world o'er and never find."
"Alas, alas," wept the Princess, "He
Would have been good and kind to me."

STORYTELLER: Chapter Three. King Kindly's Kitchen.

In King Kindly's kitchen excitement reigned,
For the King most royally entertained

> *Cook is mixing something in a bowl. Page enters with long scroll containing royal order.*

And word had come to the Cook, "Prepare
New and wonderful dishes of royal fare
With plenty of spices and onions fine
For guests come soon with the King to dine!"
The Cook in distress tore out his hair,
And wailed and shrieked in his high despair.
"The kitchen maids have enough to do!
Who will peel the onions to season the stew?"

> *Here beggar brings in Princess, explaining she is a new kitchen maid. Cook delighted, Princess overwhelmed with horror.*

Then into the kitchen the beggar brought
The poor, tired Princess, "You might be taught
To cook and bake as a poor wife should,
Here you stay 'til your cooking is really good."
And off he strode 'though her tears fell fast,
And the Cook cried, "An onion peeler at last!"

> *Princess has a well-dipped sponge to make tears fall, or uses paper tears occasionally.*

Behold, then, the once haughty Princess sat
Peeling an onion and watering it

With tears that fall with every sigh,
"Ah, how bitterly punished for pride am I."

STORYTELLER: Chapter Four. King Kindly's Throne Room.

Here is the throne room of Kindly, the King,
Whose praises his people love to sing,
For he punishes only the haughty and proud,
Who say ill-mannered things *right out loud*.
The musicians play and the singers sing,

They do so, in pantomime, making no sound.

But the throne is empty, where is the King?
Each Court-lady powders behind her fan
For the King is a good-looking bachelor man.
Then in comes a Herald, announcing clear,
"On with the show 'til the King appear.
And for your pleasure and your delight
The Onion Peeler performs tonight!"
And the poor Princess, wearied from onion peeling,
Must perform no matter how sad she's feeling.
Then all at once there's a joyous din,
"The King!" cries the Herald and ushers in—
Clad in the kingly robes and crown
The man who had begged from town to town,
With the poor, proud Princess, who through her tears
Stares in dismay as the King appears.
But he beckons her to his royal throne
And, as meek she approaches, says low, "My own
My own dear Princess, you're cured of pride,
Come take your place at your husband's side.
To test your manners I first appeared
Disguised by a most unattractive beard
But my new electric razor took the beard off clean
And I then appeared in the humble mien
Of the beggar—and now, your trials past,
I appear in my rightful guise at last!"

Then, sitting down on the royal throne
The new Queen murmured, "I should have known
That no ordinary beggar man was he
Who could make an onion peeler of me!
And I promise, O King, for the rest of my life
To be your most loving, obedient wife!"

NOTE: In her original version, Catherine Miller Balm,
the author, has a child reading this from a story book,
at the side of the stage.

THE MOON MAIDEN[5]

STAGE SETTING

The back wall of the stage is entirely covered by a dark blue curtain hung perfectly straight without ripples. At the right, about four feet above the floor, cut a circular opening three feet in diameter, with two curtains, one in front of the other, of the same size, hung on wires behind it. The first of these curtains should be dark blue to match the stage curtain and should be so hung that it can be drawn quickly aside, revealing the second, a bright yellow curtain representing the sun.

At the left, as high as possible, cut a circle four feet in diameter with a silver gray curtain hung behind it to represent the moon. (This does not need to be far above sun.) Three stiff, conventional pine trees, about four feet high, stand close to the curtain at the left, just enough space being allowed for one person to crouch comfortably behind them. At the front of the stage, left, is a low rock or grassy mound.

When the action takes place in either the sun or moon, lights will illuminate the proper curtain (gold or silver). When the Golden Cock leaves the sun, the light behind the yellow curtain will not only be extinguished, but the dark curtain dropped in front of it in order to hide completely any sign of the sun.

A low box will be sufficient for the Cock of the Sun to stand upon, while the inhabitants of the Moon will probably require strong, steady ladders.

CHARACTERS

CH'ANG O, the Maid of the Moon
THE WHITE JADE RABBIT
THE GOLDEN COCK
THE RED RABBIT
TWO OR MORE HEAVENLY SOLDIERS
THE VOICES OF THE HUMAN ONES

COSTUMES

All the characters wear the conventional Chinese costumes throughout. Ordinary pajamas may be converted into beautiful

[5] From *Chinese Ginger*, by Catherine Atkinson Miller (Heidelberg Press, 1923). Used by permission of the author. Plot suggested by an old Chinese legend.

costumes by basting bands of color about the neck and sleeves,
for a yoke.

CH'ANG O. Pale blue, rose and silver. Elaborate headdress.

THE WHITE RABBIT. White with border of pale green. White
paper rabbit head, made on wire frame.

THE GOLDEN COCK. Bright yellow; touches of scarlet; yellow
paper head with crimson cockscomb.

THE RED RABBIT. Red costume. Red paper head.

HEAVENLY SOLDIERS. Blue costumes. Silver paper helmets pointed like stars; round silver shields; swords.

*At outset the stage is almost dark; only the moon is lighted. In
the moon you can see the White Rabbit busily mixing something
in a big bowl.*

WHITE RABBIT: I am tired of living in the moon.

CH'ANG O *(appearing beside her):* But you are needed here to
make the magic of the moonlight—the magic which hides all
the ugly things of the daytime world, the magic which makes
lovers see beauty in each other, the magic . . .

WHITE RABBIT: It's so tiresome to do just the same thing over
and over . . .

MAN'S VOICE *(from a distance):* Beloved, how beautiful thou art!

MAID'S VOICE: Dost thou really think so?

WHITE RABBIT *(throwing down her spoon):* I am tired of mixing
moonlight so that the human ones may have beauty and romance. I want joy for myself! I shall climb down the ladder of
stars until I reach the earth. Then I shall visit the Magic
Spring. When I have bathed my face in its waters and have
wished with all my soul, I shall be transformed. I shall wish
. . . I shall wish to become a beautiful maiden myself! I shall
wish. . . . *(She disappears. Moon gets dark.)*

HUMAN VOICES: Ah! Ah! The moon has gone!

*There is darkness for a moment; then the sun lights up. Golden
Cock stands on one foot within the yellow circle and looks
down at the earth. White Rabbit, passing behind the pine trees,
comes into view without rabbit head. She stands, looking up
at sun.*

WHITE RABBIT: How lovely is the world at sunrise! How glorious
is the sun!

GOLDEN COCK (*looking down upon the White Rabbit*): She is like the purest white jade. She is the flower of the white lotus. I shall leave the sun and descend to this lovely one. At the Magic Spring I shall become a human prince.

The sun darkens. A dim light from the moon, where Ch'ang O stands looking down, is the only illumination.

VOICES OF HUMAN ONES: O Glorious Appearing Sun! Condescend to shine again! Our rice grows not!

CHILD'S VOICE: I am so hungry!

The Golden Cock, coming from behind the pine trees, without his cock's head, approaches the maid. She greets him gladly. They talk together in low tones.

RED RABBIT (*coming sleepily from behind the trees*): Is it morning? No, the sun sleeps! But it cannot still be night! (*Sees the maid.*) Ho! How beautiful she is! She is like white jade! Perfect! Had I but human form! Ah, the Magic Spring. The Magic Spring will perchance give me manly beauty. (*He retires behind trees, reappears without rabbit head, but with very red face.*) The Magic Spring was almost dry—yet enough water remained for my purpose. (*He approaches White Rabbit.*) Oh, loveliest of flowers . . .

WHITE RABBIT: What an ugly red-faced man!

RED RABBIT: Then there was not enough water! (*Sadly retires behind pine trees.*)

Ch'ang O appears in the moon. She points angrily at White Rabbit. Moon soldiers appear first in the moon, then on the ground. They seize White Rabbit and carry her off. A moment later she appears—with rabbit head—in the moon, sadly and slowly mixing . . . mixing. . . .

MAN'S VOICE: Beloved, thou art fair . . .

MAID'S VOICE: I am hungry! Give me rice, not flattering words.

CH'ANG O: It is time for us to sail away to the other side of the world.

The moon grows dark.

VOICES: O honorable Sun! O Lord of Heaven! We perish unless thou return!

CHILD'S VOICE: I am so hungry!

GOLDEN COCK (*startled*): My work! Romance has fled, but I have my work! The world needs me! (*He disappears behind the cur-*

tain and in a moment reappears, with cock's head, in the lighted sun.)

VOICES: Ah! Ah! The Sun! The Sun!

CHILD'S VOICE: And shall I not be hungry any more?

CURTAIN

chapter 8

PHYSICAL

FEATS

AND

TRICKS

PHYSICAL FEATS AND TRICKS

TO SOME PEOPLE "stunt" means merely a trick or a physical feat. This kind of fun material provides just the entertainment needed in such situations as these: a camp or conference group waiting for the dining room doors to open; one of those formal, stiff moments at the table when no one can think of anything to talk about; or an occasion when a group is restless and needing a chance to "see if we can do this. . . ."

These stunts are arranged in order of the vigor of the activity. The ones which could be done almost anywhere are given first; then follow the feats which require more activity and more space, usually stunts or challenges for one person; and finally the very active stunts for two or more persons are described. Some of the last group would be especially appropriate at campfires.

Pat Head, Rub Tummy

Can you pat your head and rub your stomach with a circular motion at the same time?

Figure 8

Can you make a figure 8 in the air with your finger, and at the same time with your toe?

Zero

Can you make a large zero with your toe, a large 6 in the air with your finger, at the same time?

Can You Pull Them Apart?

Put fingers of both hands together, except that you curl the tips of the middle fingers toward the palms so that the second joints of each are touching. Try to pull ring fingers apart. Bob

Tully of the University of Indiana, says he explains this to groups on marriage and home life by calling the little fingers brother and sister, thumbs grandma and grandpa, and forefingers mama and papa, the middle fingers (now lowered as above) the roof. Any of these may be separated. But you cannot separate a newly-married couple without raising the roof! Also, a penny placed between these two fingers (ring fingers) at the tips cannot be dropped without raising the middle fingers.

Can You Move It?

Cross your wrists straight in front of you, and place hands together, palms flat. Then interlace fingers and squeeze them together, almost like a fist. Without turning loose, bring your elbows around until they touch your waist. This leaves the fingers interlaced, but in a somewhat awkward position. Now, have someone point to the finger they want you to move and see if you can do it. Usually you will move the opposite finger or an adjacent one.

Touch Wrist with Thumb

Can you touch your right wrist with your right thumb?

Wiggle Middle Finger

Can you put the tips of your first and third fingers on one hand together and wiggle the middle finger back and forth behind them?

Recite the Alphabet

Recite the alphabet like an old-time orator; like someone teaching a class, or like a candidate making a political speech.

Putting Your Body Through a Keyhole

You simply write the words, "my body," on a slip of paper and put it through a keyhole.

Poking Head Through

"I can poke my head through a ring," you say, and, sticking your finger through the ring, do so. (Poke your head, that is.)

High Jump

Get someone to stack high a number of objects, and tell the group that you can take off your shoes and jump over them. (Then take off your shoes and jump over them—your shoes.)

Getting Up by Yourself

Have a person sit on the floor and tell him that he cannot get up by himself, after you have said the magic words. When he tries to get up, you simply get up with him, so he cannot get up "by himself."

Locating the Peanut

Take a peanut and three hats, place it obviously under one of the hats. Ask the group to show you under which of the other hats they would like to have you transfer it. When they indicate, you eat the peanut and put the hat on.

Trick Photographer

You take pictures of people with a boxlike arrangement, covered with a black cloth like a professional photographer, and immediately deliver to them their picture (a funny one, previously made or drawn).

Touch Your Wrist

Can you press your hand forward and make the fingertips touch your wrist?

Upside Down Hands

Can you put your palms together, then keeping them together, turn the joined hands toward you and down? Can you start behind you with palms together and change fingers from pointing down to pointing up?

Open a Knife

Can you bend over, reach both arms inside of knees, around ankles, and then open a knife?

Drawing Different Pictures

Can you draw different pictures of the same object with both hands at once?

Drawing with Feet

With a stick strapped to each foot and chalk or crayon on the end of the stick, can you draw with both feet at the same time?

Scissors Fingers

See if you can open and close your forefinger and middle finger on one hand, scissors style, while on the other hand you are doing similar action, but with forefinger going forward (stiff) and middle finger going back.

Twirling Thumb

Can you twirl one thumb forward, and the other backward (clockwise, counterclockwise motions)?

Trick Writing

Can you write the same words—or different words—with both hands at the same time?

Touch First and Fourth

Can you touch the first and fourth fingers of your hand behind the other two?

Straighten the Thumb

Can you encircle the thumb with your other fingers, put the fist into its own armpit and release the thumb? Now in the same position grasp the thumb the same way again.

Musicians

Can you direct 3/4 time with one hand, and 2/4 or 4/4 time with the other? It can be done.

Write and Act

Can you write a sentence, and at the same time with the other hand put coins into a cup or jar?

Write Your Name

Try putting a paper on your forehead, and writing your name on the paper there!

Find the Watch

Blindfold someone and see if he can find a watch by its ticks. Do the same with clock or other noise-making object.

Feel the Bag

Put some objects into a cloth bag of some sort, and see who can figure out what they are. (In order to let everybody have a chance, the answers might be written down.)

Face Feel

With a blindfold on someone, see if he can tell who a person is by feeling his face.

Hold the Most

See who can hold the most in one hand . . . pebbles, beans, etc. Make distinction for girls and boys.

Back of Hand

Who can hold the most beans on the back of his hand?

Double Handful of Water

Using a jar for measure, see who can hold the most water in a double handful.

Inverted Glass

With a card over the mouth of a glassful of water, see if you can turn it upside down without spilling. Place on a smooth table or glass and see if you can get the card out without spilling water.

Pass Through a Post Card

Can you pass through a post card? This trick is not tricky, really. About 1" from the narrow end, insert pointed scissors and cut the card down the long way to about 1" from the other end. Starting from this middle slit, about every ½", cut out from the middle toward the side, ending about ½" from the side. Go all along both sides. Then, cut from the outside edge in toward the middle, directly between the cuts which came out from the middle. Continue this all the way around. When this is finished, you can stretch the card out and pass it over your body, easily.

Guess Who Spoke

Have a blindfolded person guess who spoke to him, or who sang. Person speaking or singing tries to disguise voice, of course.

Pass the Quarter Through

If you cut a hole in a piece of paper the round size of a quarter, you can put a half-dollar through it by folding the paper across the hole and putting the half-dollar between the folds!

Balancing the Quarter

Can you put a quarter on a card balanced on the point of a finger, and flip the card away, leaving the coin balanced there?

Rising Hands

While standing in a door, press out with both hands against the sides of the door, counting to 30 slowly, then let arms hang down by your sides. They will rise up, involuntarily.

Crawling Penny

Put a penny on a table which has a cloth cover on it, and point three wooden matches at the penny. Invert a glass over the display, scratch on the tablecloth, and the penny will come to you. The matches hold the glass up so that the penny can come out.

Coathanger Silhouettes

With each person equipped with at least one coathanger (wire) and a pair of pliers, let each one draw the profile of a neighbor.

Ink Blotting

Fold a piece of paper in the middle, and put a blob of ink in the fold, then press down. Interesting figures result. See who can make the most interesting explanation of his own particular figure.

Jug Knotting

Each person sits on a large jug turned sidewise. He extends his legs, holds knees straight, puts the heel of one foot on the up-turned toes of the other foot. In this position he must tie a handkerchief. If he does not keep his knees straight until the knot is finished, he is disqualified.

Candle Lighting

Same procedure as above, but light a candle in this position.

Needle Threading

Same as above, but try to thread a needle while sitting on the jug or large bottle.

The Hard Pull

Put your elbows out to your sides, hold fingers close together, and ask anyone to try to pull them apart. Even the strong are amazed at how difficult, if not impossible, this is. Hold the fingers a few inches under your chin, for greatest leverage.

Picking Up a Coin

With your back against a wall and your heels touching the wall, try to bend over and pick up an object, such as a coin, without moving your heels away from the wall.

Lift Your Leg

Put your side against the wall, touching it all the way up with your body (including head). Now try to lift the free leg out and away from the wall. Being off balance it's tricky!

Bear Dance

Squat, fold arms, and raise them level with shoulders. Give a slight hop on the right foot and at the same time quickly extend the left leg forward perfectly straight, heel touching floor, and toes up. Hop on the right foot again and exchange the positions of the legs, bringing the left leg back to squat position and extending right leg out in front. (Like the Hopak)

Frog Dance

Same as bear dance, except that the legs are extended out to the side, instead of in front.

Balance on Knee

Can you balance your weight on one knee and then light a candle?

Pole Balance

This is almost like pillow fight on a pole. Try sitting astride on a pole (its ends suspended from ceiling by rope or chain, or on backs of two chairs) and put your feet in a basket suspended from the pole. (Tumbling mats or something soft underneath.)

Walking Straight

See who can be turned around five times, and then walk a straight line.

Balancer

Stand, clasp your left wrist with your right hand behind your back. Keep trunk and head erect, bend knees deeply to a squat position. Touch left fingers to the floor.

Balance the Stick

Who can balance a broomstick on his chin? On his finger?

Spin the Ball

Who can spin a volleyball, basketball or large playground ball on his thumb?

Seed Snap for Distance

If you have had watermelon or canteloupe and the seeds are still moist, see who can squeeze them in fingers and snap them the greatest distance.

Throw the Rider

Jim goes down on his knees, and Tom tries to get on his back. Without rolling or wrestling, Jim tries to throw Tom off his back.

Lift His Hand

Jim puts his hand on his head firmly, and Tom tries to lift the hand off his head.

Jump the Stick

Can you take a broomstick in both hands and jump over it (putting it behind you)?

Pick Up the Handkerchief

Try putting both hands on the floor, with your knees at your elbows, then pick up a handkerchief from the floor with your teeth!

Barrel Stand

Put a barrel on its side and see who can stand on it without rolling it or falling off.

Touch the Wall

Can you stand with your back two feet from wall, arms at sides, and bend backward, touching the wall?

Corkscrew

Stand with your feet together, reach right hand across front and around left knee, back of heels, and touch floor beside your right ankle.

Strait Jacket

Lie on your back with your arms folded on chest. Rise to stand, keeping your arms folded all the time.

Stick Balance

Make a bridge by laying a broomstick on the seats of two chairs, a slight distance apart. With the aid of a cane the player seats himself on the broomstick and crosses his legs. When he is nicely balanced, he tries to remove with his cane two handkerchiefs that have been hung on the back of the chair behind him. If he has three falls, he is disqualified.

Ankle Throw

Using a soft ball or bean bag, player stands, holding object firmly between feet. Making a sudden spring, he kicks feet back and up, jerks the object up over his head, and catches it coming down in front. This takes some practice, particularly to throw it over the head just so that it comes down to be caught in front.

Turn the Stick

Both Jim and Tom take firm grasp on a broomstick. Each tries to pull it down, at same time making it turn in hands of his opponent.

Bend His Wrist

Jim and Tom interlace fingers on right hands, and each tries to bend the other's wrist backward.

Elbow Wrestle

Jim and Tom interlace fingers of right hands, elbows on the table. Each is trying to bend the other's elbow down to the table.

Bend Him

Jim and Tom stand back to back, elbows locked, and each is trying to bend sideward or forward, pulling opponent off his feet (in case of forward).

Straighten Your Legs

Jim and Tom sit facing, back braced, knees bent, feet on each other's feet. Each is trying to straighten his legs out before him.

Three Legs

Bill and Pete stand facing each other, their right legs tied together with rope or belt. Each tries to pull the joined leg backward.

Slap Him Over

Bob and Joe stand facing each other, right feet touching. By slapping hands, each tries to tip the other over.

Slap Slap, Clap Clap

This is just a "show off" stunt. While Bob claps twice, Bill makes swats at his left ear, right ear (but doesn't connect). Then they reverse, Bill clapping and Bob swatting. Keep this up, getting faster and faster. The clapping is supposed to represent the sound of the slaps (which do not take place).

Ringing Chair Leg

Using rings 4" to 5" in diameter, can you ring the legs of a chair which has been turned bottom down so that the legs are up in the air?

Ring the Bottle Neck

With a large brass curtain rod ring or other large ring, on a string, which is tied on the end of a short stick (a foot long or so) can you place this ring on the neck of a pop bottle? (It's very tricky!)

Funnel Catch

Can you bounce a small rubber ball on the floor, on the wall, and then catch it on the rebound with a funnel?

Swing the Bucket

Fill a bucket fairly full of water, and try to swing the pail around by the handle without losing any water.

Jump and Touch Toes

Jump into the air with legs extended straight out in front and touch your toes!

Smudge Boxing

This is a stunt that brings audience enjoyment too. Each contestant has a pair of boxing gloves which have been blackened with soot or powdered charcoal. The object is to see who can get the other the blackest. If bathing trunks or boxing trunks are worn, the blacking shows up better.

Three Trick Boxing Ideas

There are several ways this can be used for fun:

1. Have two contestants put their feet in gunnysacks, tie the sacks up under their arms, and then let them box, using gloves.

2. Have them box in bushel baskets placed close to each other.

3. Have each one box in a barrel.

Work out your own system for points, but the push-over should count a special number of points.

Measuring Worm

Player No. 1 kneels on floor. Player No. 2 (who is behind him) holds No. 1's feet firmly while No. 1 leans forward slowly and reaches as far forward as possible to mark the floor. Then they shift places and see who has made the longer mark.

As a contest, you could have several pairs of players doing this, trying to cover a specified distance in the least time.

The Walking Chair

Several players form a straight line, standing close together and facing forward. Then they bend knees to sitting position and walk forward, keeping step. Very clever. Could be one way of getting actors off the stage after a performance.

Indian Leg Wrestle

Two players lie side by side on backs with heads in opposite directions. They hook right elbows. When the referee counts "one" they raise their right legs and touch them together, also for count "two." On "three" they hook their right knees, and each tries to turn the other one over. The player who does a back somersault is the loser.

Finger Bend

Two players stand facing each other. They extend arms over heads and clasp each other's hands, interweaving the fingers. At the signal they back apart and bring their hands down. Object: to make the other player kneel, and thus become the winner.

Stick Pull

Two players sit on the ground, each pressing the soles of his feet against those of his opponent. They grasp a stick and hold it crosswise above their toes. At the signal each tries to pull the other to a standing position. The person who is pulled up or over, or who releases stick, is the loser.

Stick Wrestle

Two players grasp a stick with both hands. At the signal, each tries to get the stick away from his opponent by any twisting or pulling. To win, you must be in complete possession of the stick.

Harlequin Wrestle

Two players stand facing each other, grasping right hands, and clasping left foot in back with left hand. Each player tries to upset his opponent by pushing or pulling, without either losing balance or losing grasp of own left foot. Change, using the other foot for balancer.

Buzz

Three players stand side by side with their feet well apart, the inside foot of each end player touching a foot of the player in the middle. The end players put the backs of their outside hands over their ears nearest the middle player. The middle player wears a hat, and he tries to protect it by ducking and dodging without moving his feet. He imitates the buzzing of an insect as he makes false passes at the end players, then slaps one of them on the out-turned palm with which he protects his ear. The one who is slapped immediately tries to brush off the middle player's hat. If he succeeds, he becomes the middle man. The challenger agrees that he will stand up through three slaps or that he and a team mate will take three slaps and give three slaps.

Slap Stick

Two players face each other. A stick about the size of a pencil is placed on the hand of one player. The other tries to lift it and tap his opponent's palm before the hand can be withdrawn. He has three trials and may score a point for each tap he succeeds in giving. Then the other player tries.

Hand Push

Two contestants stand facing each other with their toes touching. They have their palms also touching on a level with their chests. In this position each pushes the other's hands until one is forced to step back. The player who forces his opponent backward is the winner.

Toe Tilt

Two players sit on the floor or ground facing each other with their knees bent, their feet flat on the ground, and their arms clasped around their legs. Under the knees and over the arms of each is thrust a wand or broomstick. At the signal each player tries to lift with his toes the feet of his opponent. The one who succeeds, thus compelling his opponent to lose his balance and roll over on his back, wins the contest.

Rooster Fight

Two players stand in a circle drawn about 6 feet in diameter. Each puts his right hand behind his back, clasps his left foot with it, and then grips his right arm with his left hand behind his back. In this position they hop at each other when a signal is given, and each tries to force the other out of the circle or out of position. As soon as a player lets go of foot or arm or leaves the circle he loses the game.

Instead of holding his left foot each player may fold his arms over his chest, grasp his own elbows, and hop after his opponent. Releasing the elbows, lowering the foot, and leaving the circle are counted against the contestants.

Chicken Fight

Two players stand in a circle drawn about 8 feet in diameter. They stoop and grasp their own ankles. At the signal each tries to push the other from the circle or out of balance. A player loses when he leaves the circle, releases either hand, or touches the ground with any part of his body except his feet.

Bulldog Pull

Two players get on their hands and knees, and a strap is placed around their heads. A line is drawn between them. At the signal each tries to pull the other over the line or to force him to lower his head so that the strap will slip off.

Hand Wrestle

Two players face each other, grasp right hands, and place the outer edges of their right feet together. They brace themselves by putting their left feet back. At the signal each player tries to throw the other out of balance. As soon as either foot is moved, a fall is counted.

The Twister

This stunt has been widely used as the basis of races and relays. Each contestant must put his head down on top of a stick (baseball or softball bat is excellent) turn around four to six times, depending on how many you want him to, and then try to continue to run or walk to some goal. It is more fun for the onlookers than for the contestant, because it is practically impossible to run straight. If used as a relay, the players run forward to the bat, make the turns, come back to place at the end of their relay line, and first team through wins.

Lift Him

Get the heaviest individual in the room and seat him in a chair. Have one person make a V of his two forefingers placed together, and put this wedge-shaped V under one of his arms. Another person does the same with the other arm, and two more people take him, one under each knee. All breathe together, and on a signal, all take a breath and at the same time lift him 'way high. It's amazing! (HE BREATHES, TOO!)

BIBLIOGRAPHY

INDEX

BIBLIOGRAPHY

MOST play publishers have a number of collections of skits and stunts. The ones given here have proved useful in a variety of situations.

Handy Stunts by Lynn Rohrbough (48 pp.) contains many stunts usable in crowded places, and from scripts. Cooperative Recreation Service, Delaware, Ohio.

The End of Your Stunt Hunt (48 pp.) and *Skit Hits* (64 pp.), both by Helen and Larry Eisenberg, contain more skits of the general type found in this collection. Fun Books, 5847 Gregory, Hollywood, Calif.

The Pleasure Chest by Helen and Larry Eisenberg also contains stunt material, though it is a general collection. Fun Books, 5847 Gregory, Hollywood, Calif.

The Fun Encyclopedia by E. O. Harbin, 1,000 pages of fun ideas including a chapter on stunts (Abingdon-Cokesbury).

Camp Fire and Council Ring Programs by Allan A. Macfarlan, *Firelight Entertainments* by Margaret K. Soifer, and *The Camp Program Book* by Catherine T. Hammett and Virginia Musselman (all published by Association Press) offer a variety of ideas and materials for use in camps.

Cokesbury Stunt Book by A. M. Depew (Abingdon-Cokesbury) has some usable material.

357 Songs We Love to Sing (Hall-McCreary, 434 S. Wabash, Chicago, Ill.) is an excellent collection of familiar songs, harmonized.

The Twice 55 Series (C. C. Birchard, 221 Columbus Ave., Boston, Mass.) has special quartet books for men's and women's voices. (Most music stores carry them in stock.)

Grandfather Tales by Richard Chase (Houghton Mifflin) is a fine collection of mountain folk stories. *The Jack Tales,* by same author, takes Jack (of Beanstalk fame) through many other experiences.

Play Publishers

Walter H. Baker Co., 569 Boylston St., Boston 16, Mass.

Children's Theatre Press, Anchorage, Ky.

T. S. Denison, 321 Fifth Ave. S., Minneapolis 5, Minn.

Dramatic Publishing Co., 1706 Prairie Ave., Chicago 16, Ill.

Eldridge Publishing Co., Franklin, Ohio, and Denver, Colo.

Samuel French, Inc., 25 W. 45th Street, New York 36, N. Y.

Northwestern Press, 315 Fifth Ave. S., Minneapolis 15, Minn.

Row, Peterson & Co., 1911 Ridge Ave., Evanston, Ill.

INDEX

FOLLOWING the Alphabetical Index are five indexes by use, including selections of material for Auditorium and Banquet Stunts; Junior High Youth; Stunt Night; Camp and Campfire; and Stunts at Home.

ALPHABETICAL INDEX

FOR AUDITORIUM AND BANQUET

THESE suggestions include things which can be done by and for people who are in crowded spaces with not much opportunity to move around.

Some of them will be of the "warm-up" variety, designed to get the group relaxed. Others might even bring in some of the purposes of the meeting, and might be used for propaganda and advertising, if adapted.

Some of the jokes might be told by the leader or toastmaster.

FOR JUNIOR HIGH YOUTH

SOME of these stunts would be appropriate for children, as you can readily see. We are making up this special suggested list of material which we think Junior-High-age youth would enjoy. In addition to the "One-Person Stunts" listed, all others in Chapter 3 would be suitable, except possibly Table Scavenger Hunt and Telephone Booth.

FOR STUNT NIGHT

DIFFERENT people might have different judgments about what would be best for stunt nights. However, here are some suggestions, just as they come as you turn through the book.

For Master of Ceremonies *(To warm up the audience):*

All of the "Impromptu Quickies" in Chapter 4, including "60 Jokes," with these possible exceptions: Magic Writing, Embarrassing Moments, Mixed Props, How Did You Get Back?, Driven Speechless, Yes and No Taboo, Collection Stunt, Advertising Slogans.

FOR CAMP AND CAMPFIRE

IF FOR Junior High age, you might want to check that list; and if for a stunt night, to check that index.

Also, it is well to have camp stunts grow out of the life of the camp. The ideas included here may suggest further development in the camp itself.

Read "How to Present Stunts," "Settings for Stunts," and "A Unifying Theme," pages 12-16.

FOR STUNTS AT HOME

SOME of the stunts call for too many people or too much preparation, but many of them could be enjoyed by a family or by a party at home. See especially "Role Playing," page 21. Suggestions are for youth and adults. You will, of course, adapt them to fit your own occasion.